What Your Sixth Grader Needs to Know

FUNDAMENTALS OF A GOOD SIXTH-GRADE EDUCATION

The Core Knowledge™ Series

Resource Books for Kindergarten Through Grade Six

DOUBLEDAY

New York   London   Toronto   Sidney   Auckland

What Your Sixth Grader Needs to Know

FUNDAMENTALS OF A GOOD SIXTH-GRADE EDUCATION

(Revised Edition)

Edited by

E. D. HIRSCH, JR.

PUBLISHED BY DOUBLEDAY
a division of Random House, Inc.

DOUBLEDAY and the portrayal of an anchor with a dolphin are registered trademarks
of Random House, Inc.

Book design by Robert Bull

Library of Congress Cataloging-in-Publication Data

What your sixth grader needs to know : fundamentals of a good sixth-grade
education / edited by E.D. Hirsch, Jr. -- Rev. ed.
p. cm. -- (The core knowledge series)
Includes index.
ISBN 0-385-49722-9
1. Sixth grade (Education)--Curricula--United States. 2. Curriculum
planning--United States. I. Hirsch, E. D. (Eric Donald), 1928- II. Series.
LB15716th .W43 2006
372.19--dc22
2005056002

To Josie

Contents

II. History and Geography

III. Visual Arts

IV. Music

V. Mathematics

VI. Science

Acknowledgments

This series has depended on the help, advice, and encouragement of more than 2,000 people. Some of those singled out here already know the depth of our gratitude; others may be surprised to find themselves thanked publicly for help they gave quietly and freely. To helpers named and unnamed we are deeply grateful.

Editor-in-Chief of the Core Knowledge Series: E. D. Hirsch, Jr.

Text Editor: Matthew Davis

Editorial Assistance: Bob Shepherd, Souzanne Wright, Diane Castro

Art, Photo, and Text Permissions: Matthew Davis, Jennifer Wheatley, Judy Ladendorf, The Permissions Group

Writers: This revised edition involved careful reconsideration and sometimes reuse of material in the first edition of this book, as well as others in the series. In that spirit we wish to acknowledge all who contributed to either edition. Writers for the revised edition: Matthew Davis (English, history), Ed Duling (music), Lynn Emerson (science), Charles F. Gritzner (geography), William Anthony Hay (European history), Carol McGehe (math), Kristen Onuf (visual arts), Michael Stanford (ancient history), John Thompson (American history), Jennifer Wheatley (English, science). Writers for the original edition: Bernadine Connelly (history), Tricia Emlet (geography, sayings), Marie Hawthorne (science), E. D. Hirsch (science), John Hirsch (math), John Holdren (English, history), Jennifer Howard (science), Blair Longwood Jones (English), Bethanne H. Kelly (English), A. Brooke Russell (geography, science), Peter Ryan (music), Lindley Shutz (English), Michael Stanford (history), Steven M. Sullivan (American history).

Expert Reviewers and Advisors on Subject Matter: Richard Anderson, Wayne Bishop, Jesse Couenhoven, Roger Dendinger, Andrew Gleason, Jorge Gonzales, Daniel Gordon, John Hintermaier, Eric Karell, Joseph Kett, Michael Lynch, Sandra Mann, Wilfred McClay, Joseph C. Miller, Margaret Redd, Jeremiah Reedy, Mark Rush, Warren Sanderson, Martha Schwartz, Richard Schwartz, Gayle Sherwood, Michael Smith, Ralph Smith, Nancy Summers, James Trefil, Nancy Wayne, and others.

Advisors on Multiculturalism: Minerva Allen, Barbara Carey, Frank de Varona, Mick

Fedullo, Dorothy Fields, Elizabeth Fox-Genovese, Marcia Galli, Dan Garner, Henry Louis Gates, Cheryl Kulas, Joseph C. Miller, Gerry Raining Bird, Connie Rocha, Dorothy Small, Sharon Stewart-Peregoy, Sterling Stuckey, Marlene Walking Bear, Lucille Watahomigie, Ramona Wilson.

Advisors on Elementary Education: Joseph Adelson, Isobel Beck, Paul Bell, Carl Bereiter, David Bjorklund, Constance Jones, Elizabeth LaFuze, J. P. Lutz, Jean Osborne, Sandra Scarr, Nancy Stein, Phyllis Wilkin.

Miscellaneous: Special thanks to past benefactors and boosters, the conferees at the March 1990 conference where the first draft of the Core Knowledge curriculum was developed, and the schools and individual teachers—too many to list here—that have offered their advice and suggestions for improving this book and the *Core Knowledge Sequence.*

Our grateful acknowledgment to these persons does not imply that we have taken their (sometimes conflicting) advice in every case or that each of them endorses all aspects of this project. Responsibility for final decisions rests with the editors alone. Suggestions for improvements are always welcome. We thank in advance those who send advice for revising and improving this series.

A Note to Parents and Teachers

Most of this book is addressed to, and intended to be read by, sixth-grade students. However, at the beginning of each chapter we have supplied a brief introduction with advice for parents and teachers. We hope these introductions will be useful for parents seeking to build on the foundation provided here and for teachers, whether or not they teach in the growing network of Core Knowledge schools.

If you are interested in learning more about the work and ideas of teachers in Core Knowledge schools, please contact the Core Knowledge Foundation for more information:

> 801 East High Street
> Charlottesville, VA 22902
> (434) 977-7550
> coreknow@coreknowledge.org
> www.coreknowledge.org

At our website you will find an online bookstore, lesson plans, a database listing additional resources, and other supporting materials.

Introduction to the Revised Edition

This is a revision of the first edition of *What Your Sixth Grader Needs to Know*, first published in 1993. Almost nothing in that earlier book, which elicited wide praise and warm expressions of gratitude from teachers and parents, has become outdated. Why, then, revise the earlier book at all?

Because good things can be made better. In the intervening years since 1993, we at the Core Knowledge Foundation have had the benefit of a great deal of practical experience. We have learned from a growing network of Core Knowledge schools. We can build on the experiences of hundreds of schools across the nation that are following the Core Knowledge curriculum guidelines. We have also received many suggestions from parents who are using the books. And we have continued to seek advice from subject-matter experts and multicultural advisors. All these activities have enabled us to field-test and refine the original *Core Knowledge Sequence*—the curriculum guidelines on which the books in this series are based.

What kind of knowledge and skills can your child be expected to learn at school in sixth grade? How can you help your child at home? These are questions we try to answer in this book. It presents a range of knowledge and skills that should be at the core of an enriching, challenging sixth-grade education.

Because children and localities differ greatly across this big, diverse country, so do sixth-grade classrooms. But all communities, including classrooms, require some common ground for communication and learning. In this book we present the specific shared knowledge that hundreds of parents and teachers across the nation have agreed upon for American sixth graders. This core is not a comprehensive prescription for everything that every sixth grader needs to know. Such a complete prescription would be rigid and undesirable. But the book does offer a solid common ground—about 50 percent of the curriculum—that will enable young students to become active, successful learners in their classrooms and later in the larger world we live in.

In this revised edition, we have included color reproductions in the Visual Arts section. Many people have worked to make the revised edition a better book than the original. As is customary with a chief editor, however, I accept responsibility for any defects that may still be found, and I invite readers to send criticisms and suggestions to the Core Knowledge Foundation.We hope you and your child will enjoy this book and that it will help lay the foundations upon which to build a lifetime of learning.

E. D. Hirsch, Jr.

General Introduction to the Core Knowledge Series

I. WHAT IS YOUR CHILD LEARNING IN SCHOOL?

A parent of identical twins sent me a letter in which she expressed concern that her children, who are in the same grade in the same school, are being taught completely different things. How can this be? Because they are in different classrooms; because the teachers in these classrooms have only the vaguest guidelines to follow; in short, because the school, like many in the United States, lacks a definite, specific curriculum.

Many parents would be surprised if they were to examine the curriculum of their child's elementary school. Ask to see your school's curriculum. Does it spell out, in clear and concrete terms, a core of specific content and skills all children at a particular grade level are expected to learn by the end of the school year?

Many curricula speak in general terms of vaguely defined skills, processes, and attitudes, often in an abstract, pseudo-technical language that calls, for example, for children to "analyze patterns and data," or "investigate the structure and dynamics of living systems," or "work cooperatively in a group." Such vagueness evades the central question: what is your child learning in school? It places unreasonable demands upon teachers and often results in years of schooling marred by repetitions and gaps. Yet another unit on dinosaurs or "pioneer days." *Charlotte's Web* for the third time. "You've never heard of the Bill of Rights?" "You've never been taught how to add two fractions with unlike denominators?"

When identical twins in two classrooms of the same school have few academic experiences in common, that is cause for concern. When teachers in that school do not know what children in other classrooms are learning on the same grade level, much less in earlier and later grades, they cannot reliably predict that children will come prepared with a shared core of knowledge and skills. For an elementary school to be successful, teachers need a common vision of what they want their students to know and be able to do. They need to have *clear, specific learning goals*, as well as the sense of mutual accountability that comes from shared commitment to helping all children achieve those goals. Lacking both specific goals and mutual accountability, too many schools exist in a state of curricular incoherence, one result of which is that they fall far short of developing the full potential of our children.

To address this problem, I started the nonprofit Core Knowledge Foundation in 1986. This book and its companion volumes in the Core Knowledge Series are designed to give parents, teachers—and through them, children—clearly defined learning goals in the form of a carefully sequenced body of knowledge, based upon the specific content guidelines developed by the Core Knowledge Foundation.

Core Knowledge is an attempt to define, in a coherent and sequential way, a body of knowledge taken for granted by competent writers and speakers in the United States. Because this knowledge is taken for granted rather than explained when used, it forms a necessary foundation for the higher-order reading, writing, and thinking skills that children need for academic and vocational success. The universal attainment of such knowledge should be a central aim of curricula in our elementary schools, just as it is currently the aim in all world-class educational systems. For reasons explained in the next section, making sure that all young children in the United States possess a core of shared knowledge is a necessary step in developing a first-rate educational system.

II. WHY CORE KNOWLEDGE IS NEEDED

Learning builds on learning: children (and adults) gain new knowledge only by building on what they already know. It is essential to begin building solid foundations of knowledge in the early grades when children are most receptive because, for the vast majority of children, academic deficiencies from the first six grades can *permanently* impair the success of later learning. Poor performance of American students in middle and high school can be traced to shortcomings inherited from elementary schools that have not imparted to children the knowledge and skills they need for further learning.

All of the highest-achieving and most egalitarian elementary school systems in the world (such as those in Sweden, France, and Japan) teach their children a specific core of knowledge in each of the grades, thus enabling all children to enter each new grade with a secure foundation for further learning. It is time American schools did so as well, for the following reasons:

(1) Commonly shared knowledge makes schooling more effective. We know that the one-on-one tutorial is the most effective form of schooling, in part because a parent or teacher can provide tailor-made instruction for the individual child. But in a non-tutorial situation—in, for example, a typical classroom with twenty-five or more students—the instructor cannot effectively impart new knowledge to all the students unless each one shares the background knowledge that the lesson is being built upon.

Consider this scenario: in third grade, Ms. Franklin is about to begin a unit on early explorers: Columbus, Magellan, and others. In her class, she has some students who were in Mr. Washington's second-grade class last year and some students who were in Ms. Johnson's class. She also has a few students who moved in from other towns. As Ms. Franklin begins the unit, she asks the children to look at a globe and use their fingers to trace a route across the Atlantic Ocean from Europe to North America. The students who had Mr. Washington look blankly at her: they didn't learn that last year. The students who had Ms. Johnson, however, eagerly point to the proper places on the globe, while two of the students who came from other towns pipe up and say, "Columbus and Magellan again? We did that last year." When all the students in a class *do* share the relevant background knowledge, a classroom can begin to approach the effectiveness of a tutorial. Even when some children in a class do not have elements of the knowledge they were supposed to acquire in previous grades, the existence of a specifically defined core makes it possible for the teacher or parent to identify and fill in the gaps, thus giving all students a chance to fulfill their potential in later grades.

   (2) Commonly shared knowledge makes schooling more fair and democratic. When all the children who enter a grade can be assumed to share some of the same building blocks of knowledge, and when the teacher knows exactly what those building blocks are, then all the students are empowered to learn. In our current system, children from disadvantaged backgrounds too often suffer from unmerited low expectations that translate into watered-down curricula. But if we specify the core of knowledge that all children should share, then we can guarantee equal access to that knowledge and compensate for the academic advantages some students are offered at home. In a Core Knowledge school, *all* children enjoy the benefits of important, challenging knowledge that will provide the foundation for successful later learning.

   (3) Commonly shared knowledge helps create cooperation and solidarity in our schools and nation. Diversity is a hallmark and strength of our nation. American classrooms are often, and increasingly, made up of students from a variety of cultural backgrounds, and those different cultures should be honored by all students. At the same time, education should create a *school-based* culture that is common and welcoming to all because it includes knowledge of many cultures and gives all students, no matter what their background, a common foundation for understanding our cultural diversity.

III. THE CONSENSUS BEHIND THE CORE KNOWLEDGE SEQUENCE

   The content in this and other volumes in the Core Knowledge Series is based on a document called the *Core Knowledge Sequence*, a grade-by-grade sequence of specific content guidelines in English, history, geography, mathematics, science, art, and music. The *Sequence* is not meant to outline the whole of the school curriculum; rather, it offers specific guidelines to knowledge that can reasonably be expected to make up about *half* of any school's curriculum, or perhaps a little more, thus leaving ample room for local requirements and emphases. Teaching a common core of knowledge, such as that articulated in the *Core Knowledge Sequence*, is compatible with a variety of instructional methods and additional subject matters.

   The *Core Knowledge Sequence* is the result of a long process of research and consensus-building undertaken by the Core Knowledge Foundation. Here is how we achieved the consensus behind the *Core Knowledge Sequence*. First we analyzed the many reports issued by state departments of education and by professional organizations—such as the National Council of Teachers of Mathematics and the American Association for the Advancement of Science—that recommend general outcomes for elementary and secondary education. We also tabulated the knowledge and skills through grade six specified in the successful educational systems of several other countries, including France, Japan, Sweden, and West Germany. In addition, we formed an advisory board on multiculturalism that proposed specific knowledge of diverse cultural traditions that American children should all share as part of their school-based common culture. We sent the resulting materials to three independent groups of teachers, scholars, and scientists around the country, asking them to create a master list of the knowledge children should have by the end of grade six. About 150 teachers (including college professors, scientists, and administrators) were involved in this initial step.

These items were amalgamated into a master plan, and further groups of teachers and specialists were asked to agree on a grade-by-grade sequence of the items. That sequence was then sent to some 100 educators and specialists who participated in a national conference that was called to hammer out a working agreement on an appropriate core of knowledge for the first six grades.

This important meeting took place in March 1990. The conferees were elementary school teachers, curriculum specialists, scientists, science writers, officers of national organizations, representatives of ethnic groups, district superintendents, and school principals from across the country. A total of twenty-four working groups decided on revisions in the *Core Knowledge Sequence*. The resulting provisional *Sequence* was further fine-tuned during a year of implementation at a pioneering school, Three Oaks Elementary in Lee County, Florida.

In only a few years many more schools—urban and rural, rich and poor, public and private—joined in the effort to teach Core Knowledge. Based largely on suggestions from these schools, the *Core Knowledge Sequence* has been significantly revised: it was extended to seventh and eighth grades; separate guidelines were added for kindergarten; and a few topics in other grades were added, omitted, or moved from one grade to another, in order to create an even more coherent sequence for learning. A *Core Knowledge Preschool Sequence* was first published in 1997. The revised edition of this and other books in the Core Knowledge Series reflect the revisions in the *Sequence*. Current editions of the *Core Knowledge Sequence* and the *Core Knowledge Preschool Sequence* may be ordered from the Core Knowledge Foundation.

IV. THE NATURE OF THIS SERIES

The books in this series are designed to give a convenient and engaging introduction to the knowledge specified in the *Core Knowledge Sequence*. These are not textbooks; they are resource books, addressed primarily to parents, but which we hope will be useful tools for teachers, too. These books are not intended to replace the local curriculum or school textbooks, but rather to serve as aids to help children gain some of the important knowledge they will need to make progress in school and be effective in society.

Although we have made these books as accessible and useful as we can, parents and teachers should understand that they are not the only means by which the *Core Knowledge Sequence* can be imparted. The books represent a single version of the possibilities inherent in the *Sequence*. We hope that publishers will be stimulated to offer educational videos, computer software, games, alternative books, websites, and other imaginative vehicles based on the *Core Knowledge Sequence*.

Although sixth graders should be able to read this book on their own, you may also wish to read some passages aloud. You and your child can read the sections of this book in any order, depending on your child's interests or depending on the topics your child is studying in school. You can skip from section to section and reread as much as your child likes.

We encourage you to think of this book as a guidebook that opens the way to many paths you and your child can explore. These paths may lead to the library, to many other good books, and, if possible, to plays, museums, concerts, and other opportunities for knowledge and enrichment. In short, this guidebook recommends places to visit and describes what is important in those places, but only you and your child can make the actual visit, travel the streets, and climb the steps.

V. WHAT YOU CAN DO TO HELP IMPROVE AMERICAN EDUCATION

The first step for parents and teachers who are committed to reform is to be skeptical about oversimplified slogans like "critical thinking" and "learning to learn." Such slogans are everywhere, and unfortunately for our schools, their partial insights have been elevated to the level of universal truths. For example: "What students learn is not important; rather, we must teach students to learn *how* to learn." "The child, not the academic subject, is the true focus of education." "Do not impose knowledge on children before they are developmentally ready to receive it." "Do not bog children down in mere facts, but rather, teach critical-thinking skills."

Who has not heard these sentiments, so admirable and humane, and—up to a point—so true? But these positive sentiments in favor of "thinking skills" and "higher understanding" have been turned into negative sentiments against the teaching of important knowledge. Those who have entered the teaching profession over the past 40 years have been taught to scorn important knowledge as "mere facts" and to see the imparting of this knowledge as somehow injurious to children. Thus it has come about that many educators, armed with partially true slogans, have seemingly taken leave of common sense.

Many parents and teachers have come to the conclusion that elementary education must strike a better balance between the development of the whole child and the more limited but fundamental duty of the school to ensure that all children master a core of knowledge and skills essential to their competence as learners in later grades. But these parents and teachers cannot act on their convictions without an agreed-upon, concrete sequence of knowledge. Our main motivation in developing the *Core Knowledge Sequence* and this book series has been to give parents and teachers something concrete to work with.

It has been encouraging to see how many teachers have responded to the Core Knowledge reform effort. If you would like more information about the growing network of Core Knowledge schools, please call or write the Core Knowledge Foundation at the address given on p. xvii.

Parents and teachers are urged to join in a grass-roots effort to strengthen our elementary schools. Start in your own school and district. Insist that your school clearly state the core of *specific* knowledge and skills that each child in a grade must learn. Whether your school's core corresponds exactly to the Core Knowledge model is less important than the existence of *some* core—which, we hope, will be as solid, coherent, and challenging as the *Core Knowledge Sequence* has proven to be. Inform members of your community about the need for such a specific curriculum, and help make sure that your local school board members are independent-minded people who will insist that children have the benefit of a solid, specific, world-class curriculum in each grade.

Share the knowledge!

E. D. Hirsch, Jr., Chairman
Core Knowledge Foundation

I.

English

Introduction

This chapter covers most of the English topics listed for sixth grade in the *Core Knowledge Sequence*. The poems are generally given in full, but the stories are excerpts from or adaptations of longer works. If a child enjoys reading or listening to one of these excerpts, he or she should be encouraged to read the larger work. The Core Knowledge Foundation sells a literature reader for sixth grade under the title *Realms of Gold*. This and other books can be purchased on our website:

www.coreknowledge.org.

The treatments of grammar and writing in this book are brief overviews. Experts say that our children already know more about grammar than we can ever teach them. But standard written language does have special characteristics that children need to learn. In the classroom, grammar instruction is an essential part, but only a part, of an effective language arts program. Sixth graders should also have frequent opportunities to write and revise their writing—with encouragement and guidance along the way.

For some children, the section on sayings and phrases may not be needed; they will have picked up these sayings by hearing them in everyday speech. But this section will be very useful for children from homes where American English is not spoken.

For additional resources to use in conjunction with this chapter, visit the Foundation's website:

www.coreknowledge.org.

POETRY

All the World's a Stage
(from *As You Like It*)

by William Shakespeare

> All the world's a stage,
> And all the men and women merely players:
> They have their exits and their entrances,
> And one man in his time plays many parts,
> His acts being seven ages. At first the infant,
> Mewling and puking in the nurse's arms.
> And then the whining school-boy, with his satchel
> And shining morning face, creeping like snail
> Unwillingly to school. And then the lover,
> Sighing like furnace, with a woeful ballad
> Made to his mistress' eyebrow. Then a soldier,
> Full of strange oaths and bearded like the pard,
> Jealous in honour, sudden and quick in quarrel,
> Seeking the bubble reputation
> Even in the cannon's mouth. And then the justice,

The Fifth Age, the Soldier: "Seeking the bubble reputation / Even in the cannon's mouth."

In fair round belly with good capon lined,
With eyes severe and beard of formal cut,
Full of wise saws and modern instances;
And so he plays his part. The sixth age shifts
Into the lean and slipper'd pantaloon,
With spectacles on nose and pouch on side,
His youthful hose, well saved, a world too wide
For his shrunk shank; and his big manly voice,
Turning again toward childish treble, pipes
And whistles in his sound. Last scene of all,
That ends this strange eventful history,
Is second childishness and mere oblivion,
Sans teeth, sans eyes, sans taste, sans everything.

Apostrophe to the Ocean
(from *Childe Harold's Pilgrimage*, Canto 4)

by Lord Byron

There is a pleasure in the pathless woods,
There is a rapture on the lonely shore,
There is society, where none intrudes,
By the deep Sea, and music in its roar:
I love not Man the less, but Nature more,
From these our interviews, in which I steal
From all I may be, or have been before,
To mingle with the Universe, and feel
What I can ne'er express, yet can not all conceal.

Roll on, thou deep and dark blue Ocean—roll!
Ten thousand fleets sweep over thee in vain;
Man marks the earth with ruin—his control
Stops with the shore; upon the watery plain
The wrecks are all thy deed, nor doth remain
A shadow of man's ravage, save his own,
When, for a moment, like a drop of rain,
He sinks into thy depths with bubbling groan,
Without a grave, unknell'd, uncoffin'd, and unknown.

His steps are not upon thy paths,—thy fields
Are not a spoil for him,—thou dost arise
And shake him from thee; the vile strength he wields
For earth's destruction thou dost all despise,
Spurning him from thy bosom to the skies,
And send'st him, shivering in thy playful spray
And howling, to his Gods, where haply lies
His petty hope in some near port or bay,
And dashest him again to earth:—there let him lay.

The armaments which thunderstrike the walls
Of rock-built cities, bidding nations quake,
And monarchs tremble in their capitals,
The oak leviathans, whose huge ribs make
Their clay creator the vain title take
Of lord of thee, and arbiter of war—
These are thy toys, and, as the snowy flake,
They melt into thy yeast of waves, which mar
Alike the Armada's pride, or spoils of Trafalgar.

Thy shores are empires, changed in all save thee—
Assyria, Greece, Rome, Carthage, what are they?
Thy waters wash'd them power while they were free,
And many a tyrant since; their shores obey
The stranger, slave, or savage; their decay
Has dried up realms to deserts:—not so thou;—
Unchangeable, save to thy wild waves' play,
Time writes no wrinkle on thine azure brow:
Such as creation's dawn beheld, thou rollest now.

Thou glorious mirror, where the Almighty's form
Glasses itself in tempests; in all time,—
Calm or convulsed—in breeze, or gale, or storm,
Icing the pole, or in the torrid clime
Dark-heaving—boundless, endless, and sublime,
The image of eternity,—the throne
Of the Invisible; even from out thy slime
The monsters of the deep are made; each zone
Obeys thee; thou goest forth, dread, fathomless, alone.

Byron.

And I have loved thee, Ocean! and my joy
Of youthful sports was on thy breast to be
Borne, like thy bubbles, onward: from a boy
I wanton'd with thy breakers—they to me
Were a delight; and if the freshening sea
Made them a terror—'twas a pleasing fear,
For I was as it were a child of thee,
And trusted to thy billows far and near,
And laid my hand upon thy mane—as I do here.

I Wandered Lonely as a Cloud
by William Wordsworth

I wandered lonely as a cloud
That floats on high o'er vales and hills,
When all at once I saw a crowd,
A host, of golden daffodils;
Beside the lake, beneath the trees,
Fluttering and dancing in the breeze.

Continuous as the stars that shine
And twinkle on the milky way,
They stretched in never-ending line
Along the margin of a bay:
Ten thousand saw I at a glance,
Tossing their heads in sprightly dance.

The waves beside them danced; but they
Out-did the sparkling waves in glee;
A poet could not but be gay,
In such a jocund company;
I gazed—and gazed—but little thought
What wealth the show to me had brought:

For oft, when on my couch I lie
In vacant or in pensive mood,
They flash upon that inward eye
Which is the bliss of solitude;
And then my heart with pleasure fills,
And dances with the daffodils.

Wordsworth.

If—

by Rudyard Kipling

If you can keep your head when all about you
    Are losing theirs and blaming it on you,
If you can trust yourself when all men doubt you,
    But make allowance for their doubting too,
If you can wait and not be tired by waiting,
    Or being lied about, don't deal in lies,
Or being hated, don't give way to hating,
    And yet don't look too good, nor talk too wise;

If you can dream—and not make dreams your master,
    If you can think—and not make thoughts your aim,
If you can meet with Triumph and Disaster
    And treat those two impostors just the same,
If you can bear to hear the truth you've spoken
    Twisted by knaves to make a trap for fools,
Or watch the things you gave your life to broken,
    And stoop and build 'em up with worn-out tools;

If you can make one heap of all your winnings
    And risk it all on one turn of pitch-and-toss,
And lose, and start again at your beginnings
    And never breathe a word about your loss,
If you can force your heart and nerve and sinew
    To serve your turn long after they are gone,
And so hold on when there is nothing in you
    Except the Will which says to them: "Hold on!"

If you can talk with crowds and keep your virtue,
    Or walk with kings—nor lose the common touch,
If neither foes nor loving friends can hurt you;
    If all men count with you, but none too much,
If you can fill the unforgiving minute
    With sixty seconds' worth of distance run,
Yours is the Earth and everything that's in it,
    And—which is more—you'll be a Man, my son!

Mother to Son
by Langston Hughes

Well, son, I'll tell you:
Life for me ain't been no crystal stair.
It's had tacks in it,
And splinters,
And boards torn up,
And places with no carpet on the floor—
Bare.
But all the time
I'se been a-climbin' on,
And reachin' landin's,
And turnin' corners,
And sometimes goin' in the dark
Where there ain't been no light.
So boy, don't you turn back.
Don't you set down on the steps.
'Cause you finds it's kinder hard.
Don't you fall now—
For I'se still goin', honey,
I'se still climbin',
And life for me ain't been no crystal stair.

Lift Ev'ry Voice and Sing

by James Weldon Johnson

Lift ev'ry voice and sing,
Till earth and heaven ring,
Ring with the harmonies of Liberty;
Let our rejoicing rise
High as the list'ning skies,
Let it resound loud as the rolling sea.
Sing a song full of the faith that the dark past has taught us,
Sing a song full of the hope that the present has brought us.
Facing the rising sun of our new day begun,
Let us march on till victory is won.

Stony the road we trod,
Bitter the chast'ning rod,
Felt in the days when hope unborn had died;
Yet with a steady beat
Have not our weary feet
Come to the place for which our fathers sighed?
We have come over a way that with tears has been watered,
We have come, treading our path through the blood of the slaughtered,
Out from the gloomy past,
Till now we stand at last
Where the white gleam of our bright star is cast.

God of our weary years,
God of our silent tears,
Thou who hast brought us thus far on the way;
Thou who hast by Thy might
Led us into the light,
Keep us forever in the path, we pray.
Lest our feet stray from the places, our God, where we met Thee,
Lest, our hearts drunk with the wine of the world, we forget Thee;
Shadowed beneath Thy hand,
May we forever stand,
True to our God,
True to our native land.

A narrow fellow in the grass
by Emily Dickinson

A narrow Fellow in the Grass
Occasionally rides—
You may have met Him—did you not
His notice sudden is—

The Grass divides as with a Comb—
A spotted shaft is seen—
And then it closes at your feet
And opens further on—

He likes a Boggy Acre
A Floor too cool for Corn—
Yet when a Boy, and Barefoot—
I more than once, at Noon,
Have passed, I thought, a Whip lash
Unbraiding in the Sun
When stooping to secure it
It wrinkled, and was gone—

Several of Nature's People
I know, and they know me—
I feel for them a transport
Of cordiality—

But never met this Fellow,
Attended, or alone
Without a tighter breathing,
And Zero at the Bone—

There is no Frigate like a Book
by Emily Dickinson

There is no Frigate like a Book
To take us Lands away
Nor any Coursers like a Page
Of prancing Poetry—
This Travel may the poorest take
Without offense of Toll—
How frugal is the Chariot
That bears the Human soul.

A Psalm of Life
by Henry Wadsworth Longfellow

Tell me not, in mournful numbers,
    Life is but an empty dream!—
For the soul is dead that slumbers,
    And things are not what they seem.

Life is real! Life is earnest!
    And the grave is not its goal;
Dust thou art, to dust returnest,
    Was not spoken of the soul.

Not enjoyment, and not sorrow,
    Is our destined end or way;
But to act, that each tomorrow
    Find us farther than today.

Art is long, and Time is fleeting,
    And our hearts, though stout and brave,
Still, like muffled drums, are beating
    Funeral marches to the grave.

In the world's broad field of battle,
    In the bivouac of Life,
Be not like dumb, driven cattle!
    Be a hero in the strife!

Trust no Future, howe'er pleasant!
    Let the dead Past bury its dead!
Act,—act in the living Present!
    Heart within, and God o'erhead!

Lives of great men all remind us
    We can make our lives sublime,
And, departing, leave behind us
    Footprints on the sands of time;

Footprints, that perhaps another,
    Sailing o'er life's solemn main,
A forlorn and shipwrecked brother,
    Seeing, shall take heart again.

Let us, then, be up and doing.
    With a heart for any fate;
Still achieving, still pursuing,
    Learn to labor and to wait.

The Raven
by Edgar Allan Poe

Once upon a midnight dreary, while I pondered, weak and weary,
Over many a quaint and curious volume of forgotten lore—
While I nodded, nearly napping, suddenly there came a tapping,
As of some one gently rapping, rapping at my chamber door.
"'Tis some visitor," I muttered, "tapping at my chamber door—
    Only this and nothing more."

Ah, distinctly I remember it was in the bleak December,
And each separate dying ember wrought its ghost upon the floor.
Eagerly I wished the morrow;—vainly I had sought to borrow
From my books surcease of sorrow—sorrow for the lost Lenore—
For the rare and radiant maiden whom the angels name Lenore—
    Nameless here for evermore.

And the silken, sad, uncertain rustling of each purple curtain
Thrilled me—filled me with fantastic terrors never felt before;
So that now, to still the beating of my heart, I stood repeating,
"'Tis some visitor entreating entrance at my chamber door—
Some late visitor entreating entrance at my chamber door;
    This it is and nothing more."

Presently my soul grew stronger; hesitating then no longer,
"Sir," said I, "or Madam, truly your forgiveness I implore;
But the fact is I was napping, and so gently you came rapping,
And so faintly you came tapping, tapping at my chamber door,
That I scarce was sure I heard you"—here I opened wide the door;—
    Darkness there and nothing more.

Deep into that darkness peering, long I stood there wondering, fearing,
Doubting, dreaming dreams no mortal ever dared to dream before;
But the silence was unbroken, and the stillness gave no token,
And the only word there spoken was the whispered word, "Lenore?"
This I whispered, and an echo murmured back the word, "Lenore!"
  Merely this, and nothing more.

Back into the chamber turning, all my soul within me burning,
Soon again I heard a tapping somewhat louder than before.
"Surely," said I, "surely that is something at my window lattice;
Let me see, then, what thereat is, and this mystery explore—
Let my heart be still a moment and this mystery explore;—
  'Tis the wind and nothing more."

Open here I flung the shutter, when, with many a flirt and flutter,
In there stepped a stately Raven of the saintly days of yore;
Not the least obeisance made he; not a minute stopped or stayed he;
But, with mien of lord or lady, perched above my chamber door—
Perched upon a bust of Pallas just above my chamber door—
  Perched, and sat, and nothing more.

Then this ebony bird beguiling my sad fancy into smiling,
By the grave and stern decorum of the countenance it wore,
"Though thy crest be shorn and shaven, thou," I said, "art sure no craven,
Ghastly grim and ancient Raven wandering from the Nightly shore—
Tell me what thy lordly name is on the Night's Plutonian shore!"
  Quoth the Raven, "Nevermore."

Much I marvelled this ungainly fowl to hear discourse so plainly,
Though its answer little meaning—little relevancy bore;
For we cannot help agreeing that no living human being
Ever yet was bless'd with seeing bird above his chamber door—
Bird or beast upon the sculptured bust above his chamber door,
  With such name as "Nevermore."

But the Raven, sitting lonely on the placid bust, spoke only
That one word, as if his soul in that one word he did outpour.
Nothing farther then he uttered—not a feather then he fluttered—
Till I scarcely more than muttered, "Other friends have flown before—
On the morrow *he* will leave me, as my hopes have flown before."
  Then the bird said, "Nevermore."

Startled at the stillness broken by reply so aptly spoken,
"Doubtless," said I, "what it utters is its only stock and store,
Caught from some unhappy master whom unmerciful Disaster
Followed fast and followed faster till his songs one burden bore—
Till the dirges of his Hope that melancholy burden bore
      Of 'Never—nevermore.' "

But the Raven still beguiling my sad fancy into smiling,
Straight I wheeled a cushioned seat in front of bird, and bust and door;
Then, upon the velvet sinking, I betook myself to linking
Fancy unto fancy, thinking what this ominous bird of yore—
What this grim, ungainly, ghastly, gaunt, and ominous bird of yore
      Meant in croaking "Nevermore."

This I sat engaged in guessing, but no syllable expressing
To the fowl whose fiery eyes now burned into my bosom's core;
This and more I sat divining, with my head at ease reclining
On the cushion's velvet lining that the lamplight gloated o'er,
But whose velvet violet lining with the lamplight gloating o'er,
        She shall press, ah, nevermore!

Then, methought, the air grew denser, perfumed from an unseen censer
Swung by Seraphim whose foot-falls tinkled on the tufted floor.
"Wretch," I cried, "thy God hath lent thee—by these angels he hath sent thee
Respite—respite and nepenthe—from thy memories of Lenore!
Quaff, oh quaff this kind nepenthe and forget this lost Lenore!"
        Quoth the Raven, "Nevermore."

"Prophet!" said I, "Thing of evil!—prophet still, if bird or devil!—
Whether Tempter sent, or whether tempest tossed thee here ashore,
Desolate yet all undaunted, on this desert land enchanted—
On this home by horror haunted—tell me truly, I implore—
Is there—*is* there balm in Gilead?—Tell me—tell me, I implore!"
        Quoth the Raven, "Nevermore."

"Prophet!" said I, "Thing of evil—prophet still, if bird or devil!
By that Heaven that bends above us—by that God we both adore—
Tell this soul with sorrow laden if, within the distant Aidenn,
It shall clasp a sainted maiden whom the angels name Lenore—
Clasp a rare and radiant maiden whom the angels name Lenore."
        Quoth the Raven, "Nevermore."

"Be that word our sign in parting, bird or fiend!" I shrieked, upstarting—
"Get thee back into the tempest and the Night's Plutonian shore!
Leave no black plume as a token of that lie thy soul hath spoken!
Leave my loneliness unbroken!—quit the bust above my door!
Take thy beak from out my heart, and take thy form from off my door!"
        Quoth the Raven, "Nevermore."

And the Raven, never flitting, still is sitting, *still* is sitting
On the pallid bust of Pallas just above my chamber door;
And his eyes have all the seeming of a demon's that is dreaming,
And the lamplight o'er him streaming throws his shadow on the floor;
And my soul from out that shadow that lies floating on the floor
   Shall be lifted—nevermore!

A Song of Greatness

(A Native-American song
translated by Mary Austin)

When I hear the old men,
Telling of heroes,
Telling of great deeds of ancient days,
When I hear that telling,
Then I think within me
I, too, am one of these.

When I hear the tribesmen
Praising great ones,
Praising warriors of ancient days,
When I hear that praising
Then I know that I, too,
Shall be esteemed,
I, too, when my time comes,
Shall do mightily.

A Chippewa Chief.

Sympathy
by Paul Laurence Dunbar

I know what the caged bird feels, alas!
    When the sun is bright on the upland slopes;
When the wind stirs soft through the springing grass,
And the river flows like a stream of glass;
    When the first bird sings and the first bud opes,
And the faint perfume from its chalice steals—
I know what the caged bird feels!

I know why the caged bird beats his wing
    Till its blood is red on the cruel bars;
For he must fly back to his perch and cling
When he fain would be on the bough a-swing;
    And a pain still throbs in the old, old scars
And they pulse again with a keener sting—
I know why he beats his wing!

I know why the caged bird sings, ah me,
    When his wing is bruised and his bosom sore,—
When he beats his bars and he would be free;
It is not a carol of joy or glee,
    But a prayer that he sends from his heart's deep core,
But a plea, that upward to Heaven he flings—
I know why the caged bird sings!

The Walloping Window-Blind

by Charles E. Carryl

A capital ship for an ocean trip
   Was the Walloping Window-Blind—
No gale that blew dismayed her crew
   Or troubled the captain's mind.
The man at the wheel was taught to feel
   Contempt for the wildest blow,
And it often appeared, when the weather had cleared,
   That he'd been in his bunk below.

The boatswain's mate was very sedate,
   Yet fond of amusement, too;
And he played hopscotch with the starboard watch,
   While the captain tickled the crew.
And the gunner we had was apparently mad,
   For he stood on the after-rail,
And fired salutes with the captain's boots
   In the teeth of the booming gale.

The captain sat in a commodore's hat
   And dined, in a royal way,
On toasted pigs and pickles and figs
   And gummery bread each day.
But the cook was Dutch and behaved as such;
   For the food that he gave the crew
Was a number of tons of hot cross buns
   Chopped up with sugar and glue.

And we all felt ill as mariners will,
   On a diet that's cheap and rude;
And we shivered and shook as we dipped the cook
   In a tub of his gluesome food.
Then nautical pride we laid aside,
   And we cast the vessel ashore
On the Gulliby Isles, where the Poohpooh smiles,
   And the Anagzanders roar.

Composed of sand was that favored land,
   And trimmed with cinnamon straws;
And pink and blue was the pleasing hue
   Of the Tickletoeteaser's claws.
And we sat on the edge of a sandy ledge
   And shot at the whistling bee;
And the Binnacle-bats wore waterproof hats
   As they danced in the sounding sea.

On rubagub bark, from dawn to dark,
   We fed, till we all had grown
Uncommonly shrunk,—when a Chinese junk
   Came by from the torriby zone.
She was stubby and square, but we didn't much care,
   And we cheerily put to sea;
And we left the crew of the junk to chew
   The bark of the rubagub tree.

Woman Work
by Maya Angelou

I've got the children to tend
The clothes to mend
The floor to mop
The food to shop
Then the chicken to fry
The baby to dry
I got company to feed
The garden to weed
I've got the shirts to press
The tots to dress
The cane to be cut
I gotta clean up this hut
Then see about the sick
And the cotton to pick.

Shine on me, sunshine
Rain on me, rain
Fall softly, dewdrops
And cool my brow again.

Storm, blow me from here
With your fiercest wind
Let me float across the sky
'Til I can rest again.

Fall gently, snowflakes
Cover me with white
Cold icy kisses and
Let me rest tonight.

Sun, rain, curving sky
Mountain, oceans, leaf and stone
Star shine, moon glow
You're all that I can call my own.

STRUCTURE IN POETRY

Stanzas

When you listen to a song, you might notice that often the performer sings a group of related lines, then pauses to play some music, and then sings another group of lines. Similarly, in poetry, related lines are grouped together in stanzas. Usually one stanza is separated from another by a space on the page. For example, if you look at "The Walloping Window-Blind," on pages 19–20, you'll notice it has six stanzas, each containing eight lines.

Couplets

There's a special kind of stanza that's generally not separated from other stanzas by any space, because each stanza is so short. This kind of stanza is called a *couplet*, and it consists of two lines that rhyme with one another. Maya Angelou's "Woman Work" begins with a series of couplets:

> I've got the children to tend
> The clothes to mend
> The floor to mop
> The food to shop
> Then the chicken to fry
> The baby to dry . . .

Many poems written in England during the seventeenth and eighteenth centuries consisted almost entirely of couplets. The rhyming lines in a couplet often tend to tie together a thought in a nice, neat package. Many couplets are still remembered and quoted today, such as this definition of "wit" by the English poet Alexander Pope:

> True wit is nature to advantage dressed,
> What oft was thought, but ne'er so well expressed.

Rhyme Scheme

Not all poems rhyme, but those that do will often repeat rhymes in a regular pattern within each stanza. This pattern of rhyming words makes up a poem's *rhyme scheme*. In some poems, the rhyme scheme is very regular and predictable. For example, look at the first two stanzas of Lewis Carroll's humorous poem "Father William":

> "You are old, Father William," the young man said,
>   "And your hair has become very white;
> And yet you incessantly stand on your head—
>   Do you think, at your age, it is right?"

> "In my youth," Father William replied to his son,
>   "I feared it might injure the brain;
> But now that I'm perfectly sure I have none,
>   Why, I do it again and again."

To describe the pattern in a rhyme scheme, we use the letters of the alphabet and assign a new letter to each rhyme within a stanza. Let's assign a letter to the rhyming words in the first stanza of "Father William":

a	said
b	white
a	head
b	right

Now, if you look at the rhyming words in the second stanza, you'll see that the same pattern is repeated:

a	son
b	brain
a	none
b	again

So, we say that the rhyme scheme of "Father William" is a-b-a-b. See if you can find the rhyme scheme for the Byron poem that begins on page 5.

Now, let's look at a poem by Robert Frost, "Stopping by Woods on a Snowy Evening." In this poem the rhyme scheme changes from stanza to stanza and yet follows a pattern. Notice how the last word in the third line of one stanza sets up the rhymes in the following stanza.

Stopping by Woods on a Snowy Evening

Whose woods these are I think I know.	a
His house is in the village though;	a
He will not see me stopping here	b
To watch his woods fill up with snow.	a
My little horse must think it queer	b
To stop without a farmhouse near	b
Between the woods and frozen lake	c
The darkest evening of the year.	b
He gives his harness bells a shake	c
To ask if there is some mistake.	c
The only other sound's the sweep	d
Of easy wind and downy flake.	c
The woods are lovely, dark and deep,	d
But I have promises to keep,	d
And miles to go before I sleep,	d
And miles to go before I sleep.	d

If you read Frost's poem aloud, it might sound almost like casually spoken words. But by noticing the rhyme scheme, you can see that Frost was not writing casually at all: he carefully chose and arranged every word. In fact, some people think the rhyme scheme in this poem reinforces one of the key ideas in the poem, the idea of "promises to keep." Frost keeps his promises to the reader by preserving the rhyme scheme and carrying a single rhyme from each stanza over to the next one.

Meter

When you listen to music, do you ever find yourself tapping your feet or drumming your fingers in time with the beat of the music? You do that because you can feel the rhythm, the regular beat in the music.

Something similar happens in a lot of poetry. In poetry the regular beat is called the *meter*. In a way, meter is a measure of how your voice rises and falls when you read a poem. As you read, your voice rises on what are called the *stressed* syllables, while your voice falls on what are called the *unstressed* syllables. This may be hard to hear at first. One way to tune your ear to the rise and fall of your voice is to practice by exaggerating when you read aloud some lines of poetry. For example, here are the first two lines of a poem by Emily Dickinson. They are marked to signal what to do with your voice. Let your voice rise on the stressed syllables marked "/" and let your voice fall on unstressed syllables marked "U." Make it obvious; ham it up.

> U / U /U / U /
> I like to see it lap the miles,
> U / U / U /
> And lick the valleys up. . . .

Of course, you don't always want to exaggerate the meter when you read aloud, because you'll end up sounding singsongy. But by noticing the meter, you can see, again, how a poet carefully chooses words to give a poem a certain sound and rhythm.

Just as music can be played in many rhythms, so poetry can be written in many different meters. The most common meter in English poetry is called *iambic* [eye-AM-bic] and consists of an unstressed syllable followed by a stressed syllable. Much of Shakespeare's verse is iambic. The lines by Emily Dickinson quoted above are iambic, as is this line by Robert Frost:

> Whose woods these are I think I know

Although poets who write in English often use the iambic meter, they also use many others. You can hear how a meter different from iambic sounds by reading aloud this familiar line:

> 'Twas the night before Christmas and all through the house . . .

Can you mark the stressed and unstressed syllables in this line from Edgar Allan Poe's "The Raven"?

> Once upon a midnight dreary, while I pondered, weak and weary . . .

Free Verse

Many modern poems do not have a regular meter or rhyme scheme. These poems are written in what is called *free verse*. The best poets who write in free verse choose their words as carefully as poets who write in regular meter and rhyme. You can read a poem in free verse by Langston Hughes on page 9. Notice how Hughes varies the length and the rhythm of the lines.

MYTHS, STORIES, AND PLAYS

Homer's Epics

The greatest storyteller of ancient Greece was named Homer. We know very little about him. According to tradition, Homer was a blind poet who lived about 3,000 years ago. At celebrations or religious festivals, he would tell poems of great heroes in battle, of gods and goddesses, of terrible monsters, and more. Homer told two of the greatest stories of all time, the *Iliad* [ILL-ee-ud] and the *Odyssey* [ODD-uh-see]. The *Iliad* and the *Odyssey* are epics, long poems about great heroes and famous deeds.

Homer.

Homer was an oral poet—that is, he spoke and sang his poems aloud. Later, versions of these poems were written down. Today there are dozens of translations of the poems into many languages, in both poetry and prose.

Humans are not the only characters in Homer's epics. There are also many gods and goddesses. The Greek gods, as you may know, were in some respects like human beings. They liked to eat, drink, and sleep. They married, fell in love, and had children. They often quarreled and could be very jealous and vindictive. But in other respects the gods were very different from humans. They were immortal, which means they never died. They could also change themselves into various forms and even make themselves invisible. When they were not intervening in the affairs of humans on Earth, most of them lived in splendid palaces on top of Mount Olympus. These gods and goddesses play an active and important role in the *Iliad* and the *Odyssey*.

Zeus.

The Judgment of Paris

The Iliad *tells the story of the Trojan War, a long war between the Greeks and the people of Troy, called Trojans. Homer's* Iliad *begins in the middle of the Trojan War, after nine years of fighting have already occurred. Homer could assume that his Greek listeners were already familiar with the causes of the war, as told in the familiar story of the judgment of Paris.*

Paris was one of the sons of Priam and Hecuba, king and queen of the high-walled city of Troy. Shortly before Paris was born, Hecuba dreamed that her child would bring ruin upon his family and native city. So, when the baby was born, the king ordered a shepherd to take the infant to Mount Ida and leave it to die. Reluctantly, the shepherd took the baby and left him. When the shepherd returned a few days later, he found the baby alive and well. He took the baby to his home and raised the boy, whom he named Paris, as one of his own family.

Paris grew up to be strong, athletic, and handsome. He did not know he was really King Priam's son. He grew up, got married, and lived happily as a shepherd. But his happiness was not to last, for soon Paris would get involved in a quarrel among three goddesses.

The unhappy quarrel started during a wedding feast. Many gods and goddesses were at the feast, but one goddess was not invited: her name was Eris, the goddess of discord. She had caused so much quarreling among the residents of Mount Olympus that Zeus had banished her forever from the palaces of the gods. But Eris had a plan for revenge. During the wedding feast, she threw a golden apple onto a table. On the apple were written these words: "For the fairest."

At once all the goddesses began to claim the prize, each certain that she was the fairest. Soon the contest came down to three: Hera, queen of the gods; Athena, the goddess of wisdom; and Aphrodite [aff-row-DITE-ee] the goddess of love and beauty. Each claimed to be the fairest, and since no one could decide, Zeus [ZOOS], king of the gods, was called on to choose one as the fairest of all.

Zeus knew this was an impossible task: no matter whom he chose, he would be faced with two angry goddesses. So Zeus gave the task of judging to Paris, the handsome young shepherd on Mount Ida. Each of the goddesses promised Paris something if he would choose her.

"Choose me," said Hera, "and I will grant you immense power and wealth." Then Athena spoke: "If you award the apple to me, I will make you the wisest of men and great in war." Then Aphrodite, with a subtle smile in her mild eyes, spoke gently, her sweet breath warming Paris's ear: "Ah, dear Paris, give the golden apple to me, and I will give you, to be your wife, the fairest woman in the world."

Not even thinking of the wife he already had, Paris quickly made his judgment. Paris gave the golden apple to Aphrodite, and ever afterward Aphrodite was his friend and a friend of Paris's homeland, Troy. But the goddesses not chosen, Hera and Athena, would afterward look with anger upon Troy.

Paris gave the golden apple to Aphrodite.

Aphrodite would keep her promise to Paris; but first, she helped restore Paris to his place as a prince of Troy. Paris traveled from Mount Ida to take part in great athletic games being held at Troy. In the competitions he won all the first prizes, for Aphrodite had given him godlike strength and swiftness. Soon, people noticed how strikingly he resembled the sons and daughters of Priam and Hecuba. The shepherd who raised Paris, now an old man, was brought forth, and he told the story of how he had spared the infant's life. Now Priam and Hecuba welcomed their long-lost son with open arms, forgetting the prophecy that he would bring ruin upon Troy.

Paris was eager to sail to Greece, for there lived the most beautiful woman in the world, Helen. Helen, however, was already married, to a Greek king named Menelaus [men-uh-LAY-uss]. But this was no obstacle to Paris, for he had Aphrodite on his side. He set sail for Sparta, the home of Menelaus. When Paris arrived, Menelaus, little suspecting what Paris intended, received the Trojan prince with great hospitality. He held banquets in honor of Paris and invited him to stay in Sparta as long as he wished.

Soon, Menelaus left for a hunting expedition on a nearby island. He asked his beautiful queen, Helen, to see that Paris was treated graciously. When Menelaus left, Aphrodite made Helen fall in love with Paris, so he easily convinced her to leave her husband and go to Troy.

Paris carried off not only Helen but also much gold and many treasures belonging to Menelaus. When Paris and Helen arrived in Troy, they were welcomed by King Priam and Queen Hecuba with great rejoicing. But some in Troy strongly disapproved of what Paris had done. Prince Hector, another son of Priam and one of the wisest advisers of his father, urged that Helen be returned to Menelaus. But Helen remained in Troy.

The carrying off of Helen was the cause of the Trojan War. It has been said of the beautiful Helen that hers was "the face that launched a thousand ships"—for all the Greek kings and their armies were called upon to join Menelaus and sail across the sea to attack Troy and restore Helen to his side.

The Greek kings were bound to Menelaus by a promise they had made long ago, even before Menelaus and Helen were married. At that time, *all* the Greek kings had wanted to marry Helen, so Helen's father prevented conflict by having them make a promise: "All of you must swear," he said, "that you will be good friends with the man whom my daughter will choose for her husband, and that, if anyone is wicked enough to steal her away from him, you will help him get her back." They had all promised, so now they responded to the call from the brother of Menelaus, Agamemnon, the wealthy and powerful king of Mycenae. Agamemnon called upon them to join forces against Troy, both to take back Helen and to gain glory and riches for themselves.

The greatest of the Greek heroes of that time was Achilles [uh-KILL-eez], the swift-footed warrior who fought like a god in battle. He brought with him to Troy his father's famous troops, the Myrmidons, who had never been beaten in battle. He also brought wedding gifts that had been given to his father, Peleus, by Zeus: two immortal horses and a suit of armor so strong and bright that it surpassed anything ever worn by mortal man. Achilles was accompanied by his dearest friend, another hero and warrior, named Patroclus.

The Quarrel Between Agamemnon and Achilles

When the Greeks reached Troy, they found the Trojans ready for battle. The greatest of the heroes defending Troy was Hector. The Trojans, headed by Hector, came out from the city through the great gate in the high walls. They met the Greeks on the open plains between the walls of Troy and the beaches where the Greek ships had landed. They fought with swords, axes, bows and arrows, and sharp javelins. The ground ran red with the blood of many a hero whose groaning soul fled unwillingly to the realms of the dead.

The most feared of all the Greek warriors was Achilles. Clad in the shining armor that was a gift of Zeus and hurtling forth in his chariot drawn by immortal horses, he struck terror into the hearts of the Trojans, who, seeing him, would run back to their walled city.

The ground ran red with the blood
of many a hero.

Though the Trojans fought hard, they were unable to keep up a steady fight in the open against the vast numbers of Greeks. Seeing that they must depend for safety on the high walls of their city, they withdrew inside those walls.

For nine years the Greeks besieged the city of Troy. Never could they break through the high walls. As years passed, the Greeks came to need food and clothes and supplies. So they left part of the army to watch over Troy and sent part to attack other cities to get supplies and to take captives. After the raids, the spoils were divided among the chiefs, as was customary. For the Greek kings, honor and glory in battle were measured in part by the riches and captives they won.

In these raids, two maidens, named Chryseis and Briseis, were taken captive. They would soon become the cause of a bitter quarrel between Agamemnon and Achilles.

Chryseis was given to Agamemnon, while Briseis went to Achilles, who became very fond of the lovely maiden. The father of Chryseis, a priest named Chryses, came to beg Agamemnon to return his daughter. He wore his priestly garments and brought many valuable gifts as ransom for his daughter. But Agamemnon scornfully refused his plea. "Away with you, old man," he barked. "As for your daughter, I will carry her back with me when I have taken Troy."

Now Chryses prayed to Apollo, the sun god, asking him to make Agamemnon return his daughter. Apollo answered these prayers. For nine days, from his fiery chariot in the sky he shot arrows that carried death, first to the dogs and mules, then to the men. Finally, when the funeral pyres of the dead were burning day and night, Achilles called the Greek chiefs together to consider what to do.

At the meeting, the Greeks' soothsayer—a wise man who understood the ways of the gods—revealed the cause of the plague: "Apollo is angry because his priest has been dishonored by Agamemnon. Chryseis must be restored to her father, and we must offer a great sacrifice to the Archer God, if we are to appease him."

Furious, Agamemnon jumped up and growled, "You prophet from hell! Never have you spoken anything good for me. Now you say I must give up the maiden. Then so be it—I would save our army, not destroy it. But hear me! Some other prize must be given to me, at once, for Agamemnon shall not be slighted!"

Achilles responded: "What prize is there to give? All the spoils have been divided. We cannot ask our men to return what has been given to them. So, be satisfied and let the girl go for now. When we have taken the strong city of Troy, we will make it up to you, three and four times over."

"Is that your game, then, Achilles?" snapped Agamemnon. "You are to keep your prize, and I am to lose mine? No! This council must award a suitable prize to me, or else I will seize yours, or that of Ajax or Odysseus."

At this, the wrath of Achilles flared. "You greedy dog!" he shouted at Agamemnon. "How can the Greeks be expected to fight bravely under you? I have no quarrel with the

Trojans; they have done me no wrong. I have been fighting against them for your sake and your brother's. But you—you sit in your tent at ease, and then, when the spoils are divided, you take the lion's share. And now you would take the little that was given to me. I have no desire to stay here and be dishonored by you. I will take my men and go."

"Go, then," said Agamemnon. "Take your ships and your Myrmidons. But hear this: to make clear to all who is the stronger man, I will come to your tent and take the fair-cheeked Briseis, your prize, for my own."

Achilles' hand gripped the hilt of his sword. Slowly he slid the sharp blade from its scabbard. "Now I will slay this villain where he sits," he thought. But then he stopped—for at that instant the goddess Athena seized him by his long yellow hair. When he turned, he saw the goddess, who was visible only to his eyes.

"Put back your sword, swift-footed Achilles," said Athena. "Hera, queen of the gods, and I love you and Agamemnon both. Now, show your anger, though not with a blade, but with words." So saying, she disappeared.

"When an immortal speaks," thought Achilles, "a man must obey." Then turning to Agamemnon, he lashed out with angry words: "Hear this solemn oath, you drunkard with the eyes of a dog and the heart of a deer! There will come a day when every Greek soldier will beg to have Achilles back. But on that day, though a thousand perish at the hands of Hector alone, Achilles will not come to help. You will regret the dishonor you have heaped upon the bravest man in your army!"

"Put back your sword, swift-footed Achilles," said Athena.

So saying, Achilles, with his dear friend Patroclus, returned to his tent, where they were soon visited by messengers of Agamemnon, who led away the fair-cheeked Briseis. Now the Greeks would have to face the Trojans without their greatest warrior, who sat by the wine-dark sea, firm in his implacable wrath.

Hector and Andromache

At first the Greeks fought so fiercely that, even without Achilles, they pressed the Trojans hard, forcing them again behind the walls of Troy for safety. There, great Hector urged his people to offer prayers and make sacrifices so that the gods would favor the Trojans in battle.

Before returning to battle, Hector made his way to his own house to see his wife, Andromache [an-DROM-uh-key] of the white arms, and his son, yet a baby. Hector smiled when he saw his wife and child, but Andromache caught her husband by the hand and wept, saying, "O Hector, your courage will be your death. Have pity on your wife and child, and spare yourself. If I lose you, it would be better for me to die than to live. Stay here, lest you leave me a widow and your child an orphan."

"Your thoughts are mine, dear wife," Hector answered. "And yet, I would feel great shame before the Trojans if I were to shrink from battle. I have been raised always to be at the front of the fighting and to win great glory for myself and my father. Still, I care most for you, and it grieves me to think that some day some Greek may carry you away captive and say, 'See that slave woman there: she is the wife of Hector, bravest of the Trojans.' "

Then glorious Hector held out his arms to take his infant son. But the child shrank back with a cry, for he was frightened by his father's helmet, which shone so brightly, with its horsehair plumes on top. With a laugh, Hector removed the helmet from his head and took his dear son in his arms and kissed him. Then he lifted his voice in prayer to Zeus: "O Father Zeus, grant that this child may be as I am, a great man in Troy. And some day let the people say of him, 'He is an even greater man than his father, for see how he comes home from the fighting, having killed his enemy, and brings with him the bloody spoils, to delight the heart of his mother.' "

"O Father Zeus, grant that this child may be as I am, a great man in Troy."

He handed the child back to Andromache, who was still weeping. Hector gently stroked his wife's hair and said, "Do not be troubled. No man will kill me, unless it is my fate to die. And as for fate, no man, whether brave or cowardly, can escape it." Then Hector took up his helmet and left to prepare for battle.

The Combat Between Menelaus and Paris

There soon came a time when the combined forces of the Greeks, led by Agamemnon, marched across the plains to meet the massed troops of the Trojans, under the command of Hector.

The two armies advanced toward each other, the Trojans with shouts and clangs of arms, the Greeks silent and resolved. Suddenly, Paris rushed forward from the Trojan lines. Over his shoulders he wore a panther's skin; his weapons were a bow, a sword, and two sharp spears tipped with brass. Boldly, he challenged the Greeks to send their bravest warrior to fight him in single combat.

The challenge was speedily answered by Menelaus, who leaped from his chariot the moment he caught sight of Paris. At last he would have a chance to avenge himself upon the man who had so greatly wronged him by taking his wife!

When Paris saw who had come forth, he was seized with fear and ran back to the Trojan lines. There, he was rebuked by great Hector, who said, "Paris, you are worthless! You were brave enough to go across the sea and steal the fair Helen from her husband, but now, when he comes to fight you, you run away."

Paris answered, "You speak the truth, noble Hector. Now, let only Menelaus and me fight, man to man, and let him who conquers have the fair Helen and all her possessions. If he kills me, let him take her and depart; but if I kill him, then she shall stay here."

Hector announced these terms to the Greeks. Menelaus responded: "Greek and Trojan alike have suffered greatly for the sake of the wrong Paris has done me. Now, let this single combat decide: whomever fate ordains to perish, let him die. But let the rest be from this moment reconciled."

The Greeks and Trojans were happy at the prospect of a speedy end to the long war. And so the combat between the two heroes began. Paris hurled his javelin, but Menelaus warded off the blow with his strong shield. Then Menelaus, praying to Zeus to give him strength, cast his spear. It pierced the shield of Paris and might have made a fatal wound had not he bent sideways and so escaped the full force of the weapon. Instantly Menelaus rushed forward, sword in hand, and dealt a powerful blow at his enemy's head. The blade of the sword broke in pieces. Enraged, he rushed upon Paris and caught him by the helmet and began dragging him toward the army of the Greeks.

The end seemed at hand for Paris. But then Aphrodite, to whom Paris had awarded the golden apple, came to his aid. Standing invisible beside him, she broke the helmet strap from under his chin, thus releasing him from the powerful grasp of Menelaus. Then she cast a thick mist around the Trojan prince and transported him to his own house behind the walls of Troy.

With Paris nowhere to be found, the Greeks claimed victory and demanded that the Trojans return Helen and her treasures. But on Mount Olympus, the gods argued among themselves whether the war should end there. Athena and Hera—who had been denied the golden apple by Paris—wanted the fighting to continue, until such time as the high walls of Troy should tumble to the ground.

And so Athena flew down to earth and whispered a terrible thought into the ear of a Trojan soldier: "Imagine what great honor you will have, what a hero you will be, if you slay the son of Atreus. Let fly one of your sharp arrows and bring down Menelaus!" The soldier drew an arrow from his quiver, aimed, and let fly. The sharp point cut the air and would surely have killed Menelaus, had not Athena deflected it at the last moment, so that it caused only a flesh wound. Athena, after all, was friendly to the Greeks: she did not want to kill one of their heroes, only to rekindle the battle that would bring down Troy.

And so the truce was broken and the war began again. Many warriors showed themselves to be valiant men, but just as many groaning souls fled unwillingly to the realms of the dead, their bodies lying in pools of blood, to become the food of dogs and vultures.

The Arming of Achilles

As the fighting raged on, the tide began to turn against the Greeks. Their greatest heroes were all sorely wounded. Without Achilles, there was no one who could oppose the furious strength of Hector.

One night, Hector called his troops together and spoke: "Men of Troy, take your rest. Loose your horses from their chariots and give them food. Fetch cattle, sheep, wine and bread, that we may have plenty to eat and drink. For tomorrow we arm ourselves and drive these Greeks back to their ships! If the gods are willing, we will burn those ships with fire. We shall surely bring ruin upon these Greeks!" So Hector spoke, and the Trojans shouted with joy to hear such words.

While the Trojans made merry, the Greeks sat in worry and fear. And no one was more worried than Agamemnon. He called his chiefs together and spoke: "I acted as a fool the day that I sent my messengers to take the fair Briseis from Achilles. See how, when Achilles stands aside from battle, we Greeks are put to flight! As I did him wrong, so now will I make amends and give him many, many times more than what I took from him. Now, three of you go and take my message to Achilles."

The messengers were graciously received by Achilles, who listened to their moving appeals. Then he made his answer. "Long ago," he said, "my mother, Thetis of the sea, said to me, 'My son, you have two destinies, and you may choose only one. If you stay in this land and fight against Troy, then you may never go back to your own land but will die in your youth. Only your name will live forever. But if you will leave this land and go back to your home, then you shall live long, even to old age, but your name will be forgotten.' Once I thought that fame was a far better thing than life; but now that Agamemnon has shamed me before my people and taken my fame from me, my mind is changed. So, find some other way to keep Hector and the Trojans from the Greek ships, for I will depart soon."

When the battle resumed the next day, Achilles remained in his tent. At first the

Greeks did well, but then the Trojans came on more fiercely than before. Many a Greek hero fell, and the Trojans pressed closer to the ships.

Achilles was approached by that man he held dear above all others, his friend from childhood days, Patroclus. "Patroclus," asked Achilles, "why do you weep?"

"Do not be angry with me, great Achilles," said Patroclus. "The Greeks are in trouble, for all the bravest chiefs are wounded, and yet you sustain your wrath and will not help them. Now, listen: if you will not go forth to the battle, then let me go, and let your Myrmidons go with me. And let me put on your armor, for then the Trojans will think that you have come back to the battle."

So Patroclus spoke, not knowing that he asked for his own death. At first Achilles resisted, but when he saw the first of the Greek ships set afire, he bid Patroclus make haste. And so, clad in the shining armor of Achilles, the gift of Zeus, Patroclus went forth, leading the Myrmidons. The Trojans saw the armor and, thinking that Achilles had returned to battle, they turned to flee. Over and over again Patroclus charged into the ranks of the Trojans, slaying many. Then Hector, aided by Apollo, realized, "This man is not Achilles, though he wears his armor."

Suddenly, Apollo struck Patroclus from behind, and he fell to the ground, stunned. A Trojan soldier wounded him in the back with a spear. Then Hector arrived and thrust the mortal blow, driving his spear point in just above the hip. "Did you think, Patroclus," shouted Hector, "that you would take our city and carry away our wives and daughters with your ships? This you will not do, for now the fowls of the air will eat your flesh."

"Mark you, Hector," gasped Patroclus with his dying breath, "death is very near to you, at the hands of the great Achilles."

When Achilles heard the news of the death of his dear friend, he threw himself upon the ground. "Cursed be the anger that sets men to strive with one another, as it made me strive with Agamemnon," he cried out. "As for my fate—what does it matter? Let it come when it may. But I will have vengeance on Hector!"

Then Zeus sent a messenger to Achilles, saying, "Rouse yourself, or surely Patroclus will be food for the dogs of Troy. You must hurry if you wish to save his body and give it proper funeral rites."

So Achilles went forth, unarmed. Athena set about him a radiance that shone like a circle of fire. He shouted aloud, and his voice, trumpetlike, was terrible to hear, striking fear in the hearts of the Trojans, even frightening their horses. The awed Trojans retreated, and the Greeks took up the body of Patroclus, with Achilles, weeping, walking by its side.

Since the armor of Achilles had been captured by the Trojans, Achilles' mother, the sea goddess named Thetis, traveled swiftly to the forge of Hephaestus, the god who worked in gold and silver and iron. At her request, Hephaestus crafted strong and splendid armor, including a great shield upon which he inscribed images of war and peace, life and death, love and hate, work and play. It was as though the wide world were embraced within the rim of the huge, heavy shield.

When next the rosy-fingered Dawn arose, Thetis placed the great armor at the feet of her son. It dazzled the eyes of the Myrmidons, who dared not look directly at it. Only Achilles looked at it, and as he looked the wrath within him burned, and his eyes flared like the sun.

When he was fully armed, Achilles went to Agamemnon and said, "Let our foolish quarrel end. Here I make an end of my anger. Make haste, and call the Greeks to battle!"

The Death of Hector

When he returned to battle, Achilles was like a wildfire that burns everything in its path, until the trees of the forest fall in flames and the sides of the mountains are scorched black. In terror the Trojans ran like fawns to take refuge behind the high walls of the city —all except Hector, who waited to meet Achilles in mortal combat.

Hector's father and mother, old King Priam and Queen Hecuba, called out from atop the city walls, begging their son not to fight Achilles. But Hector refused, saying, "It is far better to meet in arms and see whether Zeus will give the victory to him or me."

Then Achilles approached, his armor blazing. Over his shoulder he shook a huge spear. Even brave Hector trembled at the sight, and he turned and ran. As when a hawk in the mountains swoops down upon a trembling dove, so Achilles, in fury, flew after Hector. Three times around the walls of Troy they ran. Then Athena appeared by the side of Hector, though in the form of one of his brothers. "My brother," she said to Hector, "we two will stand against Achilles." Encouraged by these words, Hector turned and faced Achilles, calling out: "Three times you have pursued me round these walls, but now I will stand and face you. Only let us agree: if Zeus gives me the victory today, I will give back your body to the Greeks; if you should be the victor, promise to do the same with me."

Achilles scowled. "Hector," he said, "lions do not make agreements with men, nor wolves with lambs." Then he threw his great spear, which Hector barely avoided. "You have missed!" cried Hector. "Now see whether my aim is true." And with all his strength he hurled his spear at Achilles. It struck full force upon the great shield and bounced off. "Give me your spear, brother!" cried Hector—only to turn and find no one there. Then he knew his fate: "The gods have decreed my doom. But let me not die without a struggle. Let me do some great thing that men will remember in years to come."

So Hector drew his sword and charged at Achilles. Achilles ran at Hector, seeking the most vulnerable spot, not protected by strong armor. He found it where the neck meets the collarbone, and there he drove his spear deep through the soft part of the neck.

Dying, Hector gasped, "O Achilles, I entreat you, do not make my body food for dogs, but give it to my father and mother that they may duly bury it. They will reward you with silver and gold."

"No amount of gold will buy you back," said Achilles. "Now, cur, die!" To shame the dead Hector, Achilles stripped him of his armor, then bent down and cut holes in the spaces between the ankles and heels. Through these holes he drew cords of ox-hide, fastened the cords to his chariot, and dragged Hector's dead body back to the Greek ships. For the next few days, in his fury, Achilles caused the dead body to be dragged about the tomb of his fallen friend, Patroclus. Yet the gods took pity on Hector and kept his dead body from harm.

The gods took pity on Hector
and kept his dead body from harm.

It was the will of the gods that Hector's body should be returned to Troy. So the gods helped old Priam make his way safely to Achilles. When he entered Achilles' tent, Priam threw himself at Achilles' feet and kissed his hands, saying, "Achilles, take pity; I kiss the hands of the man who has killed my children."

Achilles was moved. He remembered his own father and his fallen friend, Patroclus. He called upon two servants to wash and anoint the body of Hector so that it could be returned to Priam.

Priam asked, "Let there be a truce for nine days between the Greeks and Trojans, that we may bury Hector with all due ceremony."

"It shall be as you ask," replied Achilles. Then he took the aged king by the hand and led him to a place of rest. The next day Priam returned to Troy, and so began the splendid funeral for Hector, once the strong leader of the city whose high walls would soon fall.

How Troy Fell

Homer's *Iliad* ends with the funeral of Hector. Other accounts tell us of the fate of Achilles and the end of the Trojan War.

After the funeral of Hector, fighting resumed. Achilles killed many Trojans, but he was himself slain by Paris. Paris was no match for Achilles in single combat, but he was a skilled archer. He shot Achilles in the one place he could be hurt, his heel. Except for his heel, Achilles was invulnerable. When Achilles was a baby, his mother had dipped him into the river Styx, the magical waters of which protected his body from injury. But in dipping him, Thetis had held the infant by his heel, so his heel was left unprotected. Even today, we speak of a person's "Achilles' heel," meaning a person's one big weakness.

Troy eventually fell because of a clever plan on the part of the Greeks, devised by the wily Odysseus. The Greeks built an enormous, hollow horse out of wood. They left it outside the walls of the city and then pretended to sail away, though they went no farther than a nearby island. Inside, however, were hidden some of the bravest Greek warriors.

When the Trojans saw the huge wooden horse, some were suspicious, but most thought it was an offering to the gods, so they hauled it within the walls of the city. That night, the Greek warriors crept out of the horse and opened the gates of the city to the other soldiers, who had returned under cover of darkness. The Greeks set fire to Troy and conquered the great city at last.

The story of the fall of Troy is told in moving detail in an epic poem called the *Aeneid* [uh-NEE-id], written by Virgil, a great Roman poet who lived in the first century B.C.

The Trojan Horse.

The *Odyssey*

Homer's *Odyssey* is an epic poem about the adventures of the Greek hero, Odysseus, as he made his difficult journey home after the Trojan War. Odysseus was famous for his intelligence, ingenuity, and resourcefulness. It was Odysseus who came up with the plan of the Trojan Horse that won the war for the Greeks. After ten long years of war, Odysseus was looking forward to a speedy voyage home. But it was not to be: it took Odysseus ten years to reach his native island, Ithaca.

His wanderings took him to the island of Circe [SIR-see], a beautiful sorceress who turned men into swine, and to Hades, the realm of the dead, where he spoke with the sad shade of Achilles. He sailed between Scylla [SILL-uh], a six-headed monster, and Charybdis [kuh-RIB-duss], a devouring whirlpool, and past the Sirens, maidens who sang alluring songs that drew sailors to their deaths. He even matched his wits with the Cyclops [SIGH-klops].

Odysseus and the Cyclops

When Troy had been taken, Odysseus set sail for Ithaca, in twelve ships with fifty crewmen in each. Little did these mariners think that it would be ten years before any saw their home. Nor did they know that by their own recklessness, and despite the brave efforts of their king to save them, only one—Odysseus himself—would return.

Not long into their journey, a great storm fell upon the ships and carried them far to the south. Late one evening, in a dense fog, the ships' keels grazed the shore of an island. Odysseus and his crew beached the ships and then slept through the night. When the rosy fingers of Dawn touched the sky, they woke and found fresh water, as well as wild goats, which made a fine feast for the hungry sailors.

Nearby was another island. Odysseus and his men saw wisps of smoke rising from it and heard the bleating of flocks. "Friends and shipmates," announced Odysseus, "in my own ship, with my own crew, I will make the crossing to that island and find out who lives there, and whether they be good people or lawless savages."

Odysseus brought some food, as well as a big goatskin full of strong, sweet wine, a gift from a priest of Apollo. One measure of this wine could be mixed with twenty measures of water, and still it would remain wonderfully sweet and potent.

Upon reaching the island, Odysseus picked twelve of his bravest men. They set off and soon found a huge cave, apparently the home of some shepherd, as many rams and goats were walking about. The men looked inside and saw pens full of young sheep and goats, and baskets full of cheeses. "Let us take these cheeses," cried the men, "and open the pens and drive the goats and lambs aboard our ships."

Odysseus knew this was good advice. But he wanted to see what kind of man this shepherd might be. So the men built a fire, helped themselves to some cheese, and sat down to wait.

As evening neared, they were startled by a loud crash! It was the sound of a huge bundle of logs dropped into the cave from the shoulder of a great giant, one of those creatures called Cyclops. He was a brutish creature, with only one large eye in the middle of his forehead and one shaggy eyebrow above it.

Odysseus and his frightened men scrambled to the back of the cave. The Cyclops drove his flocks into the cave and then blocked the entrance with a boulder so big that twenty wagons could not move it. He milked the ewes and she-goats, setting aside half the milk to curdle for cheese and half for his own supper. He threw some logs on the fire and stirred up a great flame, the glare from which revealed Odysseus and his men.

"Who are you?" said the giant, his voice a deep rumble. "Are you men of the sea—traders or pirates?"

Odysseus replied, "We are Greeks, sailing home from Troy, where we have been fighting for King Agamemnon, whose fame is known far and wide. We are homeward bound, but great gales have blown us off course. Now, as the gods love those who show hospitality to strangers, we ask you to be hospitable to us."

"The gods!" roared the Cyclops. "We Cyclops care not for the gods. We are greater and stronger than your Zeus with all his thunder. Now, tell me, puny one—where have you left your ship?"

Odysseus knew that, if he revealed the location of the ship, the Cyclops would crush it to splinters and leave them no hope of escaping. So, with his quick and ready mind, he answered, "We have no ship, for our ship was driven upon the rocks and broken. My men and I are the only survivors."

The giant said nothing, but quickly grabbed two of the men, as a man might pick up two squirming puppies. He dashed them on the ground and then tore them limb from limb.

Like a mountain lion gnawing and crunching a fresh kill, he devoured them entirely—flesh, bones, organs, everything—and washed it all down with great swallows of milk. And when he had filled himself with this awful food, he lay down among his sheep and slept.

Odysseus drew his sharp sword and rushed to the giant's side, preparing to stab him to the heart, when a thought occurred to him. "If I kill him," he thought, "then I condemn myself and my men as well, for we could never move that great boulder from the doorway." So, sad at heart, he waited, thinking.

When morning came, the giant awoke and milked his flocks. He then seized two of the men and devoured them as before. He opened the cave and went forth with his flocks to the pastures, though before leaving he placed the great boulder over the entrance.

The giant quickly grabbed two of the men, as a man might pick up two squirming puppies.

All day Odysseus thought of how he might save himself and his companions. He noticed a great pole in the cave, the trunk of an olive tree, which the giant planned to use as a walking staff. Odysseus cut off a six-foot section and sharpened one end, then turned the pointed end in the fire to harden it.

In the evening, the Cyclops returned and once again seized two prisoners and feasted on them. Then Odysseus stepped forth, holding in his hands a bowl filled with wine from the wineskin he had brought, full of the powerful and tempting drink. "Drink, Cyclops," said Odysseus. "Wash down your scraps of flesh. I had meant to offer this to you as a gift if you would help us home."

The Cyclops greedily swallowed all that was in the bowl. "Give me more," he commanded, "and tell me your name. Then I will make you a gift as a proper host should."

Then the wily Odysseus said, "My name is No-Man. Now, give me your gift."

"My gift," laughed the one-eyed giant, "is that you shall be eaten last." Saying this, he toppled over in a drunken sleep. As he snored, drops of wine and bits of human flesh dribbled out of his mouth.

"Come, my brave friends," said Odysseus. They grabbed the sharpened stake and heated the point in the fire till it glowed red. Then, running at top speed, they thrust it into the giant's single eye and leaned with full force, twisting and turning the stake. The burning wood hissed in the eye as a red-hot iron hisses when dipped in water.

The Cyclops roared and thrashed around. Odysseus and his men fell back in fear. Blood spurted as the Cyclops tore the hot stake from his eye. He roared so loudly that other Cyclops came running from their nearby caves to see what had happened. From outside they called out, "Polyphemos!"—for that was this giant's name—"Polyphemos, what's wrong? Why do you cry out? Is someone stealing your sheep or hurting you?"

The giant bellowed, "No-Man! No-Man has hurt me! No-Man!"

"Well," replied the other Cyclops, "if no man is hurting you, then it must be yourself or the gods, and we can do nothing about that." And they returned to their caves.

Groaning, the Cyclops groped till he grabbed the boulder blocking the entrance to the cave. He removed the boulder and sat down in the entrance, feeling around him to grab any prisoners that might try to escape. Odysseus could see that there was still no easy way out. So, he called upon all his wits to devise yet another plan.

He took strips of willow from the giant's bed. With these he tied together three rams, side by side, then bound a man under the belly of the middle ram. He did this for all six of his remaining men. Then he found the largest, woolliest ram and pulled himself tight under his belly, gripping the fleece as tightly as he could.

When morning came, the Cyclops, as was his habit, let his flocks out to graze. He stroked each ram but did not feel the men hiding beneath. When he felt the biggest ram, however, he stopped it and spoke: "What is this, my sweet creature? You never lag behind but are always first out of the cave in the morning. What now keeps you back?" Odysseus remained as silent and still as possible. "Could it be," continued Cyclops, his huge fingers rubbing the ram's fleece, "that you are sad for your poor master's eye, which that villain No-Man has destroyed? I swear he will not get out alive! If only you could speak and tell me where he is—I would splatter his brains upon the ground!" Then, with a sigh, he let the ram proceed.

Once outside, Odysseus released his grip and ran to untie his companions. They rounded up as many of the giant's sheep as they could and then hurried back to their ship. Their worried companions welcomed them, and they rowed speedily away.

When they were far from shore, Odysseus could not resist shouting back, "O Cyclops!

You beast! How do you like what No-Man has done to you? May the gods punish you even more!"

The Cyclops heard Odysseus and was angered. He broke off a hilltop and heaved it in the direction from which he had heard Odysseus's voice. It struck just in front of the ship and caused a great wave, pushing the ship all the way back to the shore! "Row, men, row or die!" urged Odysseus. So they rowed, and when they were twice as far out as before, Odysseus again stood up and cupped his hands to shout. His men exclaimed, "Captain, stop! For the love of Zeus, don't make the brute angry! He'll smash us to bits!"

But Odysseus, enraged, cried out again: "Listen, Cyclops! If any man asks you who put out your eye, tell them truthfully that it was I, Odysseus of Ithaca!"

The giant took up another huge rock and threw it. This time it struck just behind the ship and propelled the craft farther away. The blind giant dropped heavily upon the ground and sobbed. "So, my fate has come," he groaned. "Long ago, a wizard predicted that I would lose my eye at the hands of Odysseus. But I always thought Odysseus would be some giant, powerful and armed—not a puny, scrawny thing."

Then the Cyclops rose and, turning his blind eye to the heavens, prayed to his father, Poseidon, god of the sea: "Hear me, father! Grant this one request: may Odysseus of Ithaca never reach home! Let him lose all his companions and taste bitterness in days to come."

Poseidon, who rules the seas, heard this request and granted it. He turned his rage upon Odysseus, sending storms, shipwrecks, and disaster at every turn, forcing Odysseus to wander for ten years before returning home.

Apollo and Daphne

This myth and the three that follow are based on stories collected by the Roman writer, Ovid. Ovid lived in the early years of the Roman Empire, at the time of the Emperor Augustus. He collected and retold stories about Greek and Roman gods and their love affairs in his long poem, Metamorphoses.

Daphne, daughter of the river god, was beautiful, strong, and agile. Like the goddess Diana, she loved to hunt. With her hair streaming wildly behind her, Daphne would run like the wind through the forest, in swift pursuit of an unlucky stag who was sure to fall when pierced by an arrow from her bow.

Daphne loved her freedom. Her father would often say, "My beautiful daughter, it is time for you to take a husband and bear me a grandson." But Daphne would laugh and reply, "I have no need of husband or marriage!"

One day while Daphne was hunting, Apollo, the sun god, caught sight of her. He admired her strength and speed. Then he felt a sharp piercing sensation, and what had been warm admiration burst into the searing flame of love.

Apollo, you see, had been struck by an arrow shot by the god of love, Cupid, whom even the gods cannot resist. Cupid struck Apollo with a golden-tipped arrow, which causes deep and burning love. At the same time, he struck Daphne with a lead-tipped arrow, which hardens the resolve to resist all love.

"Stop!" Apollo cried out to Daphne and began to run after her. But when Daphne realized she was being chased, she ran even faster. "Wait!" cried Apollo. "Do you know who you are running from? I am no servant or shepherd. I am a son of Jupiter."

Daphne had lived free all her life and did not intend to give up her freedom now. So she ran faster still. But not even the swiftest mortal can outrun a god, and soon Daphne felt her legs weakening and her breath growing short. Just when she could run no farther, she reached the banks of the river that ran through her father's forest. "Father, oh father, help me!" she cried.

The words had hardly left her lips when she felt her once swift feet begin to root themselves to the ground and her arms begin to stiffen. Then her skin turned to bark, and her hair to leaves. And where once had stood a beautiful, graceful girl, there now stood a beautiful, graceful tree—a laurel.

Apollo wrapped his arms around the trunk and felt a still beating heart inside. Then he cried out, "From this day forth, the laurel shall be my tree. Look for its shining, green leaves on my lyre and quiver. Weave it into wreaths to crown the brows of heroes and poets." And Apollo himself wore on his head a wreath made of the laurel's evergreen leaves, a sign of his love for Daphne.

Her skin turned to bark,
and her hair to leaves.

Orpheus and Eurydice

Orpheus [OR-fee-us] was a son of the Muses, the goddesses who sang so sweetly that their name has given us the word "music." The music of Orpheus was so beautiful it could soothe a savage beast. When Orpheus touched the strings of his lyre, the fiercest lion would cease his roar, the animals of the forest would gather to listen, the trees would bend their branches near, and even the rivers would turn from their beds to catch a strain of the sweet song.

People everywhere were charmed by the music of Orpheus. So when Orpheus fell in love with a maiden named Eurydice [yoo-RID-ih-see], he had only to play his lyre to win her heart. Yet even his sweetest song could not undo the terrible calamity that struck during the wedding ceremony: as his bride walked across the grass, a snake pierced her foot with its venomous bite. Orpheus swept Eurydice into his arms and cried aloud, but in vain: the spirit of Eurydice had already fled to the underworld, the cold realm of the dead.

Stricken with grief, Orpheus wandered the forests playing songs so sad that all who heard him wept. One day, as Orpheus played his doleful music, he thought, "If I can charm the souls of the living, then perhaps I can also charm the souls of the dead. I will go to the underworld and try with my music to persuade Pluto, king of that dark realm, to give Eurydice back to me."

And so Orpheus was ferried across the black waters of the river Styx, which separates the world of the living from the world of the dead. As he descended on the dark and misty path, he played such sad music that even the phantoms were moved to tears, and Cerberus, the vicious three-headed watchdog of the underworld, quietly let him pass.

Then he came to the throne of the dread king, Pluto. He touched the strings of his lyre and told of his loss of

When Orpheus touched the strings of his lyre, the fiercest lion ceased his roar and the animals of the forest would gather to listen.

Eurydice. He sang of his lasting love, of his deep grief. "I beg you," he said, "if in this dark and confused realm you know anything of love, let my Eurydice return to life." Pluto, usually merciless, was moved and granted Orpheus his request, but with one condition. "On your journey back," Pluto commanded, "you must not look back, not even once, or she will vanish from your side forever."

Eurydice was brought forth, and she and Orpheus began to climb the steep path, always looking forward. The way was hard, and Orpheus's heart was torn by the sounds of the faltering steps behind him: if only he could turn and extend a loving hand! They struggled on and were nearing the light when, who knows why, perhaps on some impulse of love, perhaps out of fear that he had already lost her, Orpheus looked back—only to see, just as Pluto had warned, Eurydice fade like a wisp of smoke carried away on the wind. Helpless, she was pulled back to the realm of the dead.

Eurydice faded like a wisp of smoke carried away on the wind.

As his beloved's farewell cry rang in his ears, Orpheus crumpled over his lyre and wept. For a second time he had lost Eurydice—for a second time, and forever.

Echo and Narcissus

When Narcissus was born, all who saw him marveled at his beauty. When he grew to be a youth, all who saw him fell in love with him. But Narcissus, vain and conceited, showed love for no one. He would not give even a glance to many a heartbroken maiden.

One day his beauty melted the heart of the lovely nymph named Echo. Once she saw Narcissus, she followed him everywhere. But she could not tell him of her love, for though she longed to speak, she could only repeat the last words of what was said to her.

How had this come to pass? It was because of Juno, queen of the gods. Juno often left Olympus to wander the hillsides in search of her husband, Jupiter, who had a fondness for the nymphs who dwelt in the woods. Just when Juno was about to find her husband, Echo would appear and take her aside to distract her with a stream of lively and amusing chatter, until the nymphs and Jupiter had gotten away. When Juno discovered what was going on, she punished Echo: "You have spoken too many words," said Juno, "and now you shall speak only the last words you hear."

And so poor Echo could follow Narcissus, but she could say nothing to him.

One day, Narcissus got lost in the forest and cried out, "Hello, is there anyone here?"

"Here, here," Echo replied, hidden behind some trees.

"Ho, there! Where are you?" Narcissus called.

"Where are you?" answered Echo.

Narcissus could see no one, so he called out again, "Are you close at hand?"

"Close at hand," came the reply.

Narcissus went toward the voice. "Are you the one who calls me?" he asked.

"Who calls me," Echo answered.

"I am Narcissus," the youth replied.

"Narcissus," said Echo, and, unable to restrain herself, she rushed toward him with open arms.

Narcissus leaped back. "Get away!" he cried. "Not one step closer. I shall go my own way, and I forbid you to stay with me!"

"Stay with me!" said Echo. Her heart broke as she watched Narcissus turn and walk away. In grief and pain, she wandered through the forest alone.

Narcissus continued to spurn all those who offered him their love. Then one day while he was hunting, he stopped to take a drink from a clear still pool. As he bent his head toward the silvery water, he saw a beautiful face looking back at him, and he fell in love— with his reflection! Now Narcissus knew the desire and longing he caused in others. He stared at the beautiful image in the water and even tried to kiss it, but the touch of his lips disturbed the surface, and the beautiful image vanished in a blur of ripples.

When the water stilled and the reflection returned, Narcissus could not tear himself away. He longed for that which he could never possess. For many days he pined away and grew weak and thin. Echo came near him but she could not help him: she could not speak, and his gaze remained fixed on his own image. Finally, with his dying breath, he gasped, "My love, my love." Echo could only reply, "My love."

Poor Echo, grief-stricken, wasted away until nothing was left of her but her voice, which still haunts dark caves and lonely hillsides.

By the side of the pool where Narcissus died, there grew a lovely flower, with a yellow center ringed by delicate white petals—it was a Narcissus, still known to this day by the name of the beautiful but foolish youth who died for love of his own reflection.

Narcissus could not tear himself away from his reflection.

Pygmalion

Once there lived a sculptor by the name of Pygmalion [Pig-MALE-ee-un] who made statues of surpassing beauty. Pygmalion had no wife: he was perfectly happy to live alone, working all day at his art and dreaming each night of the still fairer forms he would someday carve out of stone.

"You must be lonely," his friends would say. "Why don't you get married and raise a family?"

Pygmalion would always reply, "My art is wife and child to me."

Pygmalion set to work on a statue made out of the finest marble. As he chipped away at the stone, his mind began to be filled with a vision of a maiden more beautiful than any living woman. He worked on and on, never pausing for food or rest, until finally there stood before him, in smooth hard marble, the embodiment of his vision.

Pygmalion loved this statue as other men love a woman of flesh and blood. She seemed so real to him. He even spoke to her, but of course she gave no answer. He reached out to touch her, half expecting her to return the gesture, but he felt only cold, hard stone. He told her how lovely she looked and brought her presents. He draped a beautiful necklace over her and half expected, half hoped, to hear her thank him. But she remained silent and still.

His friends noticed that a change had come over the sculptor. "Tell us about your new statues," they said. But Pygmalion, driven to distraction by his own creation, only replied, "Never again shall I fashion marble into shapes of beauty."

One night, exhausted by hopeless longing, Pygmalion fell asleep at the feet of the statue. From above, Venus, the goddess of love, looked down and took pity. "Let love kindle life," she said. "Live, Galatea [gal-uh-TAY-uh], and bring joy to the heart of Pygmalion."

Something disturbed Pygmalion and he stirred from his sleep. It seemed to his tired eyes as though the statue moved. "It can not be," he cried, and slumped to the floor. Then he felt gentle arms wrap around his neck. He turned his

Venus, the goddess of love, looked down and took pity.

head and looked into the smiling eyes of Galatea, who placed her warm lips upon his.

Venus blessed the marriage of Pygmalion and Galatea. A child was soon born to them, and they lived happily for many years. Some say that when Pygmalion died and his spirit left this world, Galatea's spirit accompanied his while her body returned to the form her husband had shaped, a statue of clear white marble, placed above the sculptor's resting place in a quiet garden.

Julius Caesar

The English author William Shakespeare (1564–1616) wrote many plays about great events and famous people in history. In Julius Caesar, he dramatizes the last days and the murder of Julius Caesar [SEE-zer], one of Rome's great leaders. Here we retell Shakespeare's play in prose but quote some famous passages in the original verse.

It was mid-February, time for the Feast of the Lupercalia, in honor of the god of fertility. Ancient Rome was in a holiday mood. Many citizens had gathered along the streets in order to see the great leader Julius Caesar on his way to the festival games. Some of his wellwishers had been up early, decorating his statues with garlands in honor of Caesar's recent triumph over his enemy Pompey.

But many citizens of Rome did not hold Caesar in such high regard, for they had known and respected Pompey. They resented Caesar's attempts to glorify himself, and they feared that they would lose the freedom they cherished as Roman citizens if he became too powerful.

Soon Caesar and his retinue came along. Caesar's wife Calpurnia and the young officer Mark Antony were beside him. Suddenly a voice from the crowd called to Caesar. It was a soothsayer, one who predicts the future. "Caesar!" the soothsayer cried. "Beware the ides of March." (The ides was the fifteenth day of the month.)

"He is a dreamer," said Caesar to his companions. "Let him pass."

When Caesar's procession had moved out of sight, two noble citizens who knew Caesar well, Brutus and Cassius, remained behind and began to talk. Both were worried about Caesar's growing power. Rome was a republic, with a senate that helped make the laws; would Caesar's growing power threaten this way of government and the freedom of Roman citizens?

As Brutus and Cassius talked, they could hear shouts and applause for Caesar in the distance. "What means this shouting?" Brutus asked Cassius. "I do fear the people choose Caesar for their king."

"Ay, do you fear it?" responded Cassius. "Then must I think you would not have it so."

"I would not," said Brutus. "And yet I love him well."

Cassius became agitated and spoke to Brutus. "I know you for an honorable man, Brutus," he said. "I cannot tell what you and other men think,

"Beware the ides of March!"

but for myself, I am not in awe of Caesar. I was born free as Caesar. So were you!" There was another cheer from the people, then Cassius continued, "Why, man, Caesar doth stand like a giant and we little men walk around under his huge legs. . . . In the name of all the gods, upon what meat doth this our Caesar feed, that he is grown so great?"

Cassius's heated words seemed to trouble Brutus. He turned to Cassius and said, "For the present, say no more." Then he added, "Till we meet again, my noble friend, consider this: Brutus would rather be a slave than to call himself a son of Rome and live under a tyrant."

Now Caesar's procession returned. As they passed by, something about Cassius made Caesar uneasy, and he remarked to Antony, "Yond Cassius has a lean and hungry look. He thinks too much: such men are dangerous."

Brutus and Cassius stopped their friend Casca to ask the reason for all the shouting and applause they had heard. Casca said that Mark Antony had offered a crown to Caesar three times and that each time Caesar had refused it, which caused the people to shout their approval for his show of humility. "But, to my thinking," said Casca, "he would fain have had it." Cassius sensed that Casca too did not trust Caesar and feared his growing power.

Julius Caesar.

In the days that followed, Cassius secretly gathered a number of men who were willing to take violent steps to stop Caesar's growing power. Among the conspirators were Casca, Decius, Metellus Cimber, and other prominent men; but they still needed the support of Brutus to lend dignity to the plot, for Brutus was known throughout the city to be an honorable man. During this time, it is said that many strange signs foretold that something terrible was about to happen: fire filled the skies, lions walked the streets, and an owl hooted in the public square at midday.

One day it was rumored that the Senate was on the verge of crowning Caesar king. At last Brutus gave in. He agreed to join the conspirators at the Senate the next morning, and there they would put Caesar to death.

On the night before the bloody deed was to be done, Brutus was troubled. His wife, Portia, approached him. "Brutus," she said, "yesternight at supper you suddenly rose and walked about, musing and sighing. And when I asked you what the matter was, you stared upon me with ungentle looks. Dear, my lord, tell me the cause of your grief."

"I am not well in health, and that is all," said Brutus.

But Portia knew that something greater troubled her husband. She knelt at his feet and said, "No, my Brutus. You have some sickness within your mind. I beg you, by all your vows of love, that you unfold to me why you are so worried."

Brutus helped his wife to her feet, saying, "Kneel not, gentle Portia. Wait a while and by and by, thy bosom shall know the secrets of my heart."

The next morning, several of the conspirators went to Caesar's house to accompany him to the Senate. Before they arrived, Caesar was approached by his wife, Calpurnia. During the night she had dreamed that Caesar's statue poured forth blood like a fountain with many spouts. Now she pleaded with her husband to stay at home. "I never believed in omens," she said, "but now they frighten me. Alas, my lord, do not go forth today!"

But Caesar was determined to go. He turned to Calpurnia and said:

"Alas, my lord, do not go forth today!"

Cowards die many times before their deaths;
The valiant never taste of death but once.
Of all the wonders that I yet have heard,
It seems to me most strange that men should fear,
Seeing that death, a necessary end,
Will come when it will come.

But Calpurnia insisted until, at length, moved by his wife's fear and sorrow, Caesar relented. "For you," he said, "I will stay at home."

But shortly thereafter, when the other conspirators arrived, Caesar changed his mind. Decius told Caesar that the Senate planned to offer him a crown that day and that they would mock him for staying home because of his wife's bad dream. So Caesar dressed and went with the conspirators. As they entered the Senate House, Caesar saw the soothsayer. "The ides of March are come," Caesar said to him.

"Ay, Caesar," said the soothsayer, "but not gone."

The senators stood as Caesar took his seat. Then Metellus Cimber drew near and knelt before him. Caesar bid him rise, for he knew that Metellus was about to ask that his brother, Publius Cimber, who had been banished from Rome, be allowed to return. Brutus and Cassius came forth to support Metellus's request, but Caesar would not be persuaded.

"I am as constant as the northern star," he said. "I was constant Cimber should be banished, and constant do remain to keep him so." Other senators called upon Caesar to change his mind, but he spurned them all. Then Casca stepped behind Caesar, and saying, "Speak, hands, for me!" he struck him in the back with his dagger.

Suddenly the conspirators were upon Caesar, stabbing him on all sides. Despite their attacks Caesar stood firm—until he saw Brutus raise his hand to strike. "*Et tu, Brute?*" he said. "Even you? Then fall, Caesar!" And covering his face with his cloak, Caesar died.

The senators fled. News of Caesar's death spread quickly, and the city was in an uproar. Brutus was anxious to restore order, so when Caesar's friend Mark Antony came to him, full of humility and willing to cooperate, he was relieved. Antony promised not to oppose the new government and asked only that he be allowed to speak at Caesar's funeral. Brutus considered the request and agreed on the condition that Brutus himself speak first. In this way he could give good reason for the conspirators' bloody act, he felt, and prevent the crowd from sympathizing with Caesar. But Mark Antony had other plans: he was determined to avenge his friend's murder. He sent word to Caesar's nephew, Octavius, to keep at a safe distance and bide his time.

On the day of the funeral, Brutus ascended a pulpit in the Forum and addressed the people. "Romans, countrymen, and lovers!" he said. "Hear me for my cause, . . . and . . . believe me for mine honor. . . . If there be any in this assembly any dear friend of Caesar's, to him I say that Brutus' love to Caesar was no less than his. If then that friend demand why Brutus rose against Caesar, this is my answer: not that I loved Caesar less, but that I loved Rome more. Had you rather Caesar were living, and die all slaves, than that Caesar were dead, to live all free men? As Caesar loved me, I weep for him; . . . as he was valiant, I honor him; but as he was ambitious, I slew him. . . . Who is here so . . . vile that will not love his country? If any, speak; for him have I offended."

"None, Brutus, none," cried the people, who, though they had once cheered Caesar, were now persuaded that Caesar had threatened their freedom.

Now Mark Antony entered, dressed in mourning and helping carry Caesar's open coffin on a bier. Brutus announced that Antony had permission to give a eulogy. As Brutus departed, the crowd cheered him, some even shouting that he should be made the next Caesar. Antony entered the pulpit and spoke these words:

> Friends, Romans, countrymen, lend me your ears;
> I come to bury Caesar, not to praise him;
> The evil that men do lives after them,
> The good is oft interred with their bones,
> So let it be with Caesar. . . .

As the crowd listened, they began to think more kindly of Caesar. Antony went on:

> He was my friend, faithful and just to me:
> But Brutus says he was ambitious;
> And Brutus is an honorable man. . . .
> When that the poor have cried, Caesar hath wept:
> Ambition should be made of sterner stuff:
> Yet Brutus says he was ambitious;
> And Brutus is an honorable man.

The crowd began to get uneasy. How could this Brutus be so "honorable" if he had helped to kill a leader who was so just and kind? Antony continued:

> You all did see that on the Lupercal
> I thrice presented him a kingly crown,
> Which he did thrice refuse: was this ambition?
> Yet Brutus says he was ambitious;
> And, sure, he is an honorable man.

As Antony spoke, some people began to blame Brutus and the others for their actions. At length Antony seemed overcome with emotion. He called for the people to stand around the coffin. Then he held up Caesar's torn, bloodstained cloak for all to see. He showed them where Cassius's dagger had run it through, and Casca's. As he showed them the rip made by Brutus's dagger, he said, "This was the most unkindest cut of all." Then he pulled the cloak aside to reveal Caesar's pitiful face. This was more than the people could stand, and they began to weep sorrowfully. Some called for mutiny; some were ready to burn the house of Brutus.

Then Antony, to win the people to his cause once and for all, began to read Caesar's will. It called for every Roman citizen to be given seventy-five drachmas. "Most noble Caesar!" they cried. "We'll revenge his death." Then the angry citizens rushed forth to burn the conspirators' houses.

Cassius, Brutus, and their followers were forced to flee from Rome. They assembled troops to fight against the army of Antony and Octavius. When they were prepared to do battle, they faced a decision: should they wait for Antony and Octavius to make the first move, or should they attack? Cassius preferred to wait, but Brutus felt that the time was ripe for battle, for the enemy was growing stronger every day. "There is a tide in the affairs of men which taken at the flood leads on to fortune," he said. "On such a full sea are we now afloat, and we must take the current when it serves, or lose our ventures." Cassius agreed to Brutus's plan. The next morning they would seek the enemy at Philippi.

Brutus spent a troubled night. As he sat awake, reading, a strange sight suddenly rose before him. It was the ghost of Caesar himself! "Thou shalt see me at Philippi," warned the ghost; then it disappeared.

The next day the two armies prepared for battle. Brutus took charge of the right wing, and Cassius of the left. Brutus's soldiers fared well, but Cassius's men were driven back. Convinced that all was lost, Cassius took his own life in the old Roman way. He ordered his servant to hold his sword. Then he thrust himself against the blade, crying, "Caesar, thus thou art revenged, even with the sword that killed thee."

Brutus and the others continued to fight, but the armies of Antony and Octavius proved too strong for them. When Brutus knew at last that there was no hope of victory, he vowed to end his life as Cassius had done, rather than be captured. Brutus ran upon his sword and died.

"Thou shalt see me at Philippi," warned the ghost.

When Antony found Brutus lying dead, he was moved with admiration. "This was the noblest Roman of them all," he said to Octavius. "All the conspirators save only he did what they did in envy of great Caesar; only he acted in common good to all. His life was gentle, and the elements so mixed in him that Nature might stand up and say to all the world, 'This was a man!'"

The victorious generals buried Brutus with great dignity. Then they began restoring order to the troubled city of Rome.

The Prince and the Pauper

A selection, adapted from the novel by Mark Twain (1835–1910)

In the ancient city of London, on a certain autumn day in the sixteenth century, a boy was born to a poor family of the name of Canty, who did not want him. On the same day, another English child was born to a rich family of the name of Tudor, who did want him. All England wanted him, too. England had so longed for him, and hoped for him, and prayed God for him, that, now that he was really come, the people went nearly mad for joy. Mere acquaintances hugged and kissed each other and cried. Everybody took a holiday, and high and low, rich and poor, feasted and danced and sang and got very mellow; and they kept this up for days and nights together. There was no talk in all England but of the new baby, Edward Tudor, Prince of Wales, who lay lapped in silks and satins, unconscious of all this fuss, and not knowing that great lords and ladies were tending him and watching over him—and not caring, either. But there was no talk about the other baby, Tom Canty, lapped in his poor rags, except among the family of paupers whom he had just come to trouble with his presence.

The house in which Tom's father lived, and in which Tom grew up, was up a foul little pocket called Offal Court. It was small, decayed, and rickety, but it was packed full of wretchedly poor families. Canty's tribe occupied a room on the third floor. Tom lived with his mother and father, his twin sisters, Nan and Bet, and a grandmother. His mother loved him dearly, but his father and the grandmother were a couple of fiends. They got drunk whenever they could; then they fought each other or anybody else who came in the way. They cursed and swore always, drunk or sober. John Canty was a thief, and his mother a beggar. They made beggars of the children but failed to make thieves of them. Among, but not of, the dreadful rabble that inhabited the house, was a good old priest, and he used to get the children aside and teach them right ways secretly. Father Andrew also taught Tom a little Latin, and how to read and write.

Tom had a hard time of it but did not know it. It was the sort of time that all the Offal Court boys had; therefore he supposed it was the correct and comfortable thing. When he came

Father Andrew taught Tom a little Latin and how to read and write.

home empty-handed at night, he knew his father would curse him and thrash him first, and that when he was done the awful grandmother would do it all over again and improve on it.

Tom spent a good deal of his time listening to good Father Andrew's charming old tales and legends about giants and fairies, dwarfs and genii, gorgeous kings and princes. He read books, too, until his head grew to be full of these wonderful things, and many a night as he lay in the dark on his straw, tired, hungry, and smarting from a thrashing, he unleashed his imagination and soon forgot his aches and pains in delicious picturings to himself of the charmed life of a petted prince in a regal palace. One desire came in time to haunt him day and night—*it was to see a real prince, with his own eyes.*

By and by Tom's dreaming about princely life wrought such a strong effect upon him that he began to *act* the prince, unconsciously. His speech and manners became curiously ceremonious and courtly, to the vast admiration and amusement of his intimates. Tom even organized a royal court, with himself as the prince; his special comrades were guards, chamberlains, equerries, lords- and ladies-in-waiting, and the royal family. Daily the mock prince was received with elaborate ceremonials; daily the great affairs of the mimic kingdom were discussed in the royal council; and daily his mimic highness issued decrees to his imaginary armies, navies, and viceroyalties. After which he would go forth in his rags and beg a few farthings, eat his poor crust, take his customary cuffs and abuse, and then stretch himself upon his handful of foul straw and resume his empty grandeurs in his dreams.

One morning, as Tom wandered the city, begging, he found himself near Westminster Abbey. He stared in glad wonder at the vast pile of masonry, the frowning bastions and turrets, the huge stone gateway, with its gilded bars and its magnificent array of colossal granite lions, and the other signs and symbols of English royalty.

At each side of the gilded gate stood a living statue, that is to say, an erect and stately and motionless man-at-arms, clad from head to heel in shining steel armor. At a respectful distance were many country folk and people from the city, waiting for any chance glimpse of royalty.

Poor little Tom, in his rags, approached and was moving slowly and timidly past the sentinels, with a beating heart and a rising hope, when all at once he caught sight through the golden bars of a spectacle that almost made him shout for joy. Within was a comely boy, whose clothing was all of lovely silks and satins, shining with jewels; at his hip a little jeweled sword and dagger; dainty buskins on his feet, with red heels; and on his head a jaunty crimson cap, with drooping plumes fastened with a great sparkling gem. Oh! He was a prince—a prince, a living prince, a real prince! The pauper boy's prayer had been answered at last!

Tom's breath came quick and short with excitement, and his eyes grew big with wonder and delight. Everything gave way in his mind instantly to one desire: to get close to the prince and have a good, devouring look at him. Before he knew what he was about, he had his face against the bars of the gate. The next instant one of the soldiers snatched him rudely away and sent him spinning among the gaping crowd of country gawkers and London idlers. The soldier said: "Mind thy manners, thou young beggar!"

The crowd jeered and laughed; but the young prince sprang to the gate with his face flushed and his eyes flashing with indignation and cried out: "How dar'st thou use a poor lad like that! How dar'st thou use the king my father's meanest subject so! Open the gates, and let him in!"

You should have seen that fickle crowd snatch off their hats then. You should have heard them cheer and shout, "Long live the Prince of Wales!"

The soldiers opened the gates and presented arms as the little Prince of Poverty passed in, in his fluttering rags, to join hands with the Prince of Limitless Plenty. Edward Tudor said:

"Open the gates, and let him in!"

"Thou lookest tired and hungry; thou'st been treated ill. Come with me."

Prince Edward took Tom to a rich apartment in the palace. By his command a repast was brought such as Tom had never encountered before except in books. The prince sent away the servants; then he sat nearby and asked questions while Tom ate.

"What is thy name, lad?"

"Tom Canty, an' it please thee, sir."

"'Tis an odd one. Where dost live?"

"In the city, please thee, sir. Offal Court."

"Offal Court! Truly, 'tis another odd one. Hast parents?"

"Parents have I, sir, and a grandam likewise, and twin sisters, Nan and Bet."

"And are thy elders kind to thee?"

"My mother is, but my grandmother hath a wicked heart and worketh evil all her days."

"Doth she mistreat thee?"

"There be times that she stayeth her hand, being asleep or overcome with drink; but when she hath her judgment clear again, she maketh it up to me with goodly beatings."

A fierce look came into the little prince's eyes, and he cried out: "What! Beatings?"

"O, indeed, yes, please you, sir."

"*Beatings!*—And thou so frail and little! Hark ye: before the night come, she shall hie her to the Tower. The king my father—"

"In sooth, you forget, sir, her low degree. The Tower is for the great alone."

"True, indeed. I had not thought of that. I will consider of her punishment. Is thy father kind to thee?"

"Not more than Gammer Canty, sir."

"Fathers be alike, mayhap. Mine hath not a doll's temper. He smiteth with a heavy hand, yet spareth me; he spareth me not always with his tongue, though, sooth to say. How old be thy sisters?"

"Fifteen, an' it please you, sir."

"The Lady Elizabeth, my sister, is fourteen, and the Lady Jane Grey, my cousin, is of mine own age, and comely and gracious

"How old be thy sisters?"

withal; but my sister the Lady Mary, with her gloomy mien and—Look you: do thy sisters forbid their servants to smile, lest the sin destroy their souls?"

"They? Oh, dost think, sir, that *they* have servants?"

The little prince contemplated the little pauper gravely a moment, then said: "And prithee, why not? Who helpeth them undress at night? Who attireth them when they rise?"

"None, sir. Wouldst have them take off their garment and sleep without—like the beasts?"

"Their garment! Have they but one?"

"Ah, good your worship, what would they do with more? Truly, they have not two bodies each."

"It is a quaint and marvelous thought! Thy pardon, I had not meant to laugh. But thy good Nan and thy Bet shall have raiment and lackeys enow, and that soon, too: my cofferer shall look to it. No, thank me not; 'tis nothing. But tell me of thy Offal Court. Hast thou a pleasant life there?"

"In truth, yes, so please you, sir, save when one is hungry. There be Punch-and-Judy shows, and monkeys—and there be plays wherein they that play do shout and fight till all are slain."

"Tell me more."

"We lads of Offal Court do strive against each other with the cudgel, sometimes."

The prince's eyes flashed. Said he: "Marry, that would I not mislike. Tell me more."

"We strive in races, sir, to see who of us shall be fleetest."

"That would I like also. Speak on."

"In summer, sir, we wade and swim in the canals and in the river, and each doth duck his neighbor, and spatter him with water, and dive and shout and tumble and—"

"'Twould be worth my father's kingdom but to enjoy it once! Prithee go on."

"We dance and sing about the Maypole in Cheapside; we play in the sand, each covering his neighbor up; and times we make mud pastry—oh, the lovely mud, it hath not its like for delightfulness in all the world!—We do fairly wallow in the mud, sir, saving your worship's presence."

"Oh, prithee, say no more, 'tis glorious! If that I could but clothe me in raiment like to thine, and strip my feet, and revel in the mud once, just once, with none to rebuke me or forbid, meseemeth I could forgo the crown!"

"And if that I could clothe me once, sweet sir, as thou art clad—just once—"

"O-ho, wouldst like it? Then so shall it be. Doff thy rags, and don these splendors, lad! It is a brief happiness, but will be not less keen for that. We will have it while we may, and change again before any man knows the difference."

A few minutes later the little Prince of Wales was garlanded with Tom's fluttering odds and ends, and the little Prince of Pauperdom was tricked out in the gaudy plumage of royalty. The two went and stood side by side before a great mirror, and lo, a miracle: there did not seem to have been any change made! They stared at each other, then at the glass, then at each other again. At last the princeling said: "Thou hast the same hair, the same eyes, the same voice and manner, the same form and stature, the same face and countenance, that I bear. Fared we forth naked, there is none could say which was you, and which the Prince of Wales. And, now that I am clothed as thou wert clothed, it seemeth I should be able the more nearly to feel as thou didst when that brute soldier—Hark ye, is not this a bruise upon your hand?"

"Yes; but it is a slight thing, and your worship knoweth that the poor man-at-arms—"

"Peace! It was a shameful thing and a cruel!" cried the little prince, stamping his bare foot. "If the king—Stir not a step till I come again! It is a command!"

In a moment he was out at the door and flying through the palace grounds in his rags, with a hot face and glowing eyes. As soon as he reached the great gate, he seized the bars, and tried to shake them, shouting: "Open! Unbar the gates!"

The soldier that had maltreated Tom obeyed promptly; and as the prince burst through the portal, half smothered with royal wrath, the soldier fetched him a sounding box on the ear that sent him whirling to the roadway, and said: "Take that, thou beggar's spawn, for what thou got'st me from His Highness!"

The crowd roared with laughter. The prince picked himself out of the mud and made fiercely at the sentry, shouting:

"I am the Prince of Wales, my person is sacred; and thou shalt hang for laying thy hand upon me!"

The soldier said mockingly, "I salute Your Gracious Highness!" Then angrily, "Be off, thou crazy rubbish!"

Here the jeering crowd closed around the poor little prince and hustled him far down the road, hooting him and jeering: "Make way for His Royal Highness! Make way for the Prince of Wales!"

After hours of persistent pursuit and persecution, the little prince was at last deserted by the rabble and left to himself. He bathed his bleeding feet in a brook, then passed on, till he saw a crowd of schoolboys playing at ball and leapfrog. With native dignity, the prince said: "Good lads, say to your master that Edward Prince of Wales desireth speech with him."

"I salute Your Gracious Highness!"

A great shout went up at this, and one rude fellow said: "Marry, art thou his grace's messenger, beggar?"

Poor Edward drew himself up proudly and said: "I am the prince; and it ill beseemeth you to use me so."

This was vastly enjoyed, and there was more laughter. Someone shouted: "Hale him forth! To the horsepond, to the horsepond! Where be the dogs? Ho, there, Lion! Ho, Fangs!"

Then followed such a thing as England had never seen before— the sacred person of the heir to the throne rudely buffeted by plebeian hands and set upon and torn by dogs.

Meanwhile, Tom Canty, left alone in the prince's cabinet, turned himself this way and that

The Prince set upon and torn by dogs.

before the great mirror, admiring his finery; then walked away, imitating the prince's high-bred carriage, and still observing results in the glass. Next he drew the beautiful sword and bowed, kissing the blade and laying it across his breast.

Tom played with the jeweled dagger that hung upon his thigh; he examined the costly and exquisite ornaments of the room; he tried each of the sumptuous chairs and wondered if his relatives would believe the marvelous tale he should tell when he got home.

At the end of half an hour it suddenly occurred to him that the prince had been gone a long time; he grew uneasy, then restless, then distressed. Presently the door swung open, and a silken page said: "The Lady Jane Grey."

The door closed, and a sweet young girl, richly clad, bounded toward him calling him my lord.

Tom's breath was nearly failing him; but he made shift to stammer out: "Ah, be merciful, thou! In sooth, I am no lord, but only poor Tom Canty of Offal Court in the city. Prithee let me see the prince, and he will of his grace restore to me my rags and let me hence unhurt. Oh, be thou merciful, and save me!"

By this time the boy was on his knees and supplicating with his eyes and uplifted hands as well as with his tongue. The young girl seemed horrorstricken. She cried out: "Oh, my lord, on thy knees? and to *me*!"

Then she fled in fright; and Tom, smitten with despair, sank down, murmuring: "There is no help, there is no hope. Now will they come and take me."

Whilst he lay there benumbed with terror, dreadful tidings were speeding through the palace. The whisper, for it was whispered always, flew from menial to menial, from lord to lady, down all the long corridors, from story to story, from saloon to saloon, *The prince hath gone mad! The prince hath gone mad!*"

"Oh, be thou merciful, and save me!"

GRAMMAR AND USAGE

Is It a Sentence?

Did you ever read one of those beginner's books full of short, choppy sentences?

> See the dog. The dog barks. The dog barks at the cat. The cat runs. Run, cat, run!

Thank goodness all books aren't written like that! Short, simple sentences have their place: they can be informative and effective. But good writers use a variety of sentence structures, mixing short and long, simple and complex.

We're going to take a look at four basic kinds of sentences, but before we can do that, we need to understand what a clause is.

A *clause* is a group of words with a subject and predicate. (Remember what subjects and predicates are?) Here's a clause:

> while Felicia waited for the bus

What's the subject of that clause? It's *Felicia*. And the predicate is *waited*. Here are some more clauses. Can you find the subject and predicate in each?

> unless it rains today
> although his zipper broke
> when the teacher fainted

If someone came into the room and announced, "Unless it rains today," how would you respond? Perhaps you would say something like this: "Yes, go on. Unless it rains today . . . *what?*" Try reading each of the clauses above aloud. Do you notice how each leaves you hanging, wanting to know more? That's because none of those clauses expresses a complete thought. A clause that expresses an incomplete or partial thought is called a *dependent clause*. A dependent clause is not a complete sentence; it can't stand on its own. A dependent clause depends on another group of words to express a complete thought, and thus to make a complete sentence.

Let's complete the dependent clauses above. For example:

> While Felicia waited for the bus, she dug in her purse
> to find another quarter.
> We're going to cook hamburgers on the grill unless it
> rains today.

You try completing the others.

Now, look at the words we've used to complete the dependent clauses:

> She dug in her purse to find another quarter.
> We're going to cook hamburgers on the grill.

Those clauses can stand on their own. Each one forms a sentence that expresses a complete thought. A clause that can stand on its own and expresses a complete thought is called an *independent clause*. In the following sentence, the independent clause is italicized:

> *The Trojans were winning the war* until Achilles returned to battle.

Try identifying the dependent and independent clauses in the following sentence:

> When William Jennings Bryan spoke, his powerful words moved everyone
> in the audience.

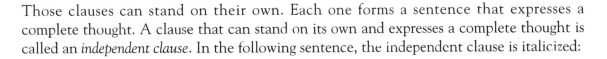

Four Kinds of Sentences

By mixing dependent and independent clauses, you can make different kinds of sentences. A sentence with one independent clause is called a *simple sentence*. For example:

> She jumped.

A simple sentence doesn't have to be so short. For example, here's another simple sentence:

> She jumped over the high bar with the grace and strength of a powerful deer.

Sometimes you can't get everything you need to say into a simple sentence. Then you might use a *compound sentence*, which has two or more independent clauses. For example:

> She jumped over the high bar with the grace and strength of a deer,
> but her teammate slipped and fell on her face.
> Jesse decided to leave the party early, and I decided to follow soon after.
> I could tell Mandy to meet us at the museum, or we could meet at a restaurant.

Notice that in the compound sentences above, the independent clauses are held together by a comma working with a *conjunction*:

> , but
> , and
> , or

You can use a comma and a conjunction to join the independent clauses in a compound sentence, or you can use the punctuation mark called a *semicolon*:

> Jesse decided to leave the party early; I decided to follow soon after.

A comma alone is *not* enough to join two independent clauses. In the example above, if you used a comma instead of a semicolon, you'd be making a mistake known as a *comma-splice*, like this:

> Jesse decided to leave the party early, I decided to follow soon after.

Here's another example of a comma-splice error:

> The teacher explained the equation, I couldn't solve it.

You can correct that comma-splice by adding a conjunction or by using a semicolon:

> The teacher explained the equation, but I couldn't solve it.
> The teacher explained the equation; I couldn't solve it.

You could also create a different kind of sentence, one that mixes a dependent clause with an independent clause, like this:

> Although the teacher explained the equation, I couldn't solve it.

A sentence with an independent clause and at least one dependent clause is called a *complex sentence*. In this case, "complex" doesn't necessarily mean "difficult." In fact, a complex sentence might be easier to understand than two simple sentences, because a complex sentence can clarify the relation between separate thoughts. For example:

1. (Two simple sentences) The coach decided to pull the star player out of the game. We won by ten points.
2. (One complex sentence) Although the coach decided to pull the star player out of the game, we won by ten points.

You can also make what is called a *compound-complex sentence* by joining two or more independent clauses with one or more dependent clauses, like this:

> Although the coach decided to pull the star player out of the game, we won by ten points, and we remained the district champions for the third year in a row.

You've learned about four different kinds of sentences: simple, compound, complex, and compound-complex. The important thing is not to label the different sentences that you read, but to use different kinds of sentences when you write. Good writers use a variety of sentence structures. Let's look at how the great writer Mark Twain varies the sentences he writes. Here's a paragraph from *The Adventures of Tom Sawyer*. It describes how Tom feels on a Monday morning when he doesn't want to go to school. Read it aloud to get a better sense of the varied length and rhythm of the sentences.

> Tom lay thinking. Presently it occurred to him that he wished he was sick; then he could stay home from school. Here was a vague possibility. He canvassed his system. No ailment was found, and he investigated again. This time he thought he could detect colicky symptoms, and he began to encourage them with considerable hope. But they soon grew feeble, and presently died wholly away. He reflected further. Suddenly he discovered something. One of his upper front teeth was loose. This was lucky; he was about to begin to groan, as a "starter," as he called it, when it occurred to him that if he came into court with that argument, his aunt would pull it out, and that would hurt. So he thought he would hold the tooth in reserve for the present, and seek further.

Like Mark Twain, you can use a variety of sentences when you write, and so give your sentences an effective rhythm and pace—almost like a good song.

Active and Passive Voice

Sentences can be written in either the active or the passive voice. Here's a sentence in the active voice:

> The senators approved the new law.

Here's a sentence that says the same thing but uses the passive voice:

> The new law was approved by the senate.

In the *active voice*, the subject of the sentence performs the action: *the senators approved*. In the *passive voice*, the subject of the sentence is acted upon by some other agent, or by something unnamed: *the new law* is acted upon (in this case approved) *by the senate*.

Sometimes passive voice is like a magician that makes the person responsible for an event disappear.

> Active: The cook prepared the roast.
> Passive: The roast was prepared.
>
> Active: I made a mistake.
> Passive: A mistake was made.

Notice that passive constructions usually include a form of the verb *to be*, such as *was* or *were*.

There are some cases in which you may want to use passive voice in your own writing, but good writers are careful not to use the passive voice too much, because a string of sentences in the passive voice tends to be less lively and interesting than a string of sentences in the active voice. See if you can change each of the following sentences from passive voice to active.

> Nuts are loved by squirrels.
> The Mets were beaten by the Yankees.
> We were entertained by the speaker.

Greek and Latin Roots

Many words in English are built up of word parts (prefixes, suffixes, and roots) that come from Latin and ancient Greek. If you study the elements listed below, they will help you understand new words. Once you've read the examples for each word, see if you can think of another word that includes the same root.

Annus is Latin for "year." *Annual* events, like *anniversaries*, happen once every year.

Ante- is Latin for "before." *Antebellum* refers to the period before a war. An *antecedent* is an event that happened before another.

Aqua means "water" in Latin. An *aquatic* animal lives in water—or in an *aquarium*.

Astro- is Greek for "star." *Astronomers* study the stars, and *astronauts* travel among the stars.

Bi- is Latin for "two." To *bisect* a line is to divide it into two parts. A *bipartisan* movement is supported by two political parties.

Bios is Greek for "life." *Biology* is the study of living organisms. A *biography* tells the history of a person's life.

Centum is Latin for "hundred." A *percent* equals one part in a hundred, and a *cent* is one one-hundreth of a dollar.

Decem is Latin for "ten." A *decade* lasts ten years. Our math system is based on *decimal* places, or groups of ten.

Dico is Latin for "say." A person who takes *dictation* writes down what someone else says. A *dictator* is a leader who tells everybody what to do.

Duo is Latin for "two." The superheroes Batman and Robin were called the "dynamic *duo*" because there were two of them. To *duplicate* means to make a copy of something.

Ge- and *geo-* come from the Greek word for "Earth." *Geologists* study Earth; *geographers* study the physical features of Earth's surface.

Hydro- comes from the Greek word for "water." A *hydrant* is a public water pipe used by firefighters. When water is used to create electricity, it is called *hydroelectric* power.

Magnus is Latin for "large" or "great." A *magnificent* object is large and impressive. *Magnification* makes a small object look larger.

Mega- means "large" or "great" in Greek. A *megaphone* makes your voice more powerful. A *megalomaniac* has an exaggerated sense of his own greatness.

Mikro- (also spelled *micro-*) means the opposite of "mega" in Greek—"small." A *microscope* is used to inspect tiny objects; a *microfilm* is a small image of a printed page.

Minus is Latin for "small." We use this word when we do subtraction: "five *minus* three equals two." If something is *minor*, it is small and unimportant.

Mono- is Greek for "single" or "one." A *monologue* is a long speech by one actor. A *monarch* is a single person who rules a kingdom.

Omni- is Latin for "all." An *omniscient* person knows all there is to know; an *omnipotent* ruler controls all the power.

Phil- means "to love" in Greek. *Philosophers* love and pursue wisdom; *philanthropists* love and help other people.

Phon- means "sound" or "voice" in Greek. A *phoneme* is a single sound, like the "*p*" sound in *pool*. A *telephone* conveys the sound of your voice to someone far away.

Photo- (from Greek) means "light." *Photographs* use light to make pictures; *photocopiers* use light to reproduce printed pages.

Poly- is Greek for "many." A *polygon* is a geometric figure with many sides. A *polytheist* believes in many gods.

Post- means "after" in Latin. A *posthumous* award is given after the recipient has died. To leave something for *posterity* means leaving it for future generations.

Pre- means "before" in Latin. A *prefix* is added before a word. To *predict* means to guess something before it happens. If you are *prepared*, you are ready for something before it happens.

Primus is Latin for "first." A *primary* goal is your first or most important goal. A *primitive* civilization is one of the first civilizations.

Proto- means first in Greek. A *prototype* for a new airplane is the first model. A *protozoan* is one of the first and simplest animals.

Psyche is Greek for "soul" or "mind." A *psychologist* studies the mind. If you *psych* yourself up, you prepare your mind for a task.

Quartus is Latin for "fourth." A *quarter* can be a fourth of a game or a fourth of a dollar. A *quartet* is a group of four musicians.

Tele- means "far away" in Greek. A *television* receives a signal from far away; a *telephone* lets you talk to people who are far away.

Thermo- is Greek for "heat." A *thermometer* tells you how hot it is; a *thermostat* regulates the temperature in a building.

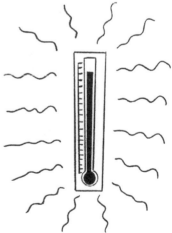

Tri- (from both Latin and Greek) means "three." A *trilogy* is a work with three parts. A *triangle* has three sides.

Unus is Latin for "one." A *unit* is one item. When all voters vote for one person, we say the vote is *unanimous*.

Video and *visus* mean "see" in Latin. A music *video* lets you see a song being performed; a *visual* aid, like a chart, helps people see what you are trying to say.

Vita is Latin for "life." *Vitality* is the life force. A *vitamin* is something important for life.

SAYINGS AND PHRASES

Every culture has sayings and phrases that can be difficult for outsiders to understand. In this section we introduce a handful of common English sayings and phrases. As you study these phrases, try to imagine a situation in which you might use each one.

All for one and one for all

This saying means that members of a team must work together.

All's well that ends well.

This saying from Shakespeare means that if something turns out okay in the end, the difficulties or mistakes along the way can be forgotten.

Bee in your bonnet

If a bee flew into your hat, wouldn't you be annoyed? When we say someone has a "bee in her bonnet," we mean she is annoyed by something.

The best-laid plans of mice and men go oft awry.

When something goes awry, it goes wrong. We use this phrase to remind others that even when you plan very carefully things can still go wrong.

A bird in the hand is worth two in the bush.

A hunter who has shot one bird is better off than a hunter who can see two birds hiding in a bush. When you tell someone "a bird in the hand is worth two in the bush," you remind them to be content with what they already have and not go chasing after something that is uncertain.

Bite the dust

When someone is defeated, we say "he bit the dust." The saying comes from ancient warfare of the sort described in Homer's *Iliad:* when a warrior was beaten, he fell facedown in the dust.

Catch-as-catch-can

We use this phrase when we don't have all the materials we'd like to have and so have to improvise: "We don't have enough uniforms for all of the players, so it'll be catch-as-catch-can this season."

Don't cut off your nose to spite your face.

Suppose you didn't like your face—would you cut off your nose to change it? That would be counterproductive. When a person takes drastic measures in a situation where something more reasonable could be done, we say the person is cutting off his nose to spite his face.

Don't lock the stable door after the horse is stolen.

We use this saying to remind each other that it is silly to take precautionary measures after the damage has already been done.

Don't look a gift horse in the mouth.

This saying means that you shouldn't find fault with something that has been given to you. If someone gave you a free bike and you complained that it wasn't your favorite color, you would be "looking a gift horse in the mouth." The saying comes from the practice of checking a horse's teeth and gums before buying it: a buyer can tell from the mouth if a horse is healthy.

Eat humble pie

If you have to "eat humble pie," it means you find yourself in an unpleasant situation in which you are forced to admit your mistakes or weaknesses.

A fool and his money are soon parted.

A foolish person won't hold on to cash for very long.

A friend in need is a friend indeed.

Some people are your friends when you are happy, but they abandon you when you are having trouble. A true friend is someone who stands by you when you are in need of help, comfort, or anything else.

Give the devil his due.

This proverb means that, even if you don't like someone, you should at least try to give that person credit for his or her strengths.

Good fences make good neighbors.

This saying suggests that by clearly marking the boundaries between yourselves and other people, you can stay on better terms. It was made famous in a poem by Robert Frost.

He who hesitates is lost.

If you wait before you do something, you may miss your chance. People use this saying to urge someone to take action without delay.

He who laughs last laughs best.

People often laugh at new ideas. But if the idea works out in the end, then the person who thought of it gets the "last laugh."

Hitch your wagon to a star.

When people tell you to "hitch your wagon to a star," they are encouraging you to aim high and try to be the best at what you do.

If wishes were horses, beggars would ride.

If wishing alone made things happen, then even the poorest people would have everything they wanted. This proverb was coined back when horses were an important means of transportation but not everyone could afford one.

The leopard can't change its spots.

It's sometimes impossible to change a particular trait, because that trait is part of a person's innermost self. Can you make a greedy person generous? Can the leopard change his spots?

Little strokes fell great oaks.

A task may seem overwhelming, but if you break it into smaller, more manageable tasks and keep at it, you can achieve great things.

Money is the root of all evil.

Greed and the desire for money can sometimes make people do things they wouldn't otherwise do. Another version of the saying, found in the King James translation of the Bible, is "the love of money is the root of all evil."

Necessity is the mother of invention.

When you really need to accomplish something, you sometimes come up with a clever way of doing it.

It's never over till it's over.

This saying means that you can never be sure what the outcome of something—a football game, a book, or even life—will be until the very end.

Nose out of joint

We say someone's nose is "out of joint" if the person is annoyed.

Nothing will come of nothing.

This saying tells us that, without effort, we can't accomplish anything.

Once bitten, twice shy

If a dog bites you, you will probably avoid dogs in the future. If you have an unpleasant experience doing something once, you are likely to be hesitant ("shy") about doing it again.

On tenterhooks

A person "on tenterhooks" is waiting nervously for something to happen.

Pot calling the kettle black

This saying means you should not blame others for something you also do yourself. If you are a loudmouth and you tell a friend she talks too much, that's an example of "the pot calling the kettle black." In the old days, pots and kettles were both made of iron— and were both black.

Procrastination is the thief of time.

Procrastination means putting things off, avoiding tasks you need to do. If you procrastinate, then you may not have time for other things. Thus, procrastination "steals" your time.

The proof of the pudding is in the eating.

This saying means that you can't really know whether a thing is good or bad until you try it. An idea may sound great, but you won't know for sure until you see how it turns out. Sometimes this is shortened to "the proof is in the pudding."

R. I. P.

This abbreviation for "Rest in Peace" is used on gravestones.

The road to hell is paved with good intentions.

Sometimes people have good intentions, but their ideas have bad consequences: "The radicals may have had the best intentions, but, you know, the road to hell is paved with good intentions."

Rome wasn't built in a day.

It took many decades to build the imperial city of Rome. We use this expression to remind each other that it takes a long time to achieve great things; we must be patient.

Rule of thumb

A "rule of thumb" is a general guideline based on experience: "As a rule of thumb, I don't like TV sitcoms."

A stitch in time saves nine.

In sewing you can sometimes fix a small hole with one stitch, whereas if you wait till the hole gets larger, you might need to make several stitches. By taking some care early on, you may save yourself much trouble later.

Strike while the iron is hot.

To work with iron, a blacksmith heats the metal and then strikes it with a mallet. Once the iron cools off, it isn't easily shaped. When someone tells you to "strike while the iron is hot," the person means that you should act now and not wait till later.

Tempest in a teapot

A teapot is a small object, and a tempest is a large storm. When someone gets overly excited about something that isn't really that important, we say, "Don't make a tempest in a teapot."

Tenderfoot

A tenderfoot is a person who has very little experience at something.

There's more than one way to skin a cat.

There are many ways to solve a problem. If one way doesn't work, try another.

Touché!

Fencers say this French word meaning "touched" when they score a point against their opponents, so when somebody scores a point against us in a discussion or an argument, we sometimes say touché!

Truth is stranger than fiction.

Things that happen in real life can sometimes be more unusual or surprising than things that writers make up in stories.

II.
History and Geography

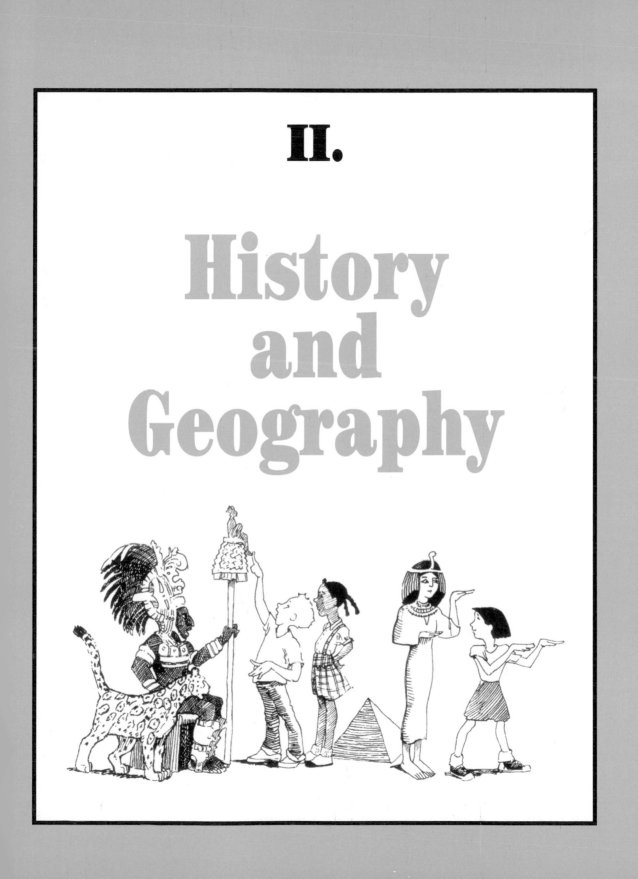

Introduction

This chapter gives a brief overview of history and geography topics for sixth grade. The geography topics include maps and deserts. The world history section begins with an account of the ancient world and stretches all the way forward in time to the Enlightenment and the Industrial Revolution. American history looks at the impact of the Industrial Revolution in the United States in the late 1800s, as well as immigration, urbanization, and reform.

Many of the topics discussed in this chapter can be connected with topics in other chapters. For example, the discussion of Ancient Greece complements the study of mythology and Homer's epics in the English chapter, and the study of classical art in the Visual Arts chapter.

Parents and teachers are encouraged to build on the foundation provided here by discussing history with children and seeking out additional books. We especially recommend the Pearson Learning/Core Knowledge history and geography series, described on our website:

www.coreknowledge.org.

WORLD GEOGRAPHY

Latitude and Longitude

If you read the previous book in this series, you learned about Earth's grid system, a system of lines called *coordinates* that measure distance in degrees of latitude and longitude. Using the grid system, any spot on Earth's surface can be located. Let's briefly review this system that is so important to finding places on maps and globes.

Parallels are imaginary lines running east-west on maps and globes. They measure degrees (°) of *latitude* north and south of the equator (0° latitude) to the North Pole (90° north latitude) and South Pole (90° south latitude). *Meridians* are imaginary lines running north-south on maps and globes. They measure degrees of *longitude* east and west of the prime meridian (0° longitude) to the 180th meridian. The prime meridian runs through Greenwich, England (near London), the site of a famous observatory. The international date line generally follows the 180th meridian.

Since parallels measure distance in both directions from the equator, they must always be clearly marked as being either north (N) or south (S). Only the equator can be indicated simply by its 0 (degree) location. So, too, must all meridians (except 0° and 180°) be indicated by their degrees either east (E) or west (W) from the prime meridian.

Use the map of the Middle East on page 83 to practice locating coordinates. What body of water would you be near at 40° N, 50°E? How about 20° N, 60° E? What peninsula would you be on at 40° N, 30° E? How about 20° N, 50° E? What city, holy to Muslims, is located near 20° N, 40°E?

Sunlight and the Seasons

Some important lines and points on Earth's surface are determined by the astronomical relationship between Earth and the sun. The location of these points and lines is determined by the way sunlight strikes Earth's surface during various seasons of the year. The equator, for example, is the midpoint between the North Pole and the South Pole. It is also the point at which the sun rises at 6:00 A.M. and sets at 6:00 P.M. (solar time) every day of the year. At the opposite extreme, at the poles, the sun remains above the horizon for six months and then sinks below the horizon for half a year.

All places on Earth's surface receive six months of daylight and six months of darkness each year, but they accumulate these totals according to very different patterns of light and darkness. The equator gets 12 hours of daylight every day, summer or winter—six months of daylight over the course of a year. The North Pole gets its six months of daylight all at once, followed by six months of darkness. Where you live, are the summer days much longer than the winter days? The farther north or south of the equator you live, the greater will be the seasonal differences.

What Is a Desert?

What do you think of when you hear the word *desert*? Most people think of deserts as being hot, dry places, but notice that the map below shows both hot and cold deserts. Many scientists define deserts based on the amount of moisture, or *precipitation*, that falls each year. Any area that gets less than ten inches of precipitation is considered a desert. Generally, few plants can grow in areas with so little precipitation.

In the Arctic and Antarctic regions, the climate is very cold, and most precipitation falls as snow. This snow stays frozen on the ground and is not available for plant growth. So these regions are considered "cold deserts."

Hot deserts, on the other hand, have high daytime temperatures, often soaring above 100° F. The highest temperature ever recorded — 136°F — occurred in the Sahara Desert in Africa. However, temperatures in hot deserts may drop sharply at night.

In hot deserts, as in cold deserts, the *aridity*, or lack of moisture, places severe limits on plant growth. However, contrary to what many people think, hot deserts are not lifeless wastelands. They are home to a fascinating variety of plants and animals that are well adapted to the hot, dry desert conditions.

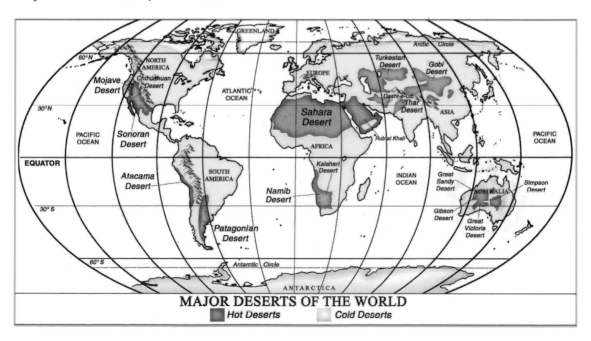

MAJOR DESERTS OF THE WORLD
■ Hot Deserts   □ Cold Deserts

When most people think of deserts, they think of shifting sand dunes. But deserts contain many different kinds of terrain. In many hot deserts, Earth's surface is covered with bare rock, boulders, and gravel. Worldwide, only about 10 percent of all desert surfaces are covered by sand. Some deserts are mountainous, such as those in the southwestern United States. Others, like vast expanses of the Sahara Desert, the Gobi Desert of Asia, and much of the desert region of Australia, are quite flat.

The Formation of Deserts

When you look at the map of the world's deserts, do you notice any patterns in their locations? Notice that there are virtually no major deserts in the tropical areas just north and just south of the equator, but there are quite a few deserts in the areas 20 to 30 degrees north and south of the equator. In order to understand why this is, you must first know something about the atmosphere, its constantly moving masses of warm and cold air, and the moisture carried by that air.

When a pan of liquid is heated on a stove, some of the water evaporates and becomes *vapor*—invisible moisture in the air. The amount of moisture air can hold is influenced by temperature. Warm air can hold more moisture than cold air. You have seen an example of this if you have ever seen droplets of water forming on the outside of a cool beverage container. When the air comes in contact with the container, it is cooled and gives off moisture, which is deposited in droplets on the side of the container. This is called *condensation*.

Our atmosphere is made up of masses of warmer and cooler air that are constantly in motion. The hot air holds more moisture than the cold air and can be pushed upward by cooler, heavier air underneath it. Air masses near the equator are hot and contain a lot of moisture that has evaporated from the oceans and other sources. Just as a hot air balloon rises, so do these warm, moist, equatorial air masses. As this hot, moist air rises, it cools, causing the moisture in the air to form huge clouds. When these clouds can hold no more water, the moisture in the clouds falls as rain. Generally, this rain falls in a broad band between the Tropic of Cancer ($23\frac{1}{2}°$ N) and the Tropic of Capricorn ($23\frac{1}{2}°$ S).

By the time these air masses reach 25 to 30 degrees north or south latitude, where many of the world's hot deserts are located, they have lost most of their moisture. Little if any is left to fall as rain. Dry air in the upper atmosphere warms up as it sinks toward the earth. As it piles up, it also forms a high-pressure system. Air within this high pressure then flows as surface wind back toward the equator. Along the way, the warm, dry air acts like a sponge, sucking up moisture. (Hot air, remember, can hold a lot of moisture.) This moisture does not fall until the warm air begins to rise again at the equator and then begins to cool. At that point the cycle starts over again, with more rain falling near the equator and more dry air passing over the areas 20 to 30 degrees north and south of the equator. Can you see how, over many centuries, this weather pattern could make a desert?

This map shows two reasons deserts are dry. First, most rain falls near the equator. By the time the air reaches areas north and south of the equator, it contains little moisture. Second, hot air can hold more moisture than cool air and tends to absorb moisture. So hot air moving from mid-latitude regions back toward the equator sucks moisture out of the desert landscape.

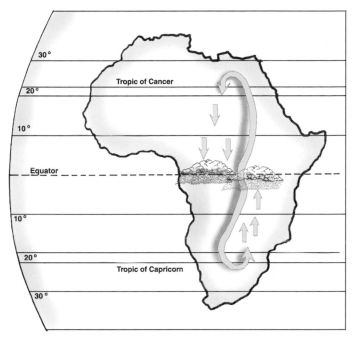

Have you ever been to a desert? Did you see many clouds? Generally speaking, there are few clouds in the desert. You've just learned why this is. By the time air masses reach the deserts, they have lost most of their moisture, so clouds rarely form. With few clouds to block sunlight, the sunlight beats down relentlessly on the already dry earth, baking it, drying it out, and keeping it a desert. The lack of clouds over deserts explains why temperatures get so hot during the day, but it also helps explain why deserts can get quite cool at night. Without a blanket of clouds to keep the heat contained, the heated air escapes very quickly into the atmosphere and the desert cools rapidly. This is why deserts often experience scorchingly hot days and surprisingly cold nights.

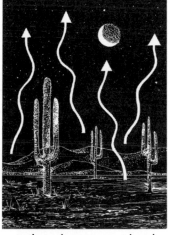

Cloud cover traps hot air and directs it back toward Earth.

When there is no cloud cover at night, deserts lose hot air and cool rapidly.

Why Deserts Are Dry

You now know that Earth's general weather patterns are responsible for the formation of some hot deserts. But there are also other factors that can keep moist air from reaching desert areas. Sometimes, deserts are located far from large bodies of water. Moisture-carrying winds simply lose most of their water vapor before they reach places that are far inland. Look back at the map on page 77 and notice how far inland the Gobi Desert is located. Winds blowing toward the Gobi Desert lose most of their moisture by the time they reach Central Asia.

You will notice that there are other deserts, such as the Atacama in South America, that are near the sea. At first, this may seem strange. If being far from the sea helps make areas like the Gobi Desert very arid, shouldn't being close to the sea make an area like the Atacama Desert moist? In the case of the Atacama, the desert conditions are partly caused by wind patterns and by the adjacent Andes Mountains. Between the equator and 30° S latitude, moisture-carrying winds blow from east to west, from the Atlantic Ocean across the eastern part of South America. However, as these winds move west, the hot, wet air is forced up by the towering Andes Mountains. As the air cools, rain falls — but most of it falls on the eastern side of the Andes. By the time the winds reach the sheltered, downwind side of the mountain, they are dry.

Deserts formed on the downwind side of a mountain are said to be in a *rain shadow*. In addition to the Atacama, much of the desert region in the western interior of the United States is located in a rain shadow, including the Sonoran Desert, which extends from northwestern Mexico into the southwestern United States. So, too, is South America's Patagonian Desert, which lies in the rain shadow of the southern Andes Mountains.

Deserts in a rain shadow: rain falls on the mountainside that faces a water source rather than on the sheltered side of the mountains.

Moist wind

Dry wind

Desert

Another factor that sometimes works to keep deserts dry is ocean currents. Again, the Atacama provides an example. A cold-water current skirts the western coast of South America. Air over the current is cooled, but as it moves inland over the very narrow coastal plain, it is warmed. Since the air is getting warmer as it passes over the Atacama, it sucks up moisture rather than releasing moisture in the form of precipitation. And so this dry place gets even drier. In fact, the Atacama is the world's driest desert. Some locations have gone several decades without receiving a drop of rain!

Sometimes several of the factors we have noted operate at once. This is the case in the Atacama. It is also the case with the deserts of the southwestern United States and northwestern Mexico. These deserts lie around 30° N latitude, a cool ocean current runs just off the coast in the Pacific Ocean, and there are tall mountains in the region that force much of the moisture out of the air before it reaches the desert. Because so many factors are at work, this is a very dry desert. Death Valley, California, receives an average of just over one inch of rain each year.

Plants and Animals in the Desert

Desert plants and animals adapt to the heat and lack of moisture in fascinating ways. For example, some trees such as the African acacia send roots down over 100 feet to reach groundwater. Trees and smaller plants also may send out a network of very shallow roots in order to capture even small amounts of moisture that gather on the surface. Many desert plants have very small leaves to cut down on water loss. Others, including most kinds of cactus, have sharp, needlelike spines that protect them from thirsty or hungry desert animals. Some desert animals do not drink water at all. Instead, they get moisture from the foods they eat. Others can go without food or water for many days. The camel, for example, can go without water for one to two weeks, and when it must go without food, it relies on the fat stored in its hump. Many desert animals also are nocturnal, becoming active only during the cooler nighttime hours.

Desertification

Deserts can grow or shrink over time, and the actions of human beings can sometimes accelerate their growth. When previously non-desert land becomes desert, as a result of climate changes, human mismanagement, or a combination of the two, the process is called *desertification*. Desertification is a global

Camels are well adapted to live in the desert. They can travel long distances on little water.

problem affecting about one-third of Earth's surface and at least parts of three-quarters of all countries.

Over many centuries, Africa's Sahara Desert has been greatly enlarged by human activities. During the early days of the Roman Empire, much of northern Africa bordering the Mediterranean Sea was a temperate area good for farming. The Romans, however, cut down forests to get firewood and to clear land for fields. They also plowed the land too much, so that when the rains came, water ran down the bare slopes and carried away the loose soil. Animals overgrazed grassy areas, which also exposed the soil to wind and rain. Soon there was no topsoil left, and most plant life vanished. Because there were few plants to hold moisture, water evaporated quickly. In only 2,000 years—a relatively short time in Earth's history—the damaged land turned to desert.

During recent decades, the Sahara Desert has also been spreading southward at an alarming rate. The southern edge of the Sahara is bordered by the Sahel, a narrow belt of land sandwiched between the desert and more humid areas to the south. Under normal conditions, the Sahel receives 10 to 20 inches of rain each year. This is enough to support pasture and cropland. But in the 1970s the rains failed. People continued to cut trees for fuel, plow the soil in order to farm the land, and tend their large herds of cattle, sheep, and goats. The results were disastrous. In some locations, the desert spread southward at a rate of 10 to 15 miles a year. Today, some of the Sahel has been reclaimed. But the pastoral nomads who once roamed the region with their flocks in search of water and good grazing conditions are gone forever.

Even the United States faces a threat of desertification. During the Great Drought of the 1930s, much of the country's semi-arid interior became a wasteland. Throughout the Great Plains, crops failed and grazing lands withered as conditions became increasingly dry. In some areas, many feet of precious topsoil were stripped away by the howling winds. Huge clouds of windborne dust were carried as far eastward as the Atlantic Coast. It took many decades and millions of dollars to restore the land to its former productivity.

The Mojave Desert in California.

JUDAISM AND CHRISTIANITY

The Middle East and Monotheism

The region we call the Middle East stretches from Egypt in northern Africa east to Mesopotamia and north to the Anatolian Peninsula. It includes the modern countries of Syria, Israel, Turkey, Egypt, Saudi Arabia, Jordan, Lebanon, and Iraq. The area has a hot, dry climate. The vast Arabian Peninsula in the heart of the region is mostly desert and has always been sparsely populated. But other, more fertile parts of the Middle East were among the earliest centers of civilization. Beginning around 5,000 years ago, cities rose on the banks of great rivers like the Nile in Egypt and the Tigris and Euphrates in Mesopotamia (today's Iraq). These cities became the centers of powerful ancient kingdoms — the empires of Egypt, Babylon, and Assyria.

One of the Middle East's most important contributions to world culture was a religious idea — the idea (called *monotheism*) that there is only one god. The region gave birth to

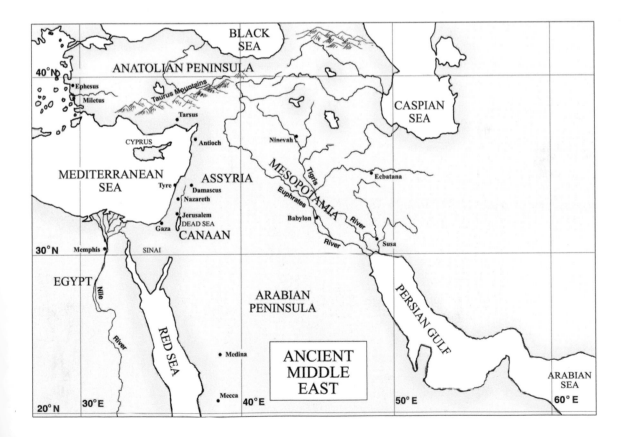

three of the world's major monotheistic faiths—Judaism, Christianity, and Islam. If you have read book four of this series, you should already know something about Islam and the prophet Muhammad. This book focuses on the two other important monotheistic religions, Judaism and Christianity.

Abraham and the Covenant

Judaism—the religion of the people called the Jews—was an early monotheistic religion. Before Judaism developed, the peoples of the ancient Middle East were *polytheists*, believers in many gods. The Egyptians, for example, believed in a god of war, a god of learning, a god of the sun, and so forth. In statues and paintings they depicted these gods in human or animal form. But the Jews came to believe that there was only one God, who ruled everyone and everything in the universe. Unlike the gods of the Egyptians, this God did not resemble a person, an animal, or any other living thing. In fact, the Jews were strictly forbidden from making any kind of image of their God.

The Jews tried to understand their God not by looking at statues but by studying their sacred scriptures, which we now call the Hebrew Bible. (Hebrew was the language of the Jews, and before the people were known as Jews they were called Hebrews or Israelites.) The Hebrew Bible consists of many different books, which were written over a long period of time, from about 1,000 B.C. to about 100 B.C., and eventually gathered into a single volume. The Torah, which includes the first five books of the Hebrew Bible, is considered especially sacred.

This engraving illustrates one of the most famous stories in the Hebrew Bible, the story of Adam and Eve. According to the book of Genesis, Adam and Eve were the first human beings. They lived in the Garden of Eden, a paradise, until they were driven out for breaking God's commandment that they not eat the fruit of a forbidden tree. Here Eve is offering the forbidden fruit to Adam.

The Hebrew Bible contains books of law as well as proverbs, poems, and stories. It also tells the story of the Jewish nation. According to the Bible, the father of the Jewish people was a man named Abraham who came from Mesopotamia. One day God spoke to Abraham, commanding him to journey to the land of Canaan, far to the west. God promised Abraham that, if he obeyed him, he would be rewarded: "I will make of you a great nation, and I will bless you and make your name great."

Abraham moved to Canaan, the land that his descendants would rename Israel. This country, which the Bible describes as beautiful and fertile ("flowing with milk and honey"), became the homeland of the Hebrew people. The Hebrew people interpreted God's words to Abraham as a *covenant*, or agreement, between God and themselves. As long as the people obeyed God, they would be blessed. But if they became disobedient, or broke his laws, they would be punished.

According to the Bible, God tested Abraham's own obedience in an especially stern way. When Abraham was an old man, his wife gave birth to a son, Isaac. The old couple, who had always longed for a child, doted on their son. Then one day God spoke to Abraham, giving him a terrible order: "Take your son, your only son, Isaac, whom you love, and . . . offer him . . . as a burnt offering [a sacrifice] upon one of the mountains I will show you."

Like other ancient groups, the Hebrews sacrificed animals as part of religious rituals. But they did not indulge in human sacrifice, as some other peoples did. Nevertheless, Abraham believed that he had to follow God's command. The old man led his son up the mountainside. When Isaac saw an altar prepared for a sacrifice, he was puzzled, asking his father, "Where is the lamb for a burnt offering?" Abraham (who must have been in anguish) replied, "God will provide the lamb for a burnt offering." Then he tied Isaac to the altar and raised his knife, preparing to kill his son.

Suddenly an angel, a messenger of God, spoke to Abraham, saying, "Do not lay your hand on the lad or do anything to him; for now I know that you fear God." The angel went on to say that, because Abraham was willing to obey such a painful order, Abraham and his descendants would receive even more blessings from God.

Suddenly an angel, a messenger of God, spoke to Abraham, saying, "Do not lay your hand on the lad. . ."

In this story, we can notice three ideas that are very important to Judaism. One is that God's actions are not always easy for humans to understand. A second is that God must always be obeyed, even when his commands seem strange or inexplicable. And a third is that, in the end, God will never force anyone to do something evil. Jews believe that God is not only all-powerful but also entirely good and just.

Moses and the Law

According to the Bible, Abraham's descendants lived in peace and prosperity in the land of Canaan for several generations. Then famine struck the country. In search of food, the Hebrews went to settle in the neighboring kingdom of Egypt. At first they were welcomed. But then a new pharaoh came to the Egyptian throne. This pharaoh hated the Hebrews and set them to work as slaves.

The Bible writers tell us that for years the Hebrews labored in bondage. But when they pleaded with God to free them, he sent a deliverer in the form of Moses, a Hebrew who had been raised as an Egyptian prince. Moses confronted the pharaoh and, speaking in God's name, demanded, "Let my people go." But over and over again the pharaoh refused to liberate the Hebrews. Angered by the pharaoh's refusals, God inflicted a series of terrible plagues on the Egyptians: water turned to blood; the land was overrun with frogs, gnats, and flies; darkness covered the land; and all the firstborn children of Egypt died. Finally the pharaoh relented and the Hebrews were able to escape from bondage. With Moses leading them, they journeyed north to return to Canaan, the land promised to Abraham.

During the journey back to Canaan, the Bible writers say, God ordered Moses to climb a tall mountain. On the mountaintop God revealed to Moses laws governing every part of Jewish life, including the Ten Commandments. The Ten Commandments include religious rules ("You shall have no other gods before me") as well as laws regulating the behavior of people toward each other ("You shall not kill," "You shall not steal"). One commandment— "Honor your father and your mother"—reflects the great importance of family in Jewish life. The Ten Commandments are central teachings of Judaism. Later, they would be adopted by Christians and Muslims as well.

Moses with the Ten Commandments.

According to the Bible, God gave Moses a number of laws in addition to the Ten Commandments. These laws were meant to guide the Hebrews' actions in everything from marriage to agriculture. Among other things, the laws explained what the Hebrew people were allowed to eat and how they could sacrifice animals to show their gratitude to God and obtain forgiveness for their sins. At the same time, many of the laws emphasized social justice. The people of Israel were commanded to treat everyone fairly and to care for those who could not care for themselves—widows, orphans, and the poor.

Israel: Triumph, Defeat, and Rebirth

The Bible says that, after forty years of wandering in the wilderness, the Hebrews finally came to the land of Canaan. They fought many wars against other peoples who claimed the land, but eventually they conquered the whole country, renaming it Israel. Under the great King David, who ruled around 1,000 B.C., Israel became a wealthy and powerful kingdom with its capital at Jerusalem. David was succeeded by his son Solomon, whom Jewish folklore calls the wisest man who ever lived. The magnificent temple that Solomon built at Jerusalem became the religious center of Judaism. It was in this temple that the Jewish priests offered animal sacrifices to God.

But Israel did not remain wealthy or powerful for long. A small country in a region of large empires, it fell prey again and again to stronger enemies—a fate that Jewish prophets said was due to Israel's repeated unfaithfulness to God. Between the eighth century B.C. and the first century A.D., the people of Israel were successively ruled by the Assyrians, the Babylonians, the Persians, the Greeks, and the Romans. But even under foreign domination, many Jews clung to their religion and their culture.

In the year A.D. 66, the Jews revolted against their Roman rulers. It took the mighty Roman army four years to crush the rebellion. In the year A.D. 70, Jerusalem finally fell to the Romans, who slaughtered the city's inhabitants and destroyed the Temple. After this, Israel virtually ceased to exist as a nation. The sacrificial system set up by Moses and his successors had to be abandoned, and the Jewish people were scattered across the world. This Diaspora (Greek for "scattering") would not end until the founding of the state of Israel in the year 1948, when the Jewish homeland became an independent nation once again.

Although exiled from their homeland for almost 2,000 years, the Jewish people never gave up their religion or its traditions. Even when living among peoples with very different customs, they strove to follow the laws laid out by Moses. They studied the Hebrew Bible so closely and reverently that they became known as "the people of the Book." Jewish scholars, called rabbis, compiled learned commentaries on the Hebrew scriptures. These were collected in a book called the Talmud. Above all, the Jewish people never doubted the existence of a God who was single, all-powerful, and wholly just. The biblical prophet

Micah summed up many of the ideas of Judaism in a simple yet powerful sentence: "What does the Lord require of you, but to do justice, and to love kindness, and to walk humbly with your God?"

Christianity

The Hebrew Bible contains a prediction of the coming of a savior called the Messiah (or "anointed one"). According to the Bible writers, when the Messiah arrives he will unite the nations of the world in a reign of justice and peace. Even the animals will stop preying on each other: "The wolf shall dwell with the lamb, and the lion shall lie down with the goat."

In the first century A.D., while Israel was under Roman rule, a small group of Jews began proclaiming that the Messiah had already come. His name was Jesus, they said, and he was a religious teacher who had been put to death by the Romans about the year A.D. 30. Most Jews did not accept the idea that Jesus was the Messiah. (Even today, the vast majority of Jews believe that the Messiah has yet to arrive.) Nevertheless, the followers of Jesus worked hard to spread his teachings, first within Israel and then in the non-Jewish lands of the Roman Empire. Those teachings became the basis of a new religion called Christianity. The word "Christian" comes from Christ, the Greek translation of Messiah. The followers of Jesus called him Jesus Christ, meaning Jesus the Messiah.

Christians accepted the Hebrew Bible, which they called the Old Testament, as divinely inspired. But they added to it a number of books by Christian writers. These books, which they called the New Testament, describe the life and death of Jesus and set out the basic ideas of Christianity. Together, the Old and New Testaments make up the Christian Bible.

Several books in the New Testament describe the birth of Jesus. According to one story, the baby Jesus was laid in a manger, a trough for feeding animals. This illustration shows Jesus in the manger, protected by his mother, Mary. Mary's husband, Joseph, is on the left and a group of shepherds on the right. Angels look down from heaven.

The Teachings of Jesus

The first four books of the New Testament, known as the Gospels, describe the life and death of Jesus. According to the Gospels, when Jesus was about 30 he began traveling around the land of Israel spreading his ideas. Some of these ideas were clearly drawn from the Hebrew Bible; others seemed original and daring. Jesus proclaimed that God was about to come into the world in a dramatic new way. Since the Kingdom of God was coming, Jesus declared, all believers should repent of their sins and follow him.

The Gospels tell us that one day, Jesus took his followers to the top of a mountain and delivered a powerful speech about life in God's kingdom. The message he delivered that day has become known as the Sermon on the Mount. Jesus began by stressing the virtues of meekness and peacefulness:

As a young man Jesus was baptized by a Jewish prophet named John the Baptist. Later, baptism—the dipping or partial immersion of a person in water—would become an important Christian ritual symbolizing initiation into the faith.

> Blessed are the meek, for they shall
>   inherit the earth.
> Blessed are they who hunger and thirst
>   for righteousness, for they shall be
>   satisfied.
> Blessed are the merciful, for they shall obtain mercy.
> Blessed are the pure of heart, for they shall see God.
> Blessed are the peacemakers, for they shall be called children of God.

Jesus encouraged his listeners to respond to violence with love: "If anyone strikes you on the right cheek, turn to him the other also. . . . I say to you, Love your enemies and pray for those who persecute you." Jesus also warned his listeners against pursuing money and other material things: "You cannot serve God and mammon [wealth]."

Someone once asked Jesus which of God's commandments was the most important. Jesus replied by quoting from the Hebrew Bible: "'You shall love your God with all your heart, and with all your soul, and with all your mind.' This is the first and great

Jesus preaching the Sermon on the Mount.

commandment. And a second is like it, 'You shall love your neighbor as yourself.'" Many believe that these two "great commandments" sum up the teachings of Jesus.

The Death of Jesus and the Spread of Christianity

According to the Gospels, as Jesus traveled around Israel, he became more and more popular among the people. But some religious leaders disliked his teachings and resented his popularity. They reported Jesus to the Roman authorities, claiming that he was stirring up a revolution against Rome. After a last supper with his followers, Jesus was arrested, tried in front of the Roman official Pontius Pilate, and

The crucifixion of Jesus.

put to death by crucifixion—being nailed alive to a wooden cross. Later, the cross on which Jesus suffered and died became the central symbol of Christianity.

After his crucifixion, Jesus was buried in a tomb. Some followers visited this tomb three days later and found that the body of Jesus was not there. According to the Gospels, an angel spoke to them and explained that Jesus had been resurrected, or raised from the dead.

At first the Christian religion grew slowly and had only a few followers. Few Jews accepted Jesus as the Messiah. But Christians eventually began to share the gospel, or "good news," about Jesus with non-Jews, called Gentiles. Beginning about 15 years after the death of Jesus, a Jew named Paul of Tarsus came to believe that he had been called to spread the message about Jesus. He started traveling around the Roman Empire, teaching about Jesus and making many converts. Eventually Paul made it as far as Rome itself.

Paul taught that Jesus was not only the Messiah but also the son of God who had sacrificed himself to save humanity; Jesus had suffered on the cross so that those who believed in him would be saved from their sins.

When the Roman emperor began a cruel persecution of Christians, Paul was arrested and executed. After his death, his followers collected letters he had written, which, along with the life stories of Jesus in the Gospels, became part of the New Testament. By the year A.D. 100, Christian churches had been set up in most of the major cities of the Roman Empire. Christianity would continue to grow until eventually it replaced polytheism (the worship of many gods) as the official religion of the Roman Empire. Today Christianity has more followers than any other religion in the world.

This engraving shows the apostle Paul preaching the gospel (the good news) about Jesus in the Greek city-state of Athens.

ANCIENT GREECE

City-States and Democracy

The religious ideas of most modern Americans and Europeans go back to ancient times and the Middle East, which gave birth to both Judaism and Christianity. But it is to Greece — another small country in the eastern Mediterranean — that Westerners trace many of their philosophical and political ideas, as well as their way of depicting reality in art.

Greece is a country of rocky mountains divided by deep valleys. In ancient times, this geography made for a politically disunited country. Although the Greeks spoke the same

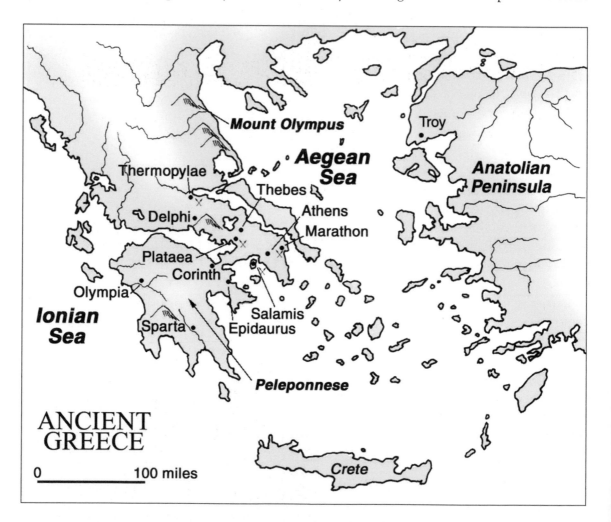

Mount Olympus

Troy

Aegean
Sea

Anatolian
Peninsula

Thermopylae

Thebes

Delphi

Athens

Marathon

Plataea

Corinth

Olympia

Ionian
Sea

Sparta

Salamis

Epidaurus

Peleponnese

ANCIENT
GREECE

0   100 miles

Crete

language and worshipped the same gods, they had no national government. Instead, each important city ruled itself as a city-state (in Greek, "polis"). There was keen rivalry between the city-states. Sometimes this rivalry showed itself in peaceful ways. Thus, every four years, athletes from all over Greece came to the town of Olympia to compete in sports

like boxing, javelin-throwing, and foot-racing. When an athlete won, his city would treat him like a hero—sometimes even setting up a statue in his honor.

The modern Olympic Games look back to these friendly competitions between the city-states. Too often, however, the rivalries between city-states were anything but friendly. Again and again, war broke out among them. Greek writers and thinkers frequently condemned the way their countrymen made war on one another, but they could do little to stop it.

One of the most intense rivalries was between the two most powerful city-states, Sparta and Athens. These two city-states had very different cultures

This jar, called an amphora, shows three runners competing in a footrace at the Panathenaic Games, a competition similar to the ancient Olympics.

and political systems. Sparta was a militaristic society; the only job of Sparta's male citizens was to train for wars and fight them. Athens, although it too produced brave warriors, was a city of merchants, sailors, and craftsmen. Like most ancient cities and countries, Sparta was ruled by kings. By contrast, Athens had a system of government unique in the ancient world—*democracy*, or "rule by the people." In democratic Athens, all male citizens came together in a great assembly to vote on important issues. Every member of the assembly had the same say in government as every other member. By modern standards, Athenian democracy was less than perfect. Women could not vote, nor could the slaves who made

up perhaps one-third of the population. Nevertheless, modern democratic governments, including that of the United States, can trace their roots to ancient Athens, the world's first democracy.

The Temple of Theseus, part of the Acropolis complex in Athens.

The Persian Wars

Although the Greek city-states frequently fought each other, they sometimes joined together in the face of an overwhelming threat from outside. This happened at the beginning of the fifth century B.C., when the united Greeks twice defeated a far more powerful enemy that was trying to conquer their country.

In those days the Persians (present-day Iranians) ruled a vast empire stretching from Egypt to India. In the year 490 B.C., Darius [darr-EYE-us], the king of Persia, decided to extend his empire to Europe by conquering Greece. He expected the small, disunited country to fall easily. But when his army landed in Greece, at a place called Marathon, it was defeated by a much smaller force of Greeks, mostly from the city-state of Athens. The Persian fleet sailed home in humiliation. Meanwhile, according to one story, a Greek runner brought the news from the battlefield at Marathon to Athens. After running nonstop for more than 20 miles, he arrived in the city. He cried out, "Rejoice! We conquer!" and then fell dead of exhaustion. The long race called the *marathon* (part of the modern Olympics) commemorates this runner's feat.

A few years after the Persian defeat at Marathon, King Darius died. He was succeeded by his son Xerxes [ZERK-sees], who yearned to avenge the humiliation of the Persians. In 480 B.C., Xerxes mounted another invasion of Greece. His army was so large, Greek historians tell us, that wherever they marched they drank the rivers dry. This is obviously an exaggeration, but it is clear that the Greeks were vastly outnumbered.

The Greek city-states came together in an alliance to resist the Persians. As Xerxes' troops marched into northern Greece, a small group of Greeks led by Spartans tried to hold them off at a mountain pass called Thermopylae. Someone warned a Spartan warrior that when the Persians shot their arrows, there were so many of them that they blotted out the sun. "This is pleasant news," the Spartan replied coolly. "If the Persians hide the sun, we will have our battle in the shade." When the Persians attacked, the Greeks fought fiercely. The small band held off Xerxes' mighty army for several days before being overwhelmed and slaughtered. Afterward the name "Thermopylae" would come to stand for great courage against overwhelming odds.

The Persians marched south, capturing Athens and burning much of the city. But then the tide of war turned in favor of the Greeks. In a great sea battle at Salamis near Athens, the Greek and Persian fleets confronted each other. The Greeks were again outnumbered, but their warships were faster and nimbler than those of the Persians. Also, as a seafaring nation, Greece had many more skilled sailors than did Persia. At Salamis, the Greeks managed to sink much of the Persian fleet. The remaining ships fled back to Persia. Fearing capture, Xerxes fled as well. Still hoping to capture Greece, he left behind a large portion of his land army. But the following year (479 B.C.), the allied Greeks crushed the Persian forces at the battle of Plataea. By coming together, the Greek city-states had defeated the most powerful empire on earth. Persia would never again threaten the independence of Greece.

The Golden Age

The defeat of the Persians left the Greeks flushed with pride and self-confidence. In the wealthy city of Athens, confidence combined with prosperity to give rise to the so-called Golden Age of Greece. In the half century after the Persian Wars, Athens produced some of the greatest works of literature, art, and architecture the world has ever seen.

In the theaters of fifth-century Athens, audiences watched the first performances of tragedies by playwrights like Aeschylus [ESS-kuh-luss] and Sophocles [SOFF-uh-klees]. Full of soaring poetry and human insight, these plays are still performed all over the world. Meanwhile, Athenian artists celebrated the beauty of the human body in magnificently realistic sculptures. (See page 175.) While artists of other ancient cultures showed humans in rigid, unrealistic poses, these Greek statues surged with life and movement. At the same time, Athenian architects designed buildings of startling beauty. Looming above Athens, on the hill called the Acropolis, was the most beautiful building of all, the

Parthenon. This marble temple, with its rhythmic rows of gently curving columns, seemed to sum up the harmony and grace of Greek architecture. (See pages 172–173.)

No one was prouder of Athens than Pericles (495–429 B.C.), the general and politician who led Athens during the Golden Age. In a famous funeral oration he gave during the Peloponnesian War against Sparta, Pericles asked what it was that had made the city of Athens so great.

An ancient Greek theater in Epidaurus.

Democracy was part of it, he said. In a democracy, anyone with talent could rise to the top. Furthermore, since everyone had a say in political decisions, everyone got involved in politics. Then, too, unlike the conservative Spartans, Athenians were adventurous and restless, constantly trying new things. They also loved being surrounded by beauty, so they always tried to make their city more beautiful. "Mighty indeed are the marks and monuments . . . which we have left," Pericles declared. "Future ages will wonder at us, as the present age wonders at us now."

But the wondrous period of Athenian glory was short lived. In 431 B.C., war broke out between Athens and Sparta. Athens had Greece's most powerful navy; Sparta had its most powerful army. Because the two sides were so evenly matched, the war ground on for decades, bringing suffering and devastation to much of Greece. The Peloponnesian War finally came to an end in 404 B.C., when Sparta defeated Athens. Although Athens would continue to be a center of learning, it never regained its former wealth, power, or cultural glory.

A bust of Pericles.

Greek Philosophy

After the defeat of Athens, the city lost its old sense of pride and self-confidence. Some Athenians asked why their city had gone down to defeat. They began to question the city's traditions and its traditional ways of doing things. The Athenian most famous for this sort of questioning was a philosopher named Socrates [SAW-kruh-teeze].

Socrates (c.470–399 B.C.) could usually be found in the marketplace, teaching groups of young Athenian men. He taught by asking questions, not by lecturing, and all of his questions were meant to get his students to think more deeply about their ideas and beliefs. Most people, he thought, pretended to know much more than they really did. Socrates liked to shock his listeners by declaring that he was the wisest man in Greece. But then he went on to explain that he was "wisest" because he was the only one wise enough to know that he didn't really know anything.

A lovable man and a brilliant teacher, Socrates attracted many students. But he also made many enemies, including the parents of some of his students (who didn't like it when their children started to question *them*). In the year 399 B.C., he was put on trial, charged with corrupting young people and disbelieving in the gods of the city. Socrates might have saved himself if he had promised to give up teaching, but this he refused to do. "I say," he told the court, "that daily to discourse about virtue . . . is the greatest good of man, and that the unexamined life is not worth living." Socrates was found guilty and sentenced to death. He was put in prison and ordered to commit suicide by drinking a powerful poison. Surrounded by his heartbroken students, Socrates carried out this act with great courage and calmness. (For a famous picture of the death of Socrates, see page 186.)

Socrates never wrote down his own thoughts and ideas. They have come down to us because one of his students, Plato (c.428–348 B.C.), wrote about them. Inspired by Socrates, Plato went on to become a great philosopher—some would say the greatest philosopher who ever lived. Plato wrote dozens of dialogues—philosophical works in the form of two or more people talking to one another. In most of these dialogues, the main speaker is Socrates (although we do not know for certain which ideas in the dialogues are Socrates' and which are Plato's).

Plato wrote about many subjects, including politics, education, and love. In all of his works, he stressed the importance of following reason rather than emotion. Plato thought that true reality lay beyond the visible world, in a realm of pure "ideas" or "forms." Most people, he thought, were too blinded by prejudice or emotion to see this ultimate reality. It could only be discovered by a true philosopher—a man who follows reason. In one of his books, Plato makes a famous comparison known as the allegory of the cave. People who are not philosophers, he says, are like a group of prisoners chained in a cave. Because the prisoners can see nothing but shadows on the walls of the cave, they mistake these shadows for reality. But sometimes one of the prisoners breaks his chains and walks out into the light of the sun. This freed prisoner is the philosopher, who sees the true reality of the forms.

Plato.

Like Socrates, Plato was a teacher. His most brilliant student, Aristotle (384–322 B.C.), became a great philosopher in his own right. Like Plato, Aristotle wanted people to follow reason rather than emotion. But he disagreed with his teacher about where true reality could be found. For Aristotle, reality was to be found not in a world of forms but right here on Earth. Unlike Plato, Aristotle was fascinated by science, especially the science of biology. (In his scientific work, he described more than 500 species of animals.) Aristotle also had down-to-earth ideas about the way people should behave. He urged his students never to go to extremes. For example, he said, it's wrong to live only for pleasure, but it's just as bad never to enjoy yourself. Similarly, it's wrong to be a coward, but it's also wrong to be brave to the point of recklessness and foolishness. True bravery, Aristotle insisted, lies between these two extremes. Aristotle thought that people should live in a balanced way, always seeking what he called *the golden mean*.

Alexander the Great

As we've seen, Aristotle was a student of Plato, who had been a student of Socrates. Aristotle's own most famous student, however, was not a philosopher but a warrior-king who conquered much of the known world. His name was Alexander the Great (356–323 B.C.).

Macedon, or Macedonia, was a country to the north of Greece that shared the same language and culture. In 343 B.C., the king of Macedonia invited Aristotle to come to his country and become the tutor of his son Alexander. The philosopher stayed in Macedonia for several years, teaching philosophy, politics, and medicine to the young prince. Alexander revered his teacher, but above all he longed to become a great ruler and conqueror. Alexander looked up to the warriors described in Homer's *Iliad*. His father encouraged his ambitions, saying, "My son, Macedonia is too small for you; seek out a larger empire."

A bust of Alexander the Great.

Alexander got his chance when his father died and he became king of Macedonia at the age of 20. First, he set out to rule all of Greece. He raised a huge army and forced the Greek city-states to swear allegiance to him. Then he announced his greatest ambition—to avenge the Persian invasions of Greece by conquering the mighty Persian Empire. At first it seemed like an impossible task. But when he attacked Persian territory in 334 B.C., he began to win victory after victory. Alexander was a brilliant general whose fanatical courage in battle earned him the devotion of his troops. Although greatly outnumbered, the Greeks and Macedonians fought more fiercely than the Persian soldiers, who felt little loyalty to their cruel and cowardly emperor.

Within three years Alexander had conquered the western part of the Persian Empire—the modern countries of Turkey, Lebanon, Israel, and Egypt. Then he invaded Persia itself (modern-day Iran) and burned its capital city to the ground. Now, although he had defeated the greatest empire on earth, Alexander yearned for yet more conquests. In 327 B.C., he invaded India. There he defeated a large Indian army whose soldiers had charged into battle on the backs of elephants. After winning this battle, Alexander wanted to push deeper into the vast subcontinent of India. But his soldiers had had enough. Tired and homesick after many years of war, they forced Alexander to turn back toward Greece. Halfway through the long journey home, Alexander died of a fever.

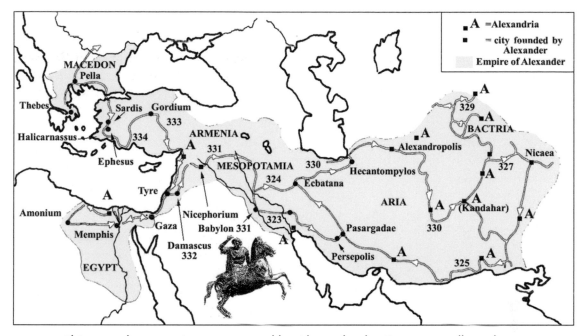

This map shows territory conquered by Alexander the Great, as well as places
he named Alexandria after himself.

When Alexander died, he left no heir. The vast realm he had conquered was divided up
by his generals, who made themselves kings. For generations their descendants would rule
the Middle East. In these Hellenistic kingdoms (from "Hellas," a name for Greece), Greek
customs and ideas dominated. Throughout the region the rulers built new cities, with
houses, theaters, and temples modeled on those in Greece. The greatest of these cities was
located in Egypt — Alexandria, named for Alexander the Great. It was here that one of
the Hellenistic kings established the most famous library in the ancient world, containing
hundreds of thousands of books. He built up such a huge collection by ordering that every
book brought into the city by a visitor should be copied and placed in the library. Scholars
from around the Mediterranean world flocked to the library to study the great works of
Greek literature and philosophy.

Alexander's empire fell apart at his death. But his conquests spread Greek culture from
Egypt to India. For this, as much as for his many successes in battle, he would be
remembered as Alexander the Great.

ANCIENT ROME

The Roman Republic

While Alexander the Great was conquering the Middle East, the city of Rome, in Italy, was just beginning to rise to prominence. Eventually it would become the capital of an empire far more long-lasting than Alexander's.

Early Rome had a *republican*, or representative, form of government. The population of the city consisted of two major groups, the *patricians* and the *plebeians*. The patricians (their name means "the fathers") were a small group of wealthy aristocrats. The plebeians were the common people. Although the plebeians could vote and hold office, most authority lay in the hands of the patricians, who dominated the powerful assembly called the *Senate* and elected leaders called *consuls*. Two thousand years later the founders of the United States would base their new government partly on the model of the Roman republic. Significantly, they created an upper (more "patrician") house of Congress called the Senate.

The Punic Wars

Like the ancient Greeks, the Romans were a warlike people who fought continually with their neighbors. By 275 B.C., they had conquered all of Italy. But as they tried to expand their conquests, they came up against a powerful enemy. Carthage, a city-state on the coast of North Africa, had a powerful navy and a desire to dominate the Mediterranean Sea. In 264 B.C., Rome and Carthage went to war over the question of who should rule Sicily, a large island off the Italian coast. The war raged for more than 20 years. Eventually, the Romans defeated the Carthaginians and took over Sicily.

In 218 B.C., however, war broke out again, this time over Carthaginian claims in Spain. The confident Romans expected an easy victory. But they did not realize how strong an opponent they faced in Hannibal, the Carthaginian commander. Hannibal unexpectedly decided to invade Italy itself. He marched his army—which included a large number of elephants—east from Spain. Then he performed the amazing feat of leading his soldiers and elephants across the Alps, the towering, icy mountain range north of Italy. After invading the Italian peninsula, Hannibal won victory after victory over the Romans. Yet, because of the city's strong fortifications and because the Romans were so fierce in its defense, he was never able to capture Rome itself. For another 15 long years, the war in Italy ground on. Then a Roman army sailed for Africa and threatened Carthage. Hannibal returned to defend his homeland. In 202 B.C., at the Battle of Zama, Hannibal's forces were defeated. The Carthaginians surrendered, signing a treaty of peace with the Romans. Under the treaty, Carthage gave Rome the right to rule Spain. It also gave up most of its navy and promised to keep its forces on the African continent.

Hannibal.

With Carthage no longer a threat, Rome was free to expand its empire around the Mediterranean. The Romans went on to conquer Greece and much of present-day Turkey. Then they decided to expand into northern Africa by conquering Carthage itself. Between 149 and 146 B.C., Rome fought yet another war against its old enemy. Once again Rome was victorious. This time the Romans utterly destroyed the city of Carthage and sowed its fields with salt so that no crops could be grown there again. This brutal act of destruction marked the end of the third and final Punic War. (The wars between Rome and Carthage were called the Punic Wars after the Roman name for the Phoenicians, the people who first settled Carthage.)

The End of the Republic

After defeating Carthage, Rome ruled most of the lands bordering the Mediterranean. Now Rome's leaders, hungry for yet more land and military glory, looked toward northern Europe. In 58 B.C., one of Rome's greatest generals, Julius Caesar (100–44 B.C.), set out to conquer the country of Gaul (today's France). After nine long years of war, he succeeded

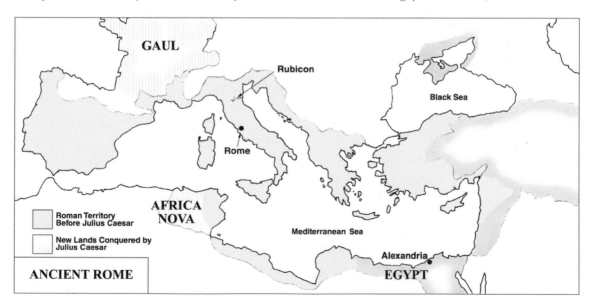

in subduing the country. Now Rome ruled an empire stretching from the English Channel to North Africa, and from the Atlantic Ocean to the Black Sea.

Caesar himself, however, wanted more than glory; he wanted political power. After his great victories he returned to Rome, where he was acclaimed by the people. He made himself even more popular by giving free food to the poor. Gradually he claimed more and more authority for himself. Some of the aristocrats in the Senate grew alarmed. Caesar wanted to abolish the republic, they whispered, and make himself king with the support of

the people. Now Caesar's enemies plotted to save the republic by assassinating him. In 44 B.C., they surrounded him in the Senate, where he had come to speak, and stabbed him to death with daggers. (See pages 47–52.)

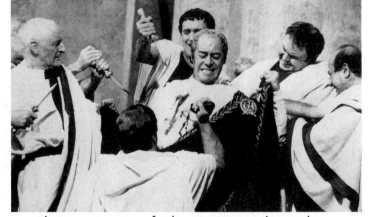

After Caesar's murder, a bloody civil war broke out between those who had supported Caesar and those who had opposed him. The conflict ended in 31 B.C., with

The assassination of Julius Caesar, as depicted in a Hollywood film.

the victory of the pro-Caesar forces led by Caesar's grand-nephew Octavian (63 B.C.– A.D. 14). Octavian seized almost total power in Rome. He took the name "Augustus," meaning "the exalted one." From this point on, although the Senate still existed, it had very little power. The Roman republic had come to an end, and power would now be concentrated in the hands of one man—the emperor. Although Augustus himself never used the term, historians agree in calling him the first emperor of Rome. Later the family name "Caesar" became another word for "emperor."

Augustus

Sick of turmoil and bloodshed, the Roman people welcomed Augustus's rise to power. His strong but mild rule brought peace and stability to Rome and her colonies. Augustus strengthened the Roman army and navy and worked to end corruption. Helped by these reforms, trade flourished and the empire grew richer than ever before. Augustus used some of this wealth to beautify the city of Rome, which had been full of crumbling and ugly old buildings. The emperor ordered these torn down and replaced with lovely new houses, temples, and theaters. Toward the end of his life, Augustus would boast, "I found Rome built of bricks; I leave her clothed in marble."

Augustus also gave generous support to artists and writers. He encouraged Virgil, the greatest Roman poet of the time, to write a long epic called the *Aeneid*. In this poem, Virgil told the legendary story of the founding of Rome by the Trojan hero Aeneas. Part of his poem praises Augustus for bringing peace and prosperity to the empire. Another part declares that it is the destiny of Rome to rule the world:

> . . . Yours will be the rulership of nations, remember, Roman, these will be your arts: to teach the ways of peace to those you conquer, to spare defeated peoples, tame the proud.

Augustus ruled the Roman Empire for more than 40 years. When he died in A.D. 14, he was deeply mourned by his subjects; more than 100,000 people marched in his funeral procession.

The Emperor Augustus.

Later Emperors

Rome had been lucky to have a man like Augustus for its first emperor. It was not so lucky with some of his successors. Several of them, corrupted by power, became bloodthirsty tyrants. One of the worst of these emperors was Nero, who reigned from A.D. 54 to 68. Nero taxed the people heavily so he could live in a vast palace whose walls were covered in gold and ivory. When a fire burned down a large part of Rome, Nero falsely blamed the Christian minority in the city. On his orders, hundreds of innocent Christians were executed. Not even his own family was safe from Nero's vicious cruelty; the emperor's mother and two of his wives were murdered because they offended him. Finally, Nero was overthrown by a rebellious general. Fearing punishment for his crimes, he committed suicide.

In the second century A.D., several wise and intelligent emperors came to the throne. The empire once again enjoyed the order and prosperity it had known under Augustus.

The period from about 29 B.C. to A.D. 180 is sometimes known as the *pax Romana*—the Roman peace. In the 1700s, the great historian Edward Gibbon would judge this era the happiest period in all of human history.

Christianity and the Roman Empire

Of course, not everyone was content to live under Roman rule. As we've seen, the Jews in Israel rose up against Rome in defense of their religion and their culture. The rebellion was crushed with great cruelty, and the Jewish capital of Jerusalem was nearly destroyed. By contrast, adherents of the other great monotheistic faith, Christianity, never rebelled against Rome. For one thing, Christians lived in small communities scattered all over the empire. Also, Jesus had taught his followers to turn the other cheek rather than to take up arms against their oppressors. Moreover, Jesus had once said, "Render unto Caesar the things that are Caesar's, and unto God the things that are God's." Many Christians took this saying to mean that, as long as the Roman government did not interfere with their religion, they should be loyal subjects of Rome.

Yet from the beginning it was often difficult to be a Christian in the Roman Empire. Most of the peoples of the empire were polytheists who looked with suspicion on this strange new faith with its single god. Because Christians believed there was only one true god, they refused to worship the traditional Roman gods. Roman officials sometimes persecuted Christians for their refusal to worship the gods of the Roman state. A Christian might be thrown in jail or even sentenced to be torn apart by wild animals in the arena. As we've seen, Nero made Christians the scapegoats when a great fire broke out in Rome.

Yet large numbers of

The Colosseum as it looked at the time of the Roman emperor Hadrian (A.D. 117–138). The Colosseum was the scene of chariot races and gladiator fights. Many early Christians suffered martyrdom in the Colosseum for refusing to worship the gods of Rome.

people continued to convert to Christianity, in part because they were moved by the courage with which Christians faced torture and execution. "The blood of the martyrs," a Christian leader declared, "is the seed of the church." Yet as conversions increased, so did persecution. The worst slaughters of Christians occurred in the third century, a time of turmoil in the empire when many people rejected the old Roman religion in favor of the new faith.

In the early fourth century, an emperor named Constantine finally brought an end to the persecution of Christians. In order to become emperor, Constantine had to defeat his enemies in a civil war. According to one story, on the day before the decisive battle, Constantine looked up in the sky and saw a huge cross (the symbol of Christianity). Underneath the cross was the phrase, "Conquer by this." Constantine had his soldiers paint crosses on their shields before they attacked the enemy. After winning the battle and becoming emperor, he showed his gratitude by making Christianity legal throughout the empire. He encouraged the spread of the faith by building churches in many different lands. He brought Christian leaders to his court to serve as advisors. From the time of Constantine on, Christianity would become the dominant religion of the Roman Empire.

The Fall of the Roman Empire

By the time of Constantine, the empire was already coming apart. Constantine found Roman politics so corrupt that he moved his capital to a new city that he founded in present-day Turkey. The emperor called the city New Rome, although future generations would know it as "Constantine's city," Constantinople. Then, at the end of the fourth century, one of Constantine's successors divided the empire in two. He created a western empire centered in Rome and an eastern empire centered in Constantinople. But the western part of the empire had grown feeble, and without the support of the stronger east, it lay exposed to its enemies. Throughout the fifth century, Italy was invaded by warlike tribes from the north and east, including the Goths and the Huns. In A.D. 410, the Visigoths sacked Rome. Finally, in A.D. 476, the last western emperor was forced to abdicate.

For centuries, historians have debated the causes of the fall of the Roman Empire. Some have argued that the empire fell because of the spread of Christianity. By making people more loyal to God than to the emperor, these historians say, Christianity undermined Roman patriotism. Other historians disagree, arguing that Rome fell because wealth and luxury had made the people soft, no longer capable of fighting or ruling. Still others argue that the empire fell because horrible diseases like smallpox and bubonic plague caused its population to dwindle. Perhaps all these factors, and more, contributed to the fall of Rome. But people will go on heatedly debating the question, because they sense that in Rome's story there are lessons to be learned about why even the mightiest nations decline and fall.

THE ENLIGHTENMENT

A New Way of Thinking

Christianity defined European society in the Middle Ages, but the Protestant Reformation divided Europe into Protestant and Catholic territories and weakened the authority of the church. During the 1600s and 1700s, some people grew more willing to question religious authority and traditional ideas. Some of them emphasized *reason*, while others emphasized *science*. The movement these people started became known as The Enlightenment, because those who were involved in it thought they were bringing the light of reason and science to people who had previously been in the dark.

Descartes

The French mathematician René Descartes (1596–1650) was one of the most famous philosophers of the Enlightenment. Descartes [day-CART] used reason to understand the world.

Descartes began by systematically doubting everything. Most of us accept that our senses present an accurate view of the world, but Descartes pointed out that sometimes our eyes play tricks on us and make us see things that are not really there. How could he be sure his senses were not deceiving him more often, or even all of the time? Descartes concluded that he could not be sure: it might be the case, he wrote, that "an evil genius of the utmost power and cunning has employed all his energies in order to deceive me."

Descartes: "I think, therefore I am."

After showing that he could not be sure that what he observed in the world was true, Descartes tried doubting his own existence. But he discovered that trying to doubt his existence only showed that he really did exist—because in order for there to be doubt, there must be a person who doubts. So Descartes' starting point for his new philosophy became the famous formula *cogito ergo sum*, which is Latin for "I think, therefore I am." From this starting point, Descartes developed an elaborate philosophy based on logic and reason. A follower of Descartes is called a Cartesian.

Newton and the Laws of Nature

Other Enlightenment thinkers disagreed with the approach taken by Descartes. They questioned whether reason and logic alone could explain the world. These thinkers placed more emphasis on scientific observation and experiment. One such thinker was the Englishman Isaac Newton (1642–1727).

Newton observed the world around him, conducted experiments, and concluded that things behave according to mathematical rules. Newton did a series of important experiments on light. He discovered that a prism breaks up white light into the colors of the rainbow. He also proved that colored light could be recombined to make white light.

Newton also made important discoveries in the field of astronomy. He designed a new, improved kind of telescope and formulated laws that explain why objects fall to the earth and why the tides come and go as they do. You can read more about Newton's laws of gravity in the science chapter, pages 327–330.

Newton's work had an enormous influence and convinced some people that *everything* could be explained by science. Even today, scientists are building on the foundation laid by Newton.

"Nasty, Brutish, and Short": The World of Hobbes

The Enlightenment also changed how people understood society and government. Thomas Hobbes (1588–1679), an English philosopher, reflected on the wars and conflicts of his time and developed a new theory of government. In his book *Leviathan* (1651), Hobbes imagined what life would be like if there were no government to keep us all in line. In such a "state of nature," Hobbes argued, you could never be sure the person who lived over the hill would keep his promises and behave fairly. If your neighbor turned out to be a bad person, he might attack you or rob you; and, if you were worried about being attacked or robbed, you might think it wise to attack your neighbor first, thus beating him to the punch. In such a world, Hobbes concluded, we would always be fighting. The state of nature would be a never-ending war of everyone against everyone else, and competition among people for scarce resources would make life "nasty, brutish, and short."

Hobbes concluded that only a strong central government could prevent this constant fighting. When people agreed to live under the authority of a government, they would have to give up some of the freedom they had in the state of nature. In exchange, however, the government would promise to protect them from other people. Hobbes called this exchange the "social contract."

Hobbes believed that only a strong government could provide security. Anybody who rebelled against this government would be breaking the social contract and threatening to plunge society into civil war and anarchy.

Locke and Natural Rights

John Locke (1632–1704), an English philosopher of the Enlightenment, also believed in the social contract, although not in the same sense as Hobbes. Locke used the social contract to argue against an idea that was still widely accepted in his day—the *divine right* of kings. Advocates of divine right believed that kings were the chosen instruments of God. They insisted that disobeying or resisting a king was just as sinful as disobeying or resisting God.

During Locke's time, the Stuart kings of Great Britain claimed to rule by divine right. But Locke argued that government was actually based on the consent of the people, and that there were certain basic rights that no government could take away, including rights to "life, liberty, and property." People form governments to protect their rights, Locke said. If a government fails to protect peoples' rights, or takes those rights away, then the people have a right to change the government.

Something like this actually happened in England during Locke's lifetime. In 1688–89, Englishmen who objected to the policies of King

John Locke.

James II started a revolution. King James was driven out and replaced by King William and Queen Mary. Locke's writings provided a justification for the revolution of 1688–89.

The Blank Slate

Locke also contributed to the Enlightenment in other ways. In *An Essay Concerning Human Understanding* (1690), he argued that all knowledge comes from experience. Locke said there are no innate ideas—no ideas that we are born knowing. On the contrary, he argued, the human mind is a blank slate, or *tabula rasa*, that gets filled in with information as a person lives in the world.

Locke's idea of the blank slate had important consequences for education. If the mind is a blank slate filled in by experiences, then it follows that education is very important.

A child whose "blank slate" is filled with good and noble ideas should grow up to be a good person, while a person whose slate is filled up with bad and ignoble ideas will almost surely turn out badly.

Montesquieu

Baron Charles de Montesquieu [MON-tess-cue] (1689–1755) was a French political philosopher who admired Locke and Newton. Montesquieu set aside the Cartesian emphasis on logic and theory and chose a more scientific approach. He studied a large number of political systems and concluded that political arrangements, or institutions, must be suited to particular societies. According to Montesquieu, the question was not "what is the best kind of government in general?" but "what is the best kind of government for this particular country?" Montesquieu believed that only small countries could govern themselves as republics. In a larger country, it would be virtually impossible for representatives to reach agreement; larger countries should therefore be ruled by kings.

In his book *The Spirit of the Laws*, Montesquieu gave a description of British government. He wrote that the British system struck a balance among different functions of government: the legislative power (parliament) could make laws; the executive power (the king) could put the laws into action; and the judicial power (judges) could judge whether the laws had been broken. Montesquieu approved of this separation of powers and said it created a balance that protected liberty by preventing any single branch from exercising too much authority.

The Enlightenment in America

Enlightenment ideas were important not only in Europe but also in America. Thomas Jefferson drew heavily on Locke when he drafted the Declaration of Independence in 1776. Locke had argued that some rights cannot be taken away, and he had listed the rights to life, liberty, and property. Jefferson wrote that "All men are endowed by their Creator with certain inalienable rights," including "life, liberty, and the pursuit of happiness." Locke argued that government was a contract based on trust; if a king violated that trust, then the people could resist his authority and alter the government. Jefferson and other American colonists argued that this was exactly what had happened with King George III. Jefferson wrote that the British government had infringed on the inalienable rights of the American people. The Americans therefore had the right "to alter or abolish" the government.

If you read the following sentences from the Declaration of Independence, you can see just how heavily Jefferson was indebted to Locke's ideas:

> We hold these truths to be self-evident, that all men are created equal, that they are endowed by their Creator with certain unalienable Rights, that among these are Life, Liberty and the pursuit of Happiness.—That to secure these rights, Governments are instituted among Men, deriving their just powers from the consent of the governed. —That whenever any Form of Government becomes destructive of these ends, it is the Right of the People to alter or to abolish it, and to institute new Government, laying its foundation on such principles and organizing its powers in such form, as to them shall seem most likely to effect their Safety and Happiness. Prudence, indeed, will dictate that Governments long established should not be changed for light and transient causes; and accordingly all experience hath shewn, that mankind are more disposed to suffer, while evils are sufferable, than to right themselves by abolishing the forms to which they are accustomed. But when a long train of abuses and usurpations, pursuing invariably the same Object evinces a design to reduce them under absolute Despotism, it is their right, it is their duty, to throw off such Government, and to provide new Guards for their future security.—Such has been the patient sufferance of these Colonies; and such is now the necessity which constrains them to alter their former Systems of Government. The history of the present King of Great Britain [George III] is a history of repeated injuries and usurpations, all having in direct object the establishment of an absolute Tyranny over these States.

The Founding Fathers of the United States, shown here drafting the Declaration of Independence, were heavily influenced by Enlightenment thinkers like Locke and Montesquieu.

The American founders were also influenced by Montesquieu's ideas about the separation of powers. When they met in Philadelphia in 1787 to draft a constitution, they divided the judicial, legislative, and executive functions among three distinct branches of government and developed a system of checks and balances to ensure that no one branch became too powerful.

THE FRENCH REVOLUTION

The Sun King

From 1643 to 1715, France was ruled by a dazzling and extravagant monarch, King Louis [LOO-ee] XIV. He called himself the Sun King. What he meant was that everything in France revolved around him in the same way the planets revolve around the sun. Under Louis XIV, France was no longer a collection of provinces ruled by various barons, but a united nation state ruled by an absolute, all-powerful king. As Louis himself put it, "The state—I am the state."

Louis XIV: "I am the state."

Louis had an enormous palace built outside Paris, at Versailles [vare-SIGH]. Versailles was decorated with dazzling mirrors, elaborate chandeliers, and beautiful works of art. At Versailles, Louis attended plays and concerts, and wealthy aristocrats called *courtiers* competed for the right to sit close to the king.

A fountain at the Palace of Versailles.

The Three Estates

Everybody in France belonged to one of three groups known as the Three Estates. The First Estate was the clergy (the church). The Second Estate was the nobility. The Third Estate included everybody else—not only peasants but also merchants, lawyers, and wealthy townspeople who did not have noble titles.

According to the law, each of the Three Estates had the right to elect representatives to send to the Estates General, an assembly that was supposed to advise the king and approve taxes. However, French kings like Louis XIV preferred to make their own decisions. No French king had called a meeting of the Estates General since 1614.

> The political order that existed in France (and other European countries) during the 1600s and 1700s, prior to the French Revolution, is known as the "Old Regime," from the French phrase *ancien regime.*

The three orders of the *ancien regime* in France: (*from left*) the clergy, the nobility, and everybody else.

Louis XV

When Louis XIV died in 1715, he was succeeded as king by his great-grandson, Louis XV. Louis XV ruled France for nearly 60 years, and during his reign serious problems began to emerge. France fought a series of expensive wars, which left the nation in debt. At the same time, the gap between the wealthy courtiers who gathered at Versailles and the rest of the nation grew even wider. Louis XV predicted that these problems would have terrible consequences following his reign, but that would be somebody else's problem. He is said to have quipped, "*Apres moi, le deluge,*" which means "after me, the flood."

Louis XVI and the Estates General

The flood predicted by Louis XV happened during the reign of Louis XVI (1774–1792). The French supported the American colonists in their war for independence, and the costs of this war drove the nation even further into debt. The queen, Marie Antoinette, made the situation worse by purchasing expensive jewels and building herself a special palace at Versailles.

During the 1780s, crops failed, bringing poverty and starvation to many peasants and townspeople. About this time a rumor began to circulate. According to the rumor, someone had told the queen that the people had no bread to eat. Marie Antoinette supposedly replied, "Then let them eat cake!" The story was probably false, but it was told and retold as evidence that the queen was cruel, or at least did not understand the sufferings of poor Frenchmen.

By 1786, France was nearing bankruptcy. Louis XVI proposed taxing the nobles and the clergy. The nobles were outraged. They insisted that any new taxes would have to be levied by an Estates General representing the Three Estates. Louis did not want to call the Estates General into session, but in 1788 he finally concluded he had no choice.

Marie Antoinette.

The Estates General met at Versailles in May of 1789. Things did not go smoothly. Representatives from the First and Second Estates treated the representatives of the Third Estate as inferiors and even forced them to enter the assembly room using a different door. Representatives of the Third Estate resented this and demanded a greater voice, on the grounds that they represented the great majority of the French people. On June 17, representatives of the Third Estate, joined by a few sympathetic nobles and clergy, left the palace and took over a nearby indoor tennis court. There, amid speeches and shouting, they declared themselves to be the National Assembly—a new assembly that replaced the old Estates General.

The Fall of the Bastille

Meanwhile, there was unrest in the capital city of Paris. Food prices were high and hunger was widespread. Poor people protested and looted. They collected weapons, pulled up cobblestones, and set up barricades in the streets. Tensions peaked on July 14, 1789, when a mob stormed the Bastille, an old fortress in Paris that served as a jail. The crowd demanded that the commander of the Bastille give them weapons, and fighting broke out when he refused. The crowd stormed the Bastille and killed the commander. In a bloody show of victory, the people stuck the commander's head on a long pole and carried it around the city.

The fall of the Bastille (shown here) is often considered the beginning of the French Revolution. Every year the French celebrate Bastille Day as a national holiday, much like July 4th in the United States.

The Women's March on Versailles

The fall of the Bastille showed that the king and his supporters were losing control of the capital. Louis XVI remained at Versailles. He ordered troops from Northern France to join men already protecting Versailles to provide more security. When news of this reached Paris, a rumor began to circulate. The rumor said that the king intended to use the soldiers against the National Assembly. Many people in the city had pinned their hopes for change on the National Assembly. They began to protest and riot once again.

On October 5, several thousand women from Paris marched out to Versailles to demand bread. The Marquis de Lafayette, who had fought with George Washington during the American Revolution, tried to prevent conflict, but the mob from Paris broke into the palace during the night and killed Marie Antoinette's servants. Lafayette eventually restored order, and Louis XVI agreed to return with him to Paris. But from this point on, the king was little more than a puppet. The real power lay with the revolutionary citizens of Paris, not the king.

Louis XVI taken into custody by a mob during the French Revolution.

Declaration of the Rights of Man

From October 1789 until September 1791, the National Assembly tried to establish a new order in France. It abolished many of the class privileges that had characterized the Old Regime and issued a document called "The Declaration of the Rights of Man and of the Citizen." This declaration gave voice to Enlightenment ideas about politics. It declared that "Men are born and remain free and equal in rights." It defined those rights as "liberty, property, security, and resistance to oppression." The declaration also promised freedom of religion and the right to a fair trial. Thousands of copies of the declaration were printed and circulated in France, as well as abroad.

France in Confusion

Despite its efforts, the National Assembly failed to solve the nation's financial problems. To make matters worse, new conflicts arose among the members of the National Assembly. Some members demanded more radical changes and appealed to the Paris mob for support. Others tried to resist proposals from the National Assembly and pressed Louis XVI to ask other countries for help in restoring the Old Regime. Nobles who had fled France called for a war against the revolution.

The countries of Europe watched the events in France with concern, particularly when French radicals urged other nations to follow their example by replacing kings with assemblies. Eventually other nations decided to take arms against the forces of revolution in France. This meant that France had to fight battles along its borders while also coping with chaos inside the country.

The National Assembly created a Committee of Public Safety to protect the new government. It also seized property of the Catholic Church to pay the costs of government. The revolutionaries feared that priests would resist the changes they sought, so they tried to prohibit Christianity altogether. This move led to resistance among ordinary people, who resented attacks on their traditional way of life.

Eventually the National Assembly was replaced by a more radical government called the Commune. The radicals punished those they considered traitors to their cause. It was a bloody time. Anyone thought to be a traitor was condemned to death, often without benefit of a trial. Jean

A French aristocrat is attacked by members of the Third Estate.

Guillotin, a French doctor, invented a machine for chopping off heads. His invention, the guillotine [GEE-uh-teen], saw plenty of use during the next few years and eventually became a symbol of the excesses of the French Revolution.

The new government had more than 1,600 people executed. One of them was King Louis XVI. On January 21, 1793, the king was brought to Paris and placed on the guillotine. Down came the blade—and off came his head. Nine months later the queen, Marie Antoinette, came to the same end.

The execution of Louis XVI and his queen shocked people across Europe. Many who had previously thought the revolution might bring reform and liberty now began to view it as a threat to social order. The British writer Edmund Burke had argued earlier that events in France would bring violence and terror instead of reform. Now many concluded that Burke had been correct. European opinion divided between those who welcomed the revolution and those who feared it.

The Terror

Meanwhile, in France, the revolution continued to grow more radical. Soon an even more radical group seized power. These new leaders promised to establish equality of all people and create a "republic of virtue." But they were also determined to protect the revolution from its enemies abroad and at home by whatever means necessary. Their actions led to what today is known as The Reign of Terror, or just the Terror. Courts were set up to "purge" the country of anyone judged an enemy to the revolution. Trials showed no respect for the rights supposedly guaranteed by the "Declaration of the Rights of Man and of the Citizen."

During this terrible time, the leaders of the revolution turned against one another. Georges-Jacques Danton went to the guillotine after losing a struggle with his former colleague Maximilien Robespierre. Robespierre led one of the most extreme political societies, the Jacobins. He called for "Liberty, Equality, and Fraternity," but he did not hesitate to send his enemies to the guillotine. Just a year after gaining power, Robespierre and his followers went to the guillotine themselves as the revolution devoured its own children.

At its conclusion in 1794, the Terror had resulted in over 40,000 deaths. There had been revolts in the countryside and the cities and harsh repression all over the nation. The French Revolution was following a path that has become all too familiar in modern history,

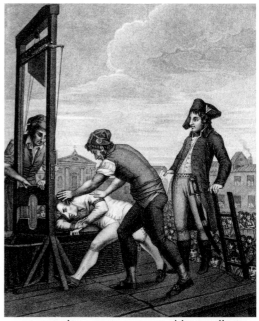

Robespierre executed by guillotine.

in which a revolution begun with noble intentions and ideals ultimately spirals out of control and leads to widespread killing and repressive government.

The Rise of Napoleon

After months of terror and chaos, a new group rose to prominence in France by calling for a restoration of order and tradition. Foremost among its members was a successful young general named Napoleon Bonaparte (1769–1821).

Napoleon was born on the Mediterranean island of Corsica. He attended military schools in France and became a French army officer. During the early stages of the French Revolution, he fought in the wars against France's enemies and won several important battles.

In 1799, when France once again fell into confusion, Napoleon seized control of the government and became First Consul. This was a title borrowed from the ancient Roman republic. It meant that Napoleon was a top leader —but not a king. In 1802, Napoleon became Consul for life, and in 1804 he had himself crowned Emperor

Napoleon.

Napoleon I. The pope presided over the ceremony, but Napoleon took the crown from the pope's hands and placed it on his own head.

Many who wanted France to be a republic were disgusted by Napoleon's decision to crown himself emperor. These people admired the Roman republic, but not the Roman Empire. They admired the spirit of the French Revolution and could not believe that the French had beheaded their king and queen only to set up an emperor.

The Napoleonic Wars

Napoleon led the French army during a series of wars against other European countries, including Austria, Russia, and Great Britain. These wars are now known as the Napoleonic Wars. Napoleon was a skilled general who won many victories. One of his most famous victories was at the battle of Austerlitz, where the French army soundly defeated the armies of Russia and Austria.

The victory at Austerlitz made Napoleon ruler of much of Europe. He placed his brothers on the thrones of European countries, including Spain and the Netherlands. Napoleon was at the height of his power. But then he made a grave mistake: he decided to invade Russia.

The Invasion of Russia

Napoleon invaded Russia in June 1812 at the head of a gigantic army. Rather than risk defeat in a major battle, the Russians made a strategic retreat. As they retreated, they destroyed crops and other resources. Napoleon's troops advanced steadily, but they advanced across a wasted land that supplied little of what they needed to survive. Napoleon led his troops all the way to Moscow, but it too had been abandoned, stripped of supplies, and set on fire. Napoleon hoped that the Russians would surrender once their capital fell. But the Russians refused.

Finally, Napoleon felt he had no choice. In late October, the French army began a long retreat. The frigid Russian winter soon began, bringing misery to Napoleon's army. Demoralized French soldiers walked barefoot through the snow. Tens of thousands died from starvation and exposure. During the retreat, Napoleon suffered over 100,000 casualties. He was left with only a tiny fragment of his original army.

Despite the terrible losses he experienced during his campaign against Russia, Napoleon was still unwilling to make peace with the other countries of Europe. He fought on against a coalition of enemies, including Russia, Austria, Prussia, and Great Britain. Eventually, in 1814, Napoleon was removed from power. The French forced him to abdicate and sent him into exile on the island of Elba, not far from his native Corsica. The French then restored the Bourbon monarchy. The new king was Louis XVIII.

Napoleon in Exile

Louis XVIII began working to bring stability after decades of war and disorder, and the leading states of Europe supported his government. European statesmen held a series of meetings to lay out the ground rules for the post-Napoleonic era. However, in the middle of their deliberations, news arrived that Napoleon had escaped from Elba and returned to France.

When Napoleon entered Paris, he was met by a cheering crowd. Many people who had accepted the restoration of the Bourbon kings now went back to supporting Napoleon. Napoleon quickly formed an army and went straight to war.

The British and other allied countries sent armies against Napoleon. The British general the Duke of Wellington commanded the allied troops and confronted Napoleon at the battle of Waterloo, in Belgium. At Waterloo, Wellington's army defeated the French army completely.

After this final defeat, Napoleon was exiled once again. This time he was sent to St. Helena, a tiny island in the South Atlantic where he was guarded night and day. There he lived in isolation until his death in 1821.

ROMANTICISM

A Revolution in the Arts

Romanticism emerged as a cultural movement during the same years as the French Revolution and the Napoleonic Wars. Artists, writers, and painters who accepted romantic ideas defined themselves in opposition to the neoclassicism that was popular during the enlightenment and the 1700s. Romanticism differs from classicism and neoclassicism in several important ways:

- Classicism emphasizes the imitation of models from ancient Greece and Rome; romanticism emphasizes originality.
- Classicism emphasizes reason, order, and balance; romanticism emphasizes emotions, feelings, and imagination.
- Classicism holds that man is made perfect only as a member of a larger society; romanticism is interested in man as an individual and thinks that man is often made worse by society.
- Classicism admires the order that man is able to impose on nature; romanticism admires nature itself.

Rousseau

One of the most famous romantic writers was the French philosopher Jean-Jacques Rousseau (1712–1778). Rousseau [roo-SOH] built a whole philosophy on his love of nature and natural ways of living.

Remember what Hobbes said about the state of nature? He said it was a war of everyone against everyone. Rousseau disagreed. He said the state of nature was beautiful, uncorrupted, and peaceful. People in the state of nature were healthier and lived in a simpler, more natural way, without artificial rules and habits.

Rousseau blamed society for creating social classes and inequality, for making one man rich and another poor, one noble and another base. He wrote that "Man is born free and everywhere he is in chains." He meant that people are

Rousseau.

free by nature but enslaved by education and society—by law and government, social classes, economic inequality, and prejudices.

Rousseau criticized the aristocrats of Europe with their artificial manners. He preferred what he called the "noble savages" (such as Native Americans). Rousseau said these people had not been corrupted by private property and social distinctions.

In his book *Emile* (1762), Rousseau laid out his philosophy of education. He argued that children should be allowed to follow their natural inclinations and make their own discoveries. He did not think children should be forced to study subjects that might bore them. Rousseau also opposed harsh discipline and memorization. He thought these things were unnatural and artificial; they stifled the imagination instead of nourishing it.

Romanticism in Literature

Romantic ideas attracted many followers in literature. Just as the French people rebelled against the old regime in politics, so romantic writers rebelled against the old regime in culture. They rejected traditional ways of writing and began to celebrate nature, the individual, and the emotions.

In 1798, the English poet William Wordsworth published an attack on poetic diction—the fancy-sounding language used by most poets of his day. Wordsworth (1770–1850) said poetry should be written not in this artificial language but in a "language really used by men." He also claimed that all good poetry is "the spontaneous overflow of powerful feelings." Many of Wordsworth's poems begin with an experience in the natural world, followed by an outpouring of emotion. You can read one such poem on page 7. In another poem Wordsworth argues that it is better to go out and experience nature than to stay inside and read books:

Up! up! my friend, and clear your looks;
    Why all this toil and trouble?   **toil:** work
Up! up! my friend, and quit your books;
    Or surely you'll grow double.   **grow double:** develop a curved spine

The sun, above the mountain's head,
    A freshening lustre mellow   **lustre:** glow
Through all the long green fields has spread,
    His first sweet evening yellow.

Books! 'tis a dull and endless strife;   **strife:** struggle
    Come, hear the woodland linnet—   **linnet:** a bird
How sweet his music! On my life,
    There's more of wisdom in it.

And hark! how blithe the throstle sings!   **blithe:** unconcernedly
   And he is no mean preacher: **throstle:** a bird
Come forth into the light of things,
   Let Nature be your teacher.

She has a world of ready wealth,
   Our minds and hearts to bless—
Spontaneous wisdom breathed by health,
   Truth breathed by cheerfulness.

One impulse from a vernal wood   **vernal:** springtime
   May teach you more of man,
Of moral evil and of good,
   Than all the sages can.   **sages:** wise men

Sweet is the lore which Nature brings;
   Our meddling intellect
Mis-shapes the beauteous forms of things:
—We murder to dissect.

Enough of Science and of Art;
   Close up those barren leaves;   **leaves:** pages
Come forth, and bring with you a heart
   That watches and receives.

The British poet Lord Byron (1788–1824) was probably the most famous romantic writer of all, for his life was as exciting as his poetry. Byron published scandalous poems and had controversial amorous relations with women. He was driven out of England and died in Greece, fighting to help the Greeks gain freedom from the Muslim Turks. Byron's poem "Childe Harold's Pilgrimage" was a smash hit in which Byron praised the beauties of nature and shared his tortured feelings and emotions with his readers. You can read a section of that poem on pages 5–7.

> Romantic ideas also influenced painters and musicians. You can read more about these movements in the Visual Arts and Music chapters of this book.

INDUSTRIALISM, CAPITALISM, SOCIALISM

The Industrial Revolution

Before 1750, most Europeans lived in the countryside and survived by growing crops and raising farm animals. People made many of the goods and tools they needed by hand. Travel meant walking, riding a horse, or rowing a boat. In many ways, life had not changed much since the Middle Ages.

By 1900, however, a great deal had changed. New forms of transportation like the train and the steamship had been invented. Many people had left the countryside and moved to the cities, where they worked in factories and operated powerful new machines. Even those who remained on the farm had to learn to use new machines or risk being driven out of business.

Historians call this great change, or set of changes, the *Industrial Revolution*. The Industrial Revolution began in Great Britain around 1750. It later spread to other European countries and the United States as those countries introduced new machinery and borrowed British techniques.

Railroads

One important part of the Industrial Revolution was the development of better and faster modes of transportation. The British built canals and better roads to help them transport goods from place to place, but the biggest changes came with the development of railroads.

Railroads used the steam engine to pull heavy wagons over rails. The first steam engines had been used to pump water out of deep mines. In the late 1700s, James Watt designed a better steam engine that could be used to power machines in factories. Then another inventor used a steam engine to pull a wagon along a track. Locomotives on rails could pull heavy loads at speeds of 20 to 40 miles per hour. Although not fast by today's standards, this was faster than anything people had seen before.

As the network of train tracks grew, it connected remote parts of the country with the great cities. Businessmen were able to use trains to ship raw materials and finished products from one place to another more quickly and inexpensively. And because railway travel was cheap, it allowed all kinds of people to travel and have new experiences.

Most people were delighted by this new form of transportation. One Englishman remembered how he would visit the countryside just to catch a glimpse of passing trains:

> I went into the country for a week. . . and saw (each day I sought to see it, each

hour of the day I could have seen it again) the white steam shooting throughout the landscape of trees, meadows and villages, and the long train, loaded with merchandise, men and women and human enterprise, rolling along under the steam. I had seen no sight like that; I have seen nothing to excel it since. In beauty and grandeur, the world has nothing beyond it.

But not everyone welcomed the railroad. The romantic poet Wordsworth saw railroads as an attack on nature and argued against plans to build a railroad where he lived. Some people insisted that trains were too noisy, too dirty, and too dangerous. They worried that a rock on the tracks might lead to a train wreck or a spark from an engine might cause a forest fire. They even worried that cows in the fields might be driven crazy by the noise of passing trains! But fears like this did not make the railroad less popular. Soon it would become England's most important form of transportation.

Textiles

One of the first industries to feel the impact of the Industrial Revolution was the English textile industry. Wool and cotton cloth for clothing were important products. The first step in making cloth is to spin cotton or wool fibers into yarn. Then the yarn is woven into cloth using a weaving machine called a loom. Each of these steps was originally done by hand or with simple, hand-operated machines. But then a whole series of inventions transformed the industry.

First, an inventor developed a loom that made weaving more efficient. These faster looms created a demand for more yarn. Then, in the 1760s, English inventors invented the spinning jenny, a machine that turned cotton and wool into yarn much faster than before. For a while the spinners were making yarn faster than the weavers could turn it into cloth. Then in the 1780s, another English inventor came up with an even better and faster loom, one that relied not only on human power but also on machine power.

Power for these new spinning and weaving machines came first from rivers. Water power had been used in mills since the Middle Ages. Falling water turned a wheel, which was connected to a grinding apparatus, which ground the flour. Later the same technique was applied to other machines, like weaving looms. Eventually water power was replaced by steam engines, which allowed people to build factories and textile mills away from streams or rivers.

As producing cotton cloth became cheaper and more efficient, demand for cotton increased. Cotton became an important crop, and more farmers grew it. But processing the harvested cotton was a challenge. Before people could use cotton, the fibers had to be separated from the seeds in each cotton boll that had been picked. This long and tedious job was done by hand until the 1790s, when an American inventor named Eli Whitney developed a machine called the cotton gin. The cotton gin made it easy to separate the seeds from the fibers and led to widespread cotton farming in places like the American South.

A 12-year-old girl working in a cotton mill in 1910.

Iron and Steel

Another industry that was transformed by a series of inventions during the Industrial Revolution was the iron industry. Before the Industrial Revolution, people made iron by using charcoal from burning wood to forge the metal. In England, however, iron producers were handicapped by a serious shortage of wood. This problem was solved when an inventor discovered how to remove impurities from coal. The purified coal produced a new fuel, called coke, which was ideal for smelting iron. Since England had large amounts of coal, the English iron industry was able to prosper in spite of the lumber shortage. Soon English factories were smelting tons of iron, and using canals and railroads to ship this iron all around the country.

A little later, manufacturers applied steam engines to iron production just as they had done with textiles. Iron mills began to use steam engines to power the blast furnaces and the rollers that flattened the iron into sheets. These steam-powered machines enabled English factories to produce even more iron.

Iron is a strong substance, but steel is even stronger. Steel is made from iron, and before the Industrial Revolution, it was made by hand, in small workshops. As a result, steel was scarce and expensive. It was generally used only for small items like knives and swords. However, during the Industrial Revolution, a series of inventions made steel easier and cheaper to produce. As a result, the nineteenth century became the great age of steel, with steel mills producing tons of steel for use in building railroads, bridges, and buildings.

Consequences of the Industrial Revolution

What happened in the textile and iron industries also happened in many other industries. Inventors developed new techniques and machines, businessmen and entrepreneurs set up large factories to house the new machines, and workers flowed to the factory towns to operate the new machines. As the Industrial Revolution swept through one industry after another and one country after another, it brought many changes, some good and some bad.

Factories produced goods more quickly, efficiently, and cheaply than ever before, and because these goods were cheaper to produce, more people were able to buy them. If you or your parents walk into a store and buy a stereo, a television set, or a dishwasher, you are enjoying the fruits of the Industrial Revolution. The Industrial Revolution also created new jobs and gave people new freedoms because it allowed people to move and change occupations much more easily.

On the other hand, the Industrial Revolution also caused new problems. In some industries, machines began doing jobs that had once been done by skilled workers. Before the Industrial Revolution, a furniture maker might have made a good living producing furniture by hand. However, once furniture-making machines were invented, unskilled workers could be hired to tend the machines, and the furniture maker might be driven out of business. Many skilled laborers were replaced by machines or unskilled laborers.

In the early 1800s, some workers who had been replaced by machines grew angry and turned to violence. They smashed machines and burned down factories. The workers who did this were called Luddites. They wanted to break the machines and return to the days when their skills were valued. The romantic poet Lord Byron spoke out in defense of the Luddites, but Luddites who were caught by the authorities were severely punished. Some were even hanged.

Factory and Living Conditions

The Luddites protested because they had been driven out of their professions, but even those workers who managed to locate jobs often lived very hard lives. In the factories of the early 1800s, the average worker worked 14 to 16 hours a day, six days a week. That's more than twice as many hours as an average American works today! Many workers had boring, tedious jobs. They just stood in one place all day running a machine. To keep workers in line, factory owners had strict rules. If a worker came to work late, he might have to pay a stiff fine. If he complained or talked back to his boss, he could be fired on the spot.

Work in the factories could also be dangerous and unhealthy. A worker who stood on his feet 16 hours a day, year after year, might wind up with crippled legs or a deformed spine. If a bored or exhausted worker let his mind wander for a moment, he might get part of an arm or a finger caught in the machine he was running. Every year, thousands of workers suffered terrible injuries this way. Some workers even lost their lives.

Smoke pours from the chimneys of a factory town, circa 1854. This factory produced cloth.

A worker who was badly injured or disabled might not be able to work anymore. Today, a disabled worker would receive a payment from the government. In the early 1800s, however, such a worker was simply out of a job, with no way to make a living.

Nor was life much safer outside the factory. Factory towns like Birmingham and Manchester could be dirty, dangerous places. Often these towns grew quickly, with no plan for how all the new people could be accommodated. Buildings were constructed rapidly, with little concern for safety. Families were crammed into tiny, dangerous apartments. The cleanliness and sanitation that we take for granted today did not exist. The air was full of smoke from factories, clean water was hard to find, and in most places there were no sewers to flush away waste. As a result, diseases became commonplace. Death rates were much higher than at present, and the poor suffered the most.

The English writer Charles Dickens described a typical factory town in his novel *Hard Times* (1854):

> It was a town of red brick, or of brick that would have been red if the smoke and ashes had allowed it. . . . It was a town of machinery and tall chimneys, out of which interminable serpents of smoke trailed . . . It had a black canal in it, and a river that ran purple with ill-smelling dye, [and buildings] where there was a rattling and a trembling all day long, and where the piston of the steam engine worked monotonously up and down . . . It contained several large streets all very like one another, and many small streets still more like one another, inhabited by people equally like one another, who all went in and out at the same hours . . . to do the same work, and to whom every day was the same as yesterday and tomorrow.

Child Labor

One of the most alarming consequences of the Industrial Revolution was the use of children as factory workers. Because adult factory workers earned such low wages, they often had to put their children to work as well. Before the Industrial Revolution children had worked, but they usually worked with family members, helping out on the farm, in the home, or in the shop. Now children—some as young as five years old—were sent off to work in the factories. There they worked the same long hours as adult workers and were exposed to the same dangers. And of course, if they were in the factory they could not be in school, so they missed out on an education.

Child laborers working in a mine.

Some factory workers were kind to their child workers, but others treated them harshly. An Englishman who had been a child worker recalled working in a factory when he was seven years old. He worked from 5 A.M. to 8 P.M., with a 30-minute break for lunch. All other meals had to be taken in snatches, without any interruption of work. The factory bosses even hired an overseer who beat the workers with a strap if they got sleepy and nodded off.

When stories like this became widely known, people were outraged. In the 1830s, the English government began making laws to protect child workers. One law said that no one under the age of nine could work in the factories. Another said that children under 13 could work no more than 36 hours a week. Gradually things became better for children who worked. Finally, in the 1900s, England and many other countries passed laws doing away with most child labor.

Laissez-Faire

The Industrial Revolution happened at about the same time a new economic idea was becoming popular. This was the idea of laissez faire. *Laissez faire* [LESS-ay FAIR] is a French phrase that means "to let alone." The idea was that the government should not try to manage the economy. Instead, the government should let things alone, allowing the market itself to create a balance of supply and demand. Laissez-faire economists claimed that laissez-faire policies would stimulate economic growth and make everyone better off than before.

Until the late 1700s, England had strict rules regulating the economy. Laws limited the amount of interest banks could charge and set strict standards for how products should be made. The government set up trade monopolies, which gave certain companies the exclusive right to trade with certain parts of the world or produce certain kinds of goods. To protect their own manufacturers, the English put high tariffs (or taxes) on goods imported from foreign countries. The idea behind this system was that only the government could order the economy in the best and most logical way.

Then in the late 1700s, a British writer named Adam Smith published a book called *The Wealth of Nations*, which argued that government controls were actually *hurting* the economy. Smith (1723–1790) said that individuals

Adam Smith.

should be free to make their own economic decisions—to decide what products to make, how to make them, what to charge for them, and so forth. If people were left alone, they would find opportunities to make money and try out new ideas. Entrepreneurs would recognize when there was a demand for a product and would find a way to meet that demand. Freedom would make people more creative and more hardworking; more products would be invented, manufactured, and traded; and society as a whole would become much wealthier. This was the basic idea of laissez-faire economics.

In the years after Smith's book was published, laissez-faire ideas became more and more popular. Many of the old laws controlling the economy were repealed. The new freedom to invent and invest helped spur the Industrial Revolution. And, as Adam Smith had predicted, this new freedom helped to create vast new wealth.

However, the same laissez-faire ideas also led to more child labor and helped to create harsh conditions in the factories. As we have seen, some employers treated their workers very badly. These employers were generally believers in laissez faire. They fought against laws intended to make things better for factory workers. It was none of the government's business, the employers said, how much their workers were paid or how many hours a day they worked.

Gradually, many people concluded that there had to be some limits to laissez faire. Not everything could just be left alone. Religious people and reformers sought to end abuses in factories and mines, including the mistreatment of children. In Britain a series of factory laws were passed to limit working hours and improve factory conditions.

Two Nations

The Industrial Revolution made some people very wealthy, but many more remained poor. The British author and politician Benjamin Disraeli (1804–1881) recognized that the growing distance between rich and poor in Great Britain had created "two nations" in the same kingdom. Workers living in harsh conditions had little contact, and little in common, with their more prosperous fellow Britons.

Disraeli wrote about the problem of the two nations in his novels, but he also tried to solve it through legislation. When he was prime minister, Disraeli passed laws designed to improve living conditions for the poor. He sought to narrow the divide between the two nations and ensure that everyone in society would benefit from the changes brought by the Industrial Revolution.

Socialism

For some people, the changes made by Disraeli and other reformers did not go far enough. In the 1800s, a number of people began to question the very idea of laissez faire and the economic system called *capitalism*. Some thinkers became critics of an economic system in which most economic decisions are made by individuals rather than the government. They argued that capitalism only benefited the people at the top of society. Entrepreneurs and businessmen got richer, but most workers remained poor. People who thought this way often argued that the government should take over the economy completely and run it for the benefit of everyone. In this way, they said, a country's wealth could be spread to all its citizens. This idea was called *socialism*.

Socialism took a variety of forms, and different writers contributed to its development. The French socialist Gracchus Babeuf (1760–1797) complained that the French Revolution had brought political equality, but differences in wealth remained. He plotted to seize control of the French government and abolish private ownership of property, but Babeuf went to the guillotine when authorities discovered his plot.

Charles Fourier (1772–1837) believed that an ideal society would be one in which people shared the responsibility for producing goods as well as the goods themselves. Each person would do his or her share of the work—and each would take a turn at the really unpleasant jobs. That way nobody would be stuck always doing the nasty jobs. Fourier and his followers believed that cooperation rather than individualism should guide how society worked. Fourier and other utopian socialists set up experimental communities based on their ideas, but most of these communities did not prosper.

Marxism

Of the socialist thinkers, one of the most extreme, and ultimately the most influential, was a German writer named Karl Marx (1818–1883). Marx believed that society was divided into two main classes—the bourgeoisie and the proletariat. The bourgeoisie was made up of the middle and upper classes; the proletariat was made up of the lower classes, or workers. According to Marx, the bourgeoisie had all the property and all the power. They oppressed and exploited the proletariat. Factory owners, Marx thought, took advantage of their workers by paying them much less than their labor was really worth.

According to Marx, the proletarian class was constantly struggling to win its rights from the bourgeoisie. Marx referred to this conflict as the class struggle. He predicted that the class struggle would end in a great revolution in

Karl Marx.

which the proletariat would overthrow the bourgeoisie and take over the government. The new government would establish a form of socialism. Private property would be abolished, and wealth would be spread around equally.

Marx's radical socialism was called Communism. In 1848, he published a book called *The Communist Manifesto*. (A manifesto is a statement of beliefs or principles.) In *The Communist Manifesto*, Marx called for workers all over Europe to rise up and overthrow the bourgeoisie.

Here are some excerpts from the last part of *The Communist Manifesto*:

> The Communists everywhere support every revolutionary movement against the existing social and political order of things.

> In all these movements, they bring to the front, as the leading question in each, the property question, no matter what its degree of development at the time.

> The Communists disdain to conceal their views and aims. They openly declare that their ends can be attained only by the forcible overthrow of all existing social conditions. Let the ruling classes tremble at a Communistic revolution. The proletarians have nothing to lose but their chains. They have a world to win.

> *Working Men of All Countries, Unite!*

The communist revolution did not occur as Marx had hoped. As the 1800s wore on, European workers did begin to win more rights. But they did so peacefully and democratically, by joining labor unions or electing leaders who favored their interests. It was not until the 1900s, long after Marx's death, that communists would seize power in certain countries. And the major communist revolutions would not occur in Western Europe, as Marx had predicted, but in Russia and China.

There are still communist countries today, but Russia and many other nations in Eastern Europe abandoned communism in the 1990s. These nations found that communism led to relatively slow economic growth, official corruption, and to the creation of police states in which those who disagreed with the government ended up in jail. They also found that communism did not eliminate differences between classes; instead, it created a new ruling class—the bureaucrats who told everybody else what to do.

LATIN AMERICAN INDEPENDENCE

Colonies in the Americas

If you've read earlier books in this series, you know that European nations set up colonies in America. North America was colonized chiefly by the British and the French, South America by the Spanish and the Portuguese.

Beginning in the late 1700s, the people of the Americas began to rebel against their European rulers. The United States was the first American country to defeat its European colonizers and become independent. It declared independence in 1776 and secured its independence by winning the Revolutionary War. Other countries soon followed the example set by the United States.

Haiti

After the United States, the next colony to win its independence was Haiti. Haiti is a country on the island of Hispaniola in the Caribbean. In the 1600s, it was colonized by the French, who brought slaves from Africa to work on sugar plantations. They brought so many slaves that the Africans outnumbered the French ten to one.

In 1791, just fifteen years after the North American colonists revolted against England, the slaves of Haiti rose up against their masters. Their leader, a former slave named Toussaint L'Ouverture [too-SAHN LOO-vair-tyur], was the son of an African king and a brilliant military leader. He abolished slavery and declared himself governor of Haiti. Later, when a French army invaded Haiti in 1802, Toussaint was captured and sent to France, where he died in prison. But his memory lived on. His followers defeated the French army, and in 1804 the rebels declared Haiti independent. Haiti became the first black republic, the first nation founded by liberated slaves.

Toussaint L'Ouverture, liberator of Haiti.

MEXICO
1810

CUBA
1895

HAITI
1804

DOMINICAN REPUBLIC
1804

BRITISH
HONDURAS
(BELIZE)
1981

PUERTO RICO

BRITISH GUIANA
(GUYANA)
1966

GUATEMALA
1821

HONDURAS
1821

EL SALVADOR
1821

NICARAGUA
1821

COSTA RICA
1821

VENEZUELA
1811

DUTCH GUIANA
(SURINAME)
1975

COLOMBIA
1810

FRENCH GUIANA

PANAMA
1821

ECUADOR
1822

PERU
1821

BRAZIL
1822

BOLIVIA
1825

CHILE
1818

ARGENTINA
1816

URAGUAY
1810

LATIN AMERICAN
INDEPENDENCE

Spanish Control

Portuguese Control

Others

This map shows when the countries of Latin America declared their independence from
European rule. In some cases independence was not actually *achieved* until several years later.

Colonial Mexico

From the 1500s to the 1800s, the land we know as Mexico was a Spanish colony called New Spain. The Spanish conquistador Hernan Cortés had conquered the great empire of the Aztecs and established New Spain as the largest and most important of all Spanish colonies. It was a huge land that included not only present-day Mexico but also the areas that became the states of California, Nevada, Arizona, Utah, New Mexico, Texas, and part of Colorado.

The population of New Spain was divided into four main groups, or classes. The group a person belonged to was determined by two things: racial background and place of birth. The most powerful group was the Spaniards, people born in Spain and sent across the Atlantic to rule the colony. Only Spaniards could hold high-level jobs in the colonial government.

Members of the second group, called creoles, were people of Spanish background who had been born in Mexico rather than Spain. Many creoles were prosperous landowners and merchants. But even the wealthiest of the creoles had very little say in the government, which was controlled by Spaniards.

The third group, the mestizos, had a much lower position in colonial society. The word *mestizo* means "mixed." A person was a mestizo if some of his ancestors were Spanish and some were Indians. The mestizos were looked down upon by both the Spaniards and the creoles, who held the racist belief that people of pure European background were superior to everyone else.

The poorest, most oppressed group in New Spain was the Indians, the original people of the land. The other groups constantly mistreated and took advantage of them. Indians were forced to work as laborers on the ranches and farms (called haciendas) of the Spaniards and creoles.

Black Africans in Mexico

In addition to the four main groups, there were also some black Africans in colonial Mexico. These black Africans were imported as laborers and shared the low status of the Indians. They made up about 4 to 5 percent of the population, and their mixed-race descendants, called mulattoes, eventually grew to represent about 9 percent.

The creoles, mestizos, and Indians often disagreed. But all three resented the small minority of Spaniards who had all the political power. By the early 1800s, many native-born Mexicans were beginning to think that Mexico should become independent of Spain, following the example of the United States. The man who finally touched off the revolt against Spain was the Catholic priest Father Miguel Hidalgo y Costilla [ee-DAHL-go ee coss-TEE-ya]. He is remembered today as the Father of Mexican Independence.

Miguel Hidalgo

Hidalgo (1753–1811) was a scholar who had studied the writings of Thomas Jefferson, Tom Paine, and the leaders of the French Revolution. These revolutionary writings helped convince him that Mexico should be free. Hidalgo also had great sympathy for the poorest, most downtrodden Mexicans. Although he himself was a creole, he lived and worked among the Indians and earned their respect and loyalty.

Miguel Hidalgo.

On September 16, 1810, Hidalgo gathered a group of his followers, most of them poor Indians. He spoke of the injustice and oppression that Spain had brought to Mexico. Then he cried, "Will you free yourselves? Will you recover the lands stolen 300 years ago from your forefathers by the hated Spaniards? We must act at once!" Today Hidalgo's speech is known to every student in Mexico, and September 16 is celebrated as Mexico's Independence Day. But there would be long years of bloodshed before the country finally won its independence.

Within months Hidalgo had gathered tens of thousands of Indians into his rebel army. At first the rebels surged across the countryside, capturing every town in their path. Several times they defeated small forces of Spaniards. But their success did not last long. The rebel forces were untrained and poorly armed, whereas the Spaniards were well trained and well equipped. The rifles, clubs, and knives of the Indians were no match for Spanish artillery. In a great battle fought in January, 1811, Hidalgo's army was beaten and dispersed.

Hidalgo and the other leaders of the rebellion tried to escape to the United States, where they hoped to win American aid for their cause. But they were ambushed and captured on the way. Hidalgo was tried for treason, found guilty, and sentenced to die by firing squad. He faced death bravely, placing his hand over his heart so that the firing squad could take better aim.

Mexican Independence

Although Hidalgo was dead, the rebellion lived on. One of Hidalgo's followers, Father José María Morelos, was determined to keep fighting. Like Hidalgo, Morelos was a Catholic priest sympathetic to the Indians. He turned a part of Hidalgo's defeated army into a tough, disciplined band of *guerrillas*, fighters who are not part of a regular, formal army. This group fought on against the Spaniards for another four years.

The rebellion was not popular with all Mexicans. Many people were shocked by the violence and disorder it brought to the country. The creoles in particular were suspicious of Morelos and his followers. Most of the rebels were Indians, a group the creoles considered inferior. The creoles worried that if the rebellion was successful, their property might be taken from them and divided among the rebels.

The rebellion was further weakened when the rebel leaders began quarreling among themselves. Then, in 1815, Morelos was captured by the Spaniards. Like Hidalgo, he was executed by a firing squad.

It seemed as if the rebellion was doomed to fail. But the people's desire for independence did not fade away. In 1820, the independence movement got a surprising new leader— Colonel Agustín de Iturbide [ee-tour-BEE-they], an officer in the Spanish army who had helped defeat the first Indian rebels. Suddenly, he turned against the Spanish government and declared that Mexico ought to be free. Unlike Hidalgo and Morelos, Iturbide appealed to the upper classes as well as the poor. And he had the power of the army behind him. In 1821, Iturbide marched into Mexico City and took control of the government from the Spanish authorities. Mexico was finally independent of Spain.

Mexico now had its own government, but at first it was not a good one. Iturbide quickly became a dictator. He even had himself proclaimed emperor of Mexico, copying the ceremony used by Napoleon when he had himself proclaimed emperor of France. No one was allowed to speak out against Iturbide. He filled his government with corrupt officials, who became rich by taking bribes and making dishonest business deals.

By 1823, Mexicans of all classes were fed up with Iturbide's corrupt and oppressive rule. They overthrew the emperor and sent him into exile. In 1824, Mexico was proclaimed a republic. The new government adopted a new constitution partly modeled on the constitution of the United States, which guaranteed basic human rights and divided the responsibilities of government between a central government and a number of smaller units known as states.

Santa Anna

Despite its newly won independence, Mexico remained a deeply divided nation. The Spaniards, creoles, mestizos, and Indians continued to quarrel with one another. And the new constitution led to arguments between those who wanted more power for the state governments and those who wanted more power for the central government.

All this quarreling made Mexico's government extremely unstable, and revolutions broke out frequently. One group of revolutionaries would overthrow the government and rule for a few months or years, and then they would be overthrown in another revolution. The Mexican army, however, remained powerful through it all. This left the country at the mercy of the *caudillos* [cow-THEE-yos], power-hungry military leaders like Iturbide.

One important caudillo was a general named Santa Anna. From the 1830s to the 1850s, Santa Anna was the most powerful man in the country. Unfortunately, he was a terrible leader. He was dishonest and used his office to make himself rich. He was also incredibly vain. He had statues of himself put up all over Mexico and forced people to address him as "Your Most Serene Highness." Santa Anna had no real beliefs or principles; all he cared about was keeping himself in power. His leadership of Mexico was a disaster for Mexico. In fact, it was partly because of his bad leadership that Mexico lost half of its total territory to the United States.

War with the United States

In the 1820s, U.S. settlers began moving into the Mexican territory of Texas. At first the settlers were happy to be living under Mexican rule. But when Santa Anna came to power, he laid down oppressive new laws, making the settlers so resentful of his government that finally, in 1836, they declared Texas to be independent of Mexico.

Santa Anna led an army into Texas to punish the rebels. At a fortress called the Alamo, his troops defeated a vastly outnumbered force of Texans. All the Texas rebels were killed, but their courage in the face of great odds inspired a rebel battle cry: "Remember the Alamo!" A few months later, the Texans got their revenge. One day, when Santa Anna's troops were resting in camp, the Texans launched a surprise attack and defeated the Mexicans.

Santa Anna.

After this defeat, Santa Anna agreed to grant Texas its independence. Meanwhile, more and more Americans were moving westward and settling in Mexican territory. They were living not just in Texas but also in California and in the area that would become the states of Arizona, Nevada, and New Mexico. Many Americans began to think that this vast region should belong to the United States rather than to Mexico. The Mexicans, of course, disagreed. The two nations grew hostile toward each other. When the United States admitted Texas into the union in 1845, Mexico was deeply angered. The following year, war broke out between the two countries.

American armies attacked Mexico by land and sea. The Mexicans fought bravely, but Santa Anna made foolish military mistakes and quarreled with other Mexican leaders. Finally, in September 1847, the Americans captured the Mexican capital of Mexico City, and the war came to an end. Mexico was forced to give up all of its territory north of the Rio Grande River—about half of its total territory.

For generations, Mexicans felt bitter and angry about this war. They were angry with Santa Anna for his incompetent leadership, but even angrier at the United States. In the United States, the war of 1846–1848 is called the Mexican-American War. But in Mexico it is called the American Invasion.

Benito Juárez

When Santa Anna was in power, many Mexicans opposed him, including a young lawyer named Benito Juárez [WAH-rez]. In 1853, Juárez was thrown in jail for speaking out against Santa Anna. But he escaped from prison and made his way to New Orleans, where he supported himself by working in a cigar factory.

Shortly after Juárez returned to Mexico in 1855, Santa Anna fell from power and a democratic government was organized. Juárez joined the government, and in 1858 he became president of Mexico.

Juárez was not at all like Santa Anna. Whereas Santa Anna was sneaky and dishonest, Juárez was famous for his sincerity and honesty. The vain Santa Anna had dressed in fancy, gaudy uniforms; Juárez dressed in plain black clothes. Santa Anna had ruled as a dictator, but Juárez governed Mexico democratically. Under Juárez, Mexicans enjoyed freedom of speech and could criticize the government without fear of harm.

Juárez also showed great concern for Mexico's poor. Juárez himself came from a poor family, and he never forgot his background. He set out to correct one of the worst injustices in Mexico at the time: most of the land was owned by a few wealthy people, while most of the workers were poor farmers who owned no land and were treated like slaves. The wealthy owners of the gigantic haciendas would not allow the workers to leave and seek work elsewhere. While the landowners lived in luxury, the workers lived in shacks without floors or windows.

Juárez was outraged by the plight of the farmworkers. He argued for new laws that would force large landowners to sell off their farms and give poor farmers a chance to own a little land of their own and work their way out of poverty.

Not everyone supported Juárez's ideas for social reform. In fact, for three years Juárez fought a civil war against those who opposed his reforms. After Juárez won the civil war, he discovered that Mexico's problems—especially poverty—were too large to solve quickly. Juárez died in 1872, but his ideals continued to inspire later generations, and today Juárez is the most honored of all of Mexico's past leaders.

Dictatorship and Revolution

After Juárez's death, his democratic government was replaced by a new dictator, a general named Porfirio Díaz, who ruled Mexico for more than 30 years. Díaz tried to make Mexico a modern, prosperous nation. He built railroads and developed natural resources such as mines and oilfields. He invited Europeans and Americans to buy land and set up businesses in Mexico. As a result, the nation as a whole became more prosperous.

But many Mexicans, especially in the countryside, were still terribly poor. Unlike Juárez, Díaz showed no concern for the landless farmworkers. Instead he allowed wealthy landowners to buy even more land, and the farmworkers became poorer and more desperate. The Indians suffered even more oppression under Díaz, too. Indian lands were stolen and given away to friends of the dictator. One group of Indians, the Yaquis, refused to give up their lands. To punish them, Díaz had thousands of Yaquis forced into slavery in a region far from their home.

Díaz ruled Mexico until 1910, when a great revolution broke out against his dictatorship. The revolution had different leaders in different parts of Mexico. Two of the most famous leaders were Pancho Villa [VEE-yah] and Emiliano Zapata [sah-PAH-tah]. As a young man, Villa had been a bandit, supporting himself by robbing trains and banks. During the revolution, he proved himself a skillful guerrilla leader. He was cruel and ruthless but also very brave, and his followers loved him. Zapata was a more idealistic leader than Villa. Like Juárez, he came from a poor family of Indian descent, and he had Juárez's concern for the landless poor. His battle cry was "Land and Liberty!"

Rebel fighters during the Mexican Revolution, 1912.

Emiliano Zapata (seated, center) with members of his staff.

In 1911, Díaz's dictatorship was overthrown, but the fighting went on. The revolution became a civil war between different groups of revolutionaries. This conflict lasted for ten years and cost almost a million lives. But it ended with the establishment of a new form of government in Mexico. The revolutionaries drew up a new constitution, one that guaranteed democracy and promised a better life for the country's poor. This constitution forms the basis of Mexico's current government.

Revolutions in South and Central America

Mexico's war of independence began in 1810. At almost the same time, the Spanish colonies in South America began their own struggles for independence.

In the northern part of South America, the revolution against Spain was led by Simón Bolívar. Bolívar, who came from a wealthy Venezuelan family, was a brilliant general and an inspiring leader. Once, in the middle of the war, Bolívar was eating dinner with some of his followers. Suddenly he leapt up on the table and began stalking back and forth. He cried, "As I cross this table from one end to the other, I shall march from the Atlantic to the Pacific, from Panama to Cape Horn, until the last Spaniard is expelled!"

Simón Bolívar.

Again and again, Bolívar's troops won victories over the larger, better-armed forces of Spain. Thanks to his leadership, a vast region in northern South America won its independence. Today, this region includes the countries of Venezuela, Colombia, Ecuador, and Peru, as well as the country named for Bolívar, Bolivia. Throughout South America, Bolívar is still referred to as the Liberator.

In the southern part of the continent, the revolution was led by another great leader, José de San Martín (1778–1850), whose forces liberated the countries of Argentina and Chile. Like Bolívar, San Martín was an awe-inspiring general. At one point, in order to attack the Spanish forces in Chile, he had to lead his army across the towering Andes Mountains.

José de San Martín.

Thanks to Bolívar and San Martín, all of the Spanish colonies in South America became independent nations. But independence from Spain did not bring democracy. Throughout the 1800s, most countries in South and Central America were ruled by a series of caudillos, or military dictators. Often one caudillo would rule for only a short time before being overthrown by another, even more ruthless leader. Simon Bolívar and José de San Martín had dreamed of a free, peaceful, prosperous South America. But the leaders who came after them betrayed that dream.

The peoples of Central America (the region of North America between Mexico and South America) also declared their independence from Spain. At first Central America was a single country, but later it broke apart into five separate nations—Costa Rica, El Salvador, Guatemala, Honduras, and Nicaragua. By 1825, Spain had been driven from the Americas.

Independence for Brazil

One important South American nation had never been colonized by Spain. This was the vast country of Brazil, which had been claimed by Portugal.

When Brazilians watched other South Americans struggling for freedom, they were inspired to fight for their own independence. Oddly enough, it was a Portuguese prince who helped them achieve it.

Prince Pedro, son of the Portuguese king, lived in Brazil, which he ruled in the name of his father. Pedro loved Brazil and was well liked by its people. As time went by, he began to sympathize more and more with the Brazilians who wanted to be independent.

In 1822, the Portuguese government ordered Prince Pedro to return to Portugal. But Pedro refused the order, crying, "I remain!" A few months later, Pedro declared the independence of Brazil. He was crowned emperor of the new country, and he promised to rule as a constitutional monarch—that is, a monarch whose powers are limited by a constitution. Thanks to Prince Pedro, Brazil achieved independence without having to suffer years of bloody warfare, as the other South American nations did.

IMMIGRATION TO THE UNITED STATES

Immigration from Ireland and Germany

From the arrival of the first English settlers until today, America has been a land of immigrants. Newcomers continued to arrive from England during the colonial period and during the early years of the republic. Starting in about 1820 to 1880, especially large numbers of people began coming from Ireland and Germany.

Living conditions in Ireland during this period went from bad to worse, making more and more people want to leave their homes and look for better opportunities in a new country. English rulers claimed ownership of Irish lands and forced farmers to pay high rents. Many poor farmers and cottage dwellers had little more to eat than potatoes and milk. Then, in 1845 and for several years afterward, the potato crops were hit by blight. Blight is a disease that weakens and kills plants. The potato blight left potatoes inedible and led to widespread famine. During the potato famine, the population of Ireland fell by one third—a million people died of disease and starvation and another million left. Many of those who left Ireland came to America. With no money to buy land, they settled in large cities like Boston and New York and took jobs as unskilled laborers, becoming street cleaners and chimney sweeps. Others went to rural areas and helped build canals and railroads.

The other nation that produced many immigrants between 1820 and 1880 was Germany. Germany had a growing population and no more land for farmers. Many Germans decided to emigrate. Unlike the Irish, the Germans often came with some money and a skill, such as baking, cabinetmaking, or printing. Some found work in factories and shops. Others bought plots of land, often in the Midwest, and started communities of German-Americans who continued to speak German and keep the traditions of the old country.

The Second Wave

A second, even larger, wave of immigrants poured into the United States over the next few decades. Between 1880 and 1924, some 26 million immigrants came ashore to begin a new life in America—the greatest movement of people in the history of the world! In 1880, the entire U.S. population was only 50 million. During the second wave, the population grew to about 115 million, and immigrants accounted for about 40 percent of the country's population growth. Many of these new arrivals came from countries in southern and eastern Europe, including Italy, Poland, Hungary, and Russia.

The earlier immigrants were like the original English settlers in many ways. The Irish spoke English, and the Germans shared much of the English culture (their music, Protestant religious beliefs, and holidays, for instance). But the new immigrants were very different. They were a varied mixture of Polish and Russian Jews, Greek Orthodox, and Italian Catholics, who spoke different languages and had different religions and customs. They even looked different from the Northern European immigrants of the first wave. Although conditions in Italy were not as bad as in Ireland, they were bad enough to make people want to leave. An Italian immigrant recalled, "We start to work on the farm from 3:00 in the morning, milk the cow, . . . plow, and then work until sundown. That's why I left and came to this country." Most of the Italian immigrants were single young men. Many of them intended to stay only long enough to make some money and then return home. But about half ended up staying and sending for their families. The Italians were very loyal to their families, and since many Italians thought the family was a better educational institution than the public schools, their children often did not advance as rapidly in American society as they might have. But they added a contagious zest for life and a strong sense of tradition that greatly enriched American culture.

Italian immigrants at
Ellis Island
circa 1910.

Jewish and Asian Immigrants

After the Italians, the Jews were the largest ethnic group in the second wave of immigration. Jews in Eastern Europe lived hard lives. Many Russians and other Eastern Europeans were anti-Semitic, meaning they distrusted and even hated the Jews. They were jealous of the Jews' hard work and success. Jews were forced to live in small villages called shtetls or in poor city neighborhoods known as ghettoes. Because they could not own land, many Jews became shoemakers or peddlers. Sometimes the shtetls and ghettoes were attacked by anti-Semites. These attacks were called pogroms. During a pogrom, houses and shops were robbed and burned, and sometimes people were killed.

Arriving in America, most Jews had no intention of ever going back. They settled for the most part in cities, arriving with their families or sending for them once they had made enough money. Because they came with business skills and because they valued education, many Jewish families prospered.

Though immigrants from Eastern and Southern Europe composed the majority of the second wave, plenty of people came from other places. Asian immigrants streamed into the western United States. Immigrant workers from China did much of the grueling work needed to build the transcontinental railroad. Japan did not allow its citizens to emigrate until the late 1880s. After that, Japanese immigrants began pouring into West Coast cities. Many settled in the San Francisco area, where they took manual jobs.

A Jewish immigrant at Ellis Island.

Ellis Island

For most immigrants, New York Harbor was the gateway to America. They arrived on a steamship, packed with passengers. Those arriving after 1886 were greeted with the sight of the Statue of Liberty, a towering symbol of their new hope and freedom. Inscribed on the base of the statue are these lines from the poem "The New Colossus," by Emma Lazarus:

> Give me your tired, your poor,
> Your huddled masses yearning to breathe free,
> The wretched refuse of your teeming shore,
> Send these, the homeless, tempest-tossed, to me:
> I lift my lamp beside the golden door.

The Statue of Liberty, a gift of the French people, was erected in 1886 and has welcomed millions of immigrants to the United States.

The message was that America, with its wide boundaries and open society, welcomed newcomers like no other country.

From 1892 until the 1950s, Ellis Island was where the immigrants disembarked. Up to 8,000 immigrants a day passed through Ellis Island. Immigrants were questioned and examined by inspectors, doctors, nurses, wardens, interpreters, and social workers. The doctors made chalk marks on the backs of immigrants—"H" meant heart disease, "F" facial rash, and the dreaded circle with a cross meant "feeble-minded," an almost certain guarantee of deportation.

Immigrants at Ellis Island.

The 80 percent who passed the physical exam went on to answer a barrage of questions: *Have you been in prison? Can you read and write? Do you have a job waiting?* Some immigrants were then given new names that the inspectors could pronounce—"Ouspenska" might become "Spensky." The lucky newcomers were given a landing card. They then exchanged whatever sort of money they had for dollars. Many immigrants arrived with little more than the name of a friend or relative living in New York, Chicago, or some other city.

Immigrants in the Cities

On arriving in this country, some immigrants pushed on westward, while others stayed in eastern cities where they could remain close to other immigrants from their old country. While the first wave of immigrants often spread out to rural areas, the newer arrivals tended to concentrate in urban centers. In such cities as New York, Chicago, Philadelphia, Detroit, Cleveland, Boston, and San Francisco, neighborhoods with names like Little Italy or Chinatown developed. By 1920, about 75 percent of all foreign-born people were living in cities.

New York was home to hundreds of thousands of Italians, Jews, Russians, and Poles. Boston was favored at first by Irish immigrants and later by French Canadians and Italians. Scandinavians went to the chilly twin cities of Minneapolis and St. Paul; Russians and Poles headed to industrial Cleveland. Chicago was home to a mixture of many races and nationalities, each with its own ethnic neighborhood. In these neighborhoods poor immigrants often crowded into run-down apartments, where they struggled to survive. But newcomers could also receive help and comfort from fellow countrymen who had settled in America before them.

These boys, aged 12 to 14, worked in textile mills in Massachusetts. The picture was taken in 1911.

The Melting Pot

In 1908, an English playwright wrote, "America is God's crucible, the great melting pot where all the races of Europe are melting and re-forming!" The idea of America as a melting pot of nationalities meant different things to different people. To some, it meant that the newcomers were assimilated into the mainstream of American life. Others thought that the newcomers changed the mixture more than they were changed by coming to America. In either case, the result was supposed to be a homogenous society, with people speaking (or learning to speak) the same language, accepting the same laws, and to some degree sharing the same culture. Public schools, newspapers, and later radio helped create a unified identity.

A crowded New York City street, 1911.

Another way to look at the rich mixture of cultures is to think of it as a salad bowl. The lettuce, carrots, tomatoes, and other ingredients each keep their own shape and color, but they blend together to form a new thing. In America, the newcomers often retained certain aspects of their old cultural identities (for example, their clothing and their food), while also adapting to the larger American culture. This American culture was much newer than that of the European countries the immigrants had left behind, and it was constantly evolving with every influx of newcomers.

The children of immigrants often found themselves caught between two worlds—the old world of their parents, and the new world of America. They learned the new language and customs more quickly than their parents, and many of them rebelled against the old ways. Unsure of where they fit in, some of them caused problems in their communities. By the third generation, the pull of the old traditions was generally much weaker. These grandchildren of immigrants, though they might celebrate some ethnic holidays, tended to be fully adjusted to American life.

Resistance to Immigrants

Immigrants sometimes encountered discrimination. Some people who were already well settled disliked the idea of more and more poor immigrants arriving, adding to already crowded cities and taking jobs that might otherwise have gone to native-born Americans. With the flood of Eastern and Southern Europeans in the late 1800s, some Americans became afraid that the country was in danger of losing its values and identity. At that time many Northern Europeans believed that Southern Europeans were racially, or genetically, inferior. Congress enacted laws to limit the numbers and nationalities of immigrants. City and state legislatures dominated by Protestants created laws to prevent Catholics from holding political office, for fear they would be too influenced by the pope.

This advertisement for the American Patriot, an anti-Catholic, nativist newspaper, shows immigrants disembarking from a boat. Native-born Americans hold protest banners that say "Beware of Foreign Influence" and "None But Americans Shall Rule America." The text reads: "Already the enemies of our dearest institutions, like the foreign spies in the Trojan horse of old, are within our gates. . . . They aim at nothing short of conquest and supremacy over us."

The Chinese Exclusion Act of 1882 attempted to keep the Chinese from immigrating to the West Coast and taking low-paying jobs. If the Eastern Europeans were considered too foreign to fit in, the Asians were considered even more so. Anti-Asian riots eventually led to the passage of more legislation to restrict the influx of Japanese and Chinese immigrants and limit their ability to own land and become citizens.

Social discrimination against Jews and other ethnic groups continued into the 1900s. They were excluded from high-paying jobs and membership in prestigious athletic and social clubs.

With each new group of immigrants, America has grappled with the question of how many is too many, and what type is the right type. One by one, various ethnic groups have managed to find a place here, though in some cases it took several generations to achieve widespread acceptance. Despite all of the difficulties, very few places in the world foster such a peaceful shoulder-to-shoulder mix of races and religions.

Land of Opportunity

Many people in countries around the world looked upon the United States as the land of opportunity, a welcoming country that offered the promise of land and prosperity for all. Some of them had built up an idealistic image of America and inevitably were disappointed by the reality. Ellis Island was sometimes called the Island of Tears, because it was where many foreigners were quarantined or rejected. It was true that the growing country needed workers, but the jobs could be almost as hard as those the immigrants had left behind. "I came to America because I heard the streets were paved with gold," goes an old Italian story. "When I got here, I found . . . they weren't paved at all; I was expected to pave them."

In addition to hard work and anti-immigrant sentiment, aliens encountered living conditions that were far different from those in their villages back home. In the 1890s, New York had 1.3 million people living in tenement buildings. Tenements were drab, dark, unventilated apartments. The buildings were four to seven stories tall, with shops on the ground floor. They were so dreary, one girl said, "It seemed as if there were no sky." There was usually one toilet per hallway, for four apartments. In these unsanitary conditions, it was not uncommon for a family of seven or more to live in a few small rooms, and they sometimes had to take in boarders to make ends meet.

Yet for all the immigrants who found that America was not what they had hoped, there were at least as many who found that it was still better than what they had left behind. One successful immigrant looked back on his arrival in New York with awe: "There *was* gold," he said. "There were markets groaning with food and clothes. There were streetcars all over town. You could watch the automobiles. There was no military on horseback and no whips."

This photograph, taken in 1911, shows a tenement apartment in New York City. The photographer described the scene: "5:15 P.M. Father hanging around the home while family works. Said, 'I not work. Got some sickness. Dunno what.' Mother; Millie, 16 yrs.; Jimmie, 11 yrs.; Mary, 12 yrs.; Camilla, 5 yrs. all work. Some of the children until 9 and 10 P.M. . . . If all work, they make $4, $5, or even $6 a week. Dirty floor. Vermin abounded."

Many new arrivals felt welcome and did quite well. The great Italian-born movie director Frank Capra migrated with his family in 1903 when he was a boy. Another Italian, Rudolph Valentino, arrived in 1913 as a young man and worked his way to Hollywood movie stardom. A young man named Marcus Rothkowitz came to America in 1913 to get away from persecution of Jews in Russia. He became world-famous painter Mark Rothko. The brilliant violinist Jascha Heifitz escaped the Russian Revolution and came to America as a teenager in 1917. And without Irving Berlin, American music would not be what it is today. The composer of "White Christmas," "Puttin' on the Ritz," and "God Bless America" fled Russian anti-Jewish violence in 1893 with his family. In America, these and countless others found opportunities they could not find at home, and they set about creating their own success stories.

Irving Berlin, composer of "God Bless America," came to the United States from Russia.

INDUSTRIALIZATION AND URBANIZATION

An Age of Industry

In the decades after the Civil War, the United States became an increasingly industrialized nation. Many Americans went from working on farms to working in factories. New railroads spurred the growth of industries. The birth of the petroleum industry created even more possibilities in efficient transportation, agriculture, and manufacturing. Gold and silver from western mines brought new wealth. Throughout this period, the government took a laissez-faire attitude toward business—that is, it did not enact regulations that might slow the pace of growth.

The writer Mark Twain called this period the Gilded Age, meaning it glittered on the surface while underneath lay base metal. A less cynical observer might have pointed to many positive changes. During this period the country grew more prosperous, secure, and confident of itself. Inventions like the lightbulb, the telephone, and the phonograph improved the quality of life. Mass production of goods allowed millions to buy things they could not previously have afforded, and rail transportation allowed workers to relocate for higher-paying jobs. On the other hand, greed and corruption were widespread, and the new wealth was not enjoyed by all. The growth of America as an industrial power produced disturbing social inequalities, including a widening gap between the rich and the poor.

The most striking gap was between those who worked in the industries and those who owned the industries. The owners were called capitalists: *capital* means money, and capitalists were those who had enough money to fund the development of businesses and industries in hope of making more money—profits— from what they produced and sold.

Mark Twain coined
the phrase the Gilded Age.

Although the gap between rich and poor was often vast, there was a core belief that those who started at the bottom of the economic ladder could, if they were persistent, climb to the top. The idea of working one's way up from rags to riches, from laborer to factory owner, made dull jobs more appealing. No one captured this American ideal better than the writer Horatio Alger, Jr. His novels featured young men who began by working hard as newspaper boys or shoeshine boys and eventually achieved success.

New Inventions

Along with advancements in industry came new inventions, which in turn did their part to make industry more efficient. Between 1860 and 1900, the U.S. Patent Office issued patents for more than half a million different inventions. A patent is a special right granted to an inventor who can show that his invention is both new and useful. Once a patent is granted, no one may use, make, or sell the invention without the inventor's permission. An inventor who holds a patent may become rich if enough people are willing to pay for the privilege of using the invention.

Perhaps no one embodied the spirit of invention more than Thomas Edison (1847–1931). Edison invented over 1,000 devices and processes. He is most famous for three of his inventions: the phonograph, the electric lamp, and the motion picture (or movie). Actually, Edison was not the first to invent an electric lamp. But he did what inventors often do: he solved problems and improved upon the ideas of others. Before Edison, no one had invented a system that would make electric light affordable. Edison and his team of researchers developed a better electric lamp and a system for generating electricity cheaply. Thanks to Edison, cities soon replaced their dim gaslights with bright electric streetlights. Today, almost every home has electric lights.

Sometimes accidents lead to new inventions. Such was the case in the invention of the telephone by Alexander Graham Bell (1847–1922). Bell was working on a new type of telegraph. One day while he was experimenting, his machine accidentally made a familiar sound—the sound of human speech! With the help of an electrical engineer named Thomas Watson, Bell developed his chance discovery into the first working telephone. On March 10, 1876, Bell spoke the first sentence ever transmitted by telephone: "Mr. Watson, come here; I want you." Soon Bell's invention had people everywhere talking on the telephone.

Thomas Edison.

Growth of Industrial Cities

During the post–Civil War period of tremendous industrial expansion, cities were growing ever bigger. People left farms and small towns for jobs in cities; immigrants came to cities and stayed. One example of an industrial city during this period is Pittsburgh, Pennsylvania. Pittsburgh's location near the ingredients for iron making—iron ore, coal, and limestone—made it ideally suited for iron and steel production. The rivers that flowed past the city made it easy to ship iron to places around the country. By 1868, Pittsburgh had 46 iron and steel foundries, 53 oil refineries, and hundreds of other production plants. In the late 1800s, half the country's steel came from Pittsburgh.

The iron and steel produced in Pittsburgh helped build railroads, locomotives, boats, and buildings. But the industrial boom also brought pollution. The air of Pittsburgh was filled with soot, buildings were blackened, and the noisy clanking of railroads and machinery could be heard around the clock. The fumes could bring tears to the eyes. Office workers who wore white shirts in the morning might find them dark by afternoon.

The nearby city of Cleveland, on Lake Erie, also expanded greatly with industry and immigration. In the second half of the nineteenth century, Cleveland's population grew more than 20 times, from 17,000 to nearly 400,000. In addition to producing locomotives and other iron products, the city became the nation's top oil refining center. In 1870, John D. Rockefeller founded the Standard Oil Company in Cleveland. It would become one of the nation's largest and most successful companies.

On the opposite shore of Lake Erie, Detroit became the leading city for the new automobile industry after Henry Ford organized the Ford Motor Company there in 1903. One of the first industrial unions, the United Auto Workers, started in Detroit. Detroit was the first city with a paved road (1909), and the first to have a traffic light (1915).

To the west on Lake Superior, Chicago was the second largest American city during this period. With its many steel mills, shipping facilities, and factories, Chicago became an industrial titan. During the 1910s, Chicago's industries grew rapidly to supply material for World War I. Along with immigrants, thousands of African Americans moved to Chicago. After the Civil War, blacks began trickling out of the South. But it was not until the 1910s that a major migration to northern cities occurred. In five years, half a million blacks moved north. Chicago's black population rose from 44,000 to 109,000; Detroit's African-American population soared from 5,700 to 41,000. These African Americans came primarily for jobs in the factories, which paid much better than most sharecropping work in the South. Racial tensions sometimes arose on neighborhood borders. In Chicago's South Side neighborhood, a huge riot broke out in 1919 when a black child swam or drifted over to a beach reserved for whites—a four-day melee between whites and blacks left 38 people dead, 500 injured, and 1,000 homes destroyed.

Urban Corruption

The immigrants and other new city dwellers depended on local politicians to help them find jobs, get food, and obtain legal aid. In return for their services, many of these politicians expected complete loyalty from their voters. Securely in office, they took advantage of their positions to gain wealth for themselves. They often accepted kickbacks, or bribes—money from business owners for favors or advantageous contracts. This illegal use of power is called *graft*. In East Coast cities like Boston and New York, many corrupt city politicians were Irish. The Irish, having arrived in the first wave of immigration, had political connections the new immigrants lacked. The laissez-faire, or non-interfering, attitude of the federal government allowed this corruption on the city level to flourish.

Among the most notorious of the city bosses was William Marcy Tweed, nicknamed Boss Tweed. He became head of Tammany Hall, a powerful New York political organization, or machine, that influenced politicians with bribes and gained lucrative contracts for construction and other municipal services. Between 1869 and 1871, he and his fellow bosses bilked the city out of tens of millions of dollars. After being exposed by political cartoons, Tweed was put in jail. Unfortunately, Tweed's successor at Tammany Hall was almost as bad. He made a small fortune through his political dealings—enough to afford a mansion and a stable of racehorses. The Tammany machine kept its power until the early 1930s.

"Boss" Tweed, head of the Tammany Hall political machine in New York City.

Labor Conditions

Until the reforms of the early 1900s, the conditions under which people labored in factories and mines were often harsh. Mine and mill workers might work a 12-hour day, six or seven days a week. The miner could earn a fairly good living at $450 a year; a mill worker might earn $250. Others made far less. In hot, airless basements called sweatshops, laborers sewed garments, shelled peanuts, or rolled cigars for barely enough to support themselves, or less. (At this time, there was no such thing as a minimum wage.)

In California fish canneries, North Carolina textile mills, Pennsylvania iron foundries, Michigan coal mines, and other workplaces, women and children often worked long hard hours, for less pay than men. Children were not as strong and skillful as adults in industrial jobs, and they suffered three times as many accidents. Fingers and limbs were often lost in the heavy, fast-moving machinery, especially when the workers were tired and not paying close attention. Falling rock posed a constant hazard in coal mines, as did coal dust, which could cause lung disease.

"Breaker boys" employed by the Pennsylvania Coal Company, photographed after a day working in a mine.

Unions

To fight for shorter hours, higher wages, and better working conditions, laborers organized themselves into *unions*. Groups of blacksmiths, printers, and other skilled workers formed local unions, which shared information and ideas with similar unions around the country. Individuals in a union had little power or money, but by joining together in a union they could bargain with factory managers and owners for better conditions. If this collective bargaining failed, the union could *strike*—that is, the members could refuse to work until their demands were met. If a large group of workers went on strike, they could disrupt or even shut down an entire company. Then, perhaps, the owners might be forced to listen to the workers.

One of the earliest national labor organizations was the American Federation of Labor (AFL), organized by Samuel Gompers (1850–1924) in the early 1880s. Gompers was a Dutch Jew who immigrated to America in 1863 when he was 13 years old. Like his father, he became a cigar maker. Seeing the powerlessness of

Samuel Gompers.

workers around him, he formed a trade union and built it into one of the strongest in the nation. With the AFL, Gompers was able to get laws passed that improved workplace sanitation and limited working hours for children, while making it harder for courts to end strikes. From 1886 until his death in 1924, the energetic Samuel Gompers served as AFL president every year except one. The AFL continues today as the combined AFL-CIO.

As the unions gained power, employers did what they could to retain control. They circulated *blacklists* of union members to keep them from getting jobs. They hired *strikebreakers*—workers who would come in during strikes to keep the business going. Sometimes employers brought in armed guards to threaten strikers and keep them off company property.

Between 1881 and 1905, there were 37,000 strikes around the country. Most of them were small and short lived. Some, however, were big and spectacular. On several occasions labor strikes led to violence. In 1886, workers gathered for a protest meeting in Chicago's Haymarket Square. During the meeting, an anarchist threw a bomb that killed several policemen. Eight labor leaders were arrested and charged with inciting violence that led to murder. Even though they were not directly responsible for the deaths, four of the men were hanged. Of the remaining four, one committed suicide and the others were imprisoned. Seven years later they were pardoned by the Illinois governor. In the aftermath of the Haymarket Riot, public opinion turned against unions.

Another ugly strike occurred in 1892 in Homestead, Pennsylvania. When the Carnegie Steel Company lowered the already low wages of its workers by nearly 20 percent, the local union called a strike. Rather than meet the workers' demands, the company locked the union workers out of the steel plant and hired new workers. The company also hired guards to protect the plant. When the guards and strikers confronted each other, angry words turned to violence. Three guards and ten workers were killed. The strike ultimately failed. Most of the workers dropped out of the union and went back to work.

Angry strikers confront Pinkerton guards hired by the owners during the Homestead Strike, 1892.

Though strikes that ended in violence often worked against the strikers, the labor movement as a whole was successful. By 1900, workers had gained the basic rights of organizing, striking, and collective bargaining. They had also made some progress toward improving the conditions and wages of laborers. In 1894, President Grover Cleveland declared a national holiday to honor America's workforce. Labor Day has been celebrated ever since.

The Great Industrialists

Many businesses and industries required a great deal of capital: for example, almost no one could afford to start a railroad with his own money. He would have to pay for locomotives, passenger cars, tracks, stations, fuel, and more. In such cases, several capitalists would combine their money to form a corporation. Each person who invested money would own a share of the corporation and would receive a share of the profits. But each also took on a share of the risk in case the venture failed.

The owners of these corporations were known as industrialists. Those who admired these men praised them for their vision and entrepreneurial spirit—for taking risks and creating new industries that made the nation stronger. Those who disapproved of them called them robber barons and blamed them for exploiting natural resources, government policies, and wage earners in order to gain great wealth.

One successful industrialist was Andrew Carnegie (1835–1919). Carnegie was a Scottish immigrant who began his career as a lowly bobbin boy in a factory. Like a character in a Horatio Alger novel, he made his way up, through hard work and entrepreneurship, until he was one of the richest and most successful men in the country. Carnegie worked in the railroad and oil businesses, but he made his greatest contributions and largest profits in the steel industry. After the Civil War, Carnegie had the vision to see that there would be a great need for steel to build railroads, so he invested in the iron and steel industry that was developing in Pittsburgh. His company helped build the nation's railroad network, and Carnegie grew fabulously wealthy in the process.

Carnegie's success in the steel business shows the way some industrialists built powerful monopolies. *Monopoly* comes from the Greek words for "one" and "sell." When someone has a monopoly, it means that person is the "one seller"

Andrew Carnegie.

—the only seller in the business. If you had a monopoly on televisions today, you would be very, very rich! A monopoly has the power to control prices in an industry and can drive other companies out of the business. That's what Carnegie did in the steel industry. He built modern steel mills to produce steel faster. To ensure a steady supply of cheap raw materials, Carnegie's company acquired control of iron ore mines and coal mines. Carnegie's company even bought the railroads and shipping companies it used to transport iron and coal from the mines to the mills. Because Carnegie controlled everything needed to make steel, his company could sell steel at low prices that other companies could not match. Whenever somebody else tried to enter the business, Carnegie soon drove the rival company out of business. Eventually, Carnegie controlled most of the steel business in this country.

Carnegie became so wealthy that he could buy up material and facilities during an economic recession, when prices were low and no one else was buying. Then a few years later, when the demand for steel returned, his profits soared. In 1901, Carnegie sold his company to another industrialist, J. P. Morgan, to form the United States Steel Corporation. Carnegie then retired. "Mr. Carnegie," Morgan said, "I want to congratulate you on being the richest man in the world." Carnegie had a total fortune of about $500 million.

The man who bought Carnegie's steel empire, J. P. Morgan (1837–1913), was a powerful banker who provided the capital that helped many major companies get started and thrive. Among the companies he helped fund were General Electric, International Harvester, and American Telephone and Telegraph (AT&T). Morgan was so rich that he lent money to banks to keep them open during financial hard times. He even helped the U.S. Treasury during a gold shortage.

The Biltmore Estate in Asheville, North Carolina, was built by members of the Vanderbilt family, who made their money running steamships and railroads. The house, which opened in 1896, had 34 bedrooms and featured new inventions including central heat, fire alarms, and a telephone.

Another industrialist, John D. Rockefeller (1839–1937), dominated the country's oil industry by controlling the processing plants, called refineries. His Standard Oil Company was a huge monopoly composed of smaller oil companies.

By 1900, a small group of powerful monopolies called *trusts* dominated America's most important industries, including copper, sugar, rubber, leather, farm machinery, and telephones.

The Industrialist as Philanthropist

The great industrialists made lots of money, but they also gave lots away. Many of them were *philanthropists*, people who devote part of their wealth to helping others.

Andrew Carnegie was almost as famous for his philanthropy as for his skill in business. He believed that others could rise from poverty—as he had—if they were willing to work hard. Carnegie donated $350 million, a large proportion of his net worth, to universities and other educational institutions. This money created more than 2,500 public libraries worldwide and financed the building of New York's Carnegie Hall. Carnegie was unusual in his determination to give away not just some of his money but most of it. He once commented, "The man who dies rich, dies disgraced."

Morgan gave generously to charities and educational institutions. He collected many priceless books and works of art and donated many of them to museums and libraries. He was one of the founders of the Metropolitan Museum of Art in New York.

Rockefeller gave away about $520 million and set up charitable foundations that continue to this day. The Rockefeller Foundation supports a variety of causes: it provides money to fight hunger, improve education, help the environment, and fund the creative arts.

Attempts to Regulate Business

At first people were afraid that monopolies would raise prices. But this generally did not happen. Like Wal-Mart and other big chain stores of today, the big companies made goods and services cheaper for consumers. The wealth of Carnegie, Morgan, and Rockefeller was approved of, even admired. But their *power* was feared. Their ability to influence the government might eventually mean that the United States would be controlled by a handful of very wealthy men. America was supposed to have a government of the people, by the people, and for the people.

Carnegie and his fellow capitalists defended their business practices. In an essay on wealth, Carnegie said that it was natural for a few people to gain great wealth. The rich man should then help his "poorer brethren" by "bringing to their service his superior wisdom, experience, and ability to administer." But many people were suspicious of the accumulation of wealth and the whole anticompetitive nature of monopolies. An author of a popular book entitled *Wealth Against Commonwealth* wrote, "Every important man in the oil, coal and many other trusts ought today to be in . . . one of our penitentiaries."

The first attempt of government to regulate big business was with the railroads. In

1887, Congress passed the Interstate Commerce Act. This law stated that all railroad charges ". . . shall be reasonable and just." It also provided for an Interstate Commerce Commission to investigate complaints. In practice, though, the law was powerless to control the railroad monopolies. In most cases it was very difficult to prove that rates were not reasonable and just. But the law did set a precedent of the federal government acting to restrain the policy of laissez faire.

The Sherman Antitrust Act of 1890 was a more general and effective tool in curbing the monopolies. Its purpose was to allow for fair competition by outlawing a monopoly in any particular market. Any combination or trust "in restraint of trade or commerce" was considered illegal. In the early 1900s, the law was used to break apart the Standard Oil Company and other large monopolies. The law allowed companies to merge with each other, but only if they did not destroy all their competition.

J. P. Morgan (right)
with another wealthy industrialist.

REFORM

Farmers and Populism

In the decades after the Civil War, Americans were proud of the country's many accomplishments. The United States had developed into a powerful industrial nation, and Americans enjoyed greater civil liberties than most other people. Free public education, which was only a dream in most parts of the world, was a reality in America.

However, Americans faced a number of difficult problems in changing from a mainly agricultural country to an industrial country with big cities and lots of factories. With the cities and factories came hard conditions for workers and the poor. Toward the end of the nineteenth century, a series of reformers tried to address new problems besetting the urban poor, as well as African Americans, women, and farmers.

After the Civil War, many American farmers found themselves in a difficult bind. The opening of new farmland and the use of modern farm machinery made it possible for American farmers to produce more crops than ever before. But there was a catch: when the supply of a commodity gets to be greater than the demand, the price drops. With new techniques, the supply of many crops increased to the point where prices went down dramatically. So, while the cost of operating a farm went up because of the cost of machinery, the prices farmers received for their crops went down because of the oversupply.

Farmers banded together to gain a more powerful, bigger voice. One of the leaders of the movement to organize farmers' alliances told farmers it was time to "raise less corn and more hell." In 1891, farmers formed a new political party to challenge the Democratic and Republican Parties. Followers of the new party were called Populists. The Populists didn't like what they saw happening to America. They saw a country moving away from Thomas Jefferson's vision of a land of independent farmers and toward domination by big corporations and industries.

William Jennings Bryan

One Populist hero was a handsome, farm-raised Nebraskan named William Jennings Bryan (1860–1925). Nicknamed the Great Commoner, Bryan was a powerful orator, with a commanding voice and a deep faith in both the Bible and the Constitution. Bryan championed the American farmer and other laborers and ultimately became one of the most popular speakers in American history. Audiences came from far and wide to hear him speak, and they cheered wildly during his speeches. "The farmer who goes forth in the

The great orator, William Jennings Bryan.

morning," Bryan thundered, "and toils all day is as much of a businessman as the man who goes upon the board and bets upon the price of grain."

In the presidential election of 1896, Bryan ran as a Democrat but favored many Populist ideas. For instance, he advocated the free-silver plan. This was a plan that farmers believed would help them pay off their debts. "Free silver" basically meant putting more money into circulation in the form of silver dollars. At the time American currency was on the gold standard—that is, the value of the dollar was tied to the price of gold and the amount of currency in circulation was backed up by reserves of gold. Many farmers argued that the gold standard helped rich bankers in the East and hurt farmers. They thought American money should be based not only on gold, but also on silver. In a famous speech, Bryan spoke out against the gold standard. He declared, "You shall not press down upon the brow of labor this crown of thorns. You shall not crucify mankind upon a cross of gold."

It was a close presidential race, but the candidate supported by big business, the Republican William McKinley, won the election. Bryan continued to speak out for the common man and the farmer. But his constituency was declining. By the 1920s, nearly three-quarters of the American population was living in cities. Farmers were losing their clout as a voting bloc. Bryan ran twice more for president and lost both times. But until his death in 1925 he remained a very popular lecturer.

The Progressive Era

The two decades following Bryan's first defeat were known as the Progressive Era. During this time a great number of reforms were enacted in business, politics, society, and other areas of American life. Americans began to sense that in the rush for material wealth, some of the core values of democracy were being trampled. Many felt that an uncontrolled laissez-faire attitude was leaving too many people out of the American dream. America was good, many people thought, but it could be even better. As a result of this desire to make a good country better, corrupt political machines were challenged and the growth of monopolies was checked.

In the late 1900s, Americans could read stories in newspapers and magazines about corrupt practices in business and government and about the suffering of poor people in big cities. President Theodore Roosevelt called the writers of these articles "muckrakers." The muckrakers exposed the corruption of public figures and prominent organizations. They wrote about the muck—the unpleasant, dirty side—of American life, in order to urge people to clean up the mess and stop the suffering. They helped deepen the country's awareness of social problems.

One of the first muckrakers was Jacob Riis (1849–1914), a Danish immigrant who settled in New York City. As a newspaper reporter, Riis witnessed life in New York's crowded, filthy slums and tenements. In 1890, Riis wrote a book entitled *How the Other Half Lives*, which described actual slums with names like Murderer's Alley and Misery Row. Riis used words to take readers into the slums: "Be a little careful, please! The hall is dark and you might stumble. . . . Here is a door. Listen! That short, hacking cough, that tiny helpless wail—what do they mean?" Riis's vivid words were reinforced by striking photographs. The pictures and photographs that we take for granted in modern newspapers and magazines first began to appear in the 1890s. When readers could actually see the crowded slums and suffering people that Riis described, many were angered and joined Riis in his demand for reforms, including better housing, better living conditions, and decent schools for the poor.

The muckrakers also tackled the abuses of big business. The journalist Ida Tarbell's *History of the Standard Oil Company* helped show how monopolies push the competition aside to dominate an industry.

Soon other writers

This photograph by Jacob Riis shows homeless boys sleeping on the streets of New York City.

joined the chorus, taking jabs at sweatshops, the insurance and drug businesses, prostitution, and a host of other targets. The publication of Upton Sinclair's novel *The Jungle* in 1906 exposed the unsanitary conditions of Chicago's slaughterhouses. Sinclair described "rivers of hot blood," "tons of garbage festering in the sun," and fertilizer tanks that stank "like the craters of hell." Appalled by what he read in Sinclair's novel, President Roosevelt pushed for a Pure Food and Drug Act.

Socialism in America

Some labor leaders and workers responded to the problems of capitalism by becoming socialists. The socialists believed that factories, land, and railroads should all be publicly owned. The government, instead of a few rich people, would then be in charge of coal mines, oil wells, and so forth. Socialism, they believed, would spread wealth around to many people and thus be a fairer economic system than capitalism. Of course, some property already was publicly owned—highways and bridges, for example—but socialists thought that more should be.

Ida Tarbell.

America's most prominent socialist in the early 1900s was Eugene V. Debs (1855–1926). He started out as a locomotive fireman. In 1893, he organized the American Railway Union. When he participated in a strike of Pullman car makers, he was sent to prison because he refused to follow a court order ending the strike. During the strike he had been such a colorful and convincing spokesman that leaders of

the socialist party visited him in prison. They tried to convert him to their cause, and they gave him an important socialist book called *Capital* by the German political philosopher Karl Marx. He found it too boring to finish. But he did read some other books, and two years later, in 1897, he announced that he was a socialist.

Socialist Eugene Debs spoke out against American involvement in World War I and exploitation of the poor: "The master class has always declared the wars; the subject class has always fought the battles. The master class has had all to gain and nothing to lose, while the subject class has had nothing to gain and all to lose—especially their lives."

Debs ran for president five times as a socialist, but he never got more than 6 percent of the popular vote. The last time he ran, in 1920, he was in prison again. He still managed to receive almost one million votes! Debs's criticism of the excesses of capitalism played a part in helping labor gain a voice, but socialism never caught on in the United States as it did in some other countries.

Jane Addams

In many of America's cities, poor people crowded into filthy slums. There were few government programs to help them. Jane Addams (1860–1935) was determined to help those who were less fortunate. On a visit to England, Addams was inspired by reformers who lived among the poor in what was called a settlement house.

Addams and a friend set up their own settlement house, called Hull House, in a poor part of Chicago. Hull House provided childcare so that mothers could go to work. Toys and games at Hull House helped to keep boys and girls out of trouble. Addams personally helped unemployed people find jobs. Hungry children and adults received hot meals at the Hull House soup kitchen. Hull House also helped new immigrants adjust to life in this country. Addams described her experiences in a book, *Twenty Years at Hull House.*

Jane Addams with some of the children who came to celebrate the 40th birthday of Hull House.

Reformers in other cities followed the example of Jane Addams and set up settlement houses. By the turn of the century there were 100 such houses in American cities. Many were staffed by young women right out of college who wanted to do something to help the less fortunate.

Theodore Roosevelt

The 26th president of the United States, Theodore Roosevelt (1858–1919)—popularly known as Teddy—was an active reformer. Roosevelt was known as a "trust buster." He set out to limit the power of the trusts—the large monopolies—that had come to dominate

American business and industry. Roosevelt ordered government lawyers to break up a huge railroad trust created by J. P. Morgan and John D. Rockefeller. The powerful trust fought the case all the way to the Supreme Court, but the government won. During Roosevelt's presidency (1901–1909), the government sued more than 40 companies for antitrust violations. In addition to the railroad trust, the government broke up Rockefeller's oil trust and Duke's tobacco trust.

Teddy Roosevelt was not against big business, but he was in favor of government regulation. He said, "We do not wish to destroy corporations, but we do wish to make them subserve the public good." He used the office of the presidency as no one had before. During a strike of the United Mine Workers in Pennsylvania, he threatened to send the army in to run the mines if the workers and owners could not come to an agreement. A compromise was worked out, with the miners getting a raise in pay. Roosevelt said he tried to give them a "square deal."

Before he became president, Teddy Roosevelt served as an officer in the Spanish-American War.

Roosevelt was also a sportsman who loved the outdoors. As president he took steps to prevent Americans from destroying too much wilderness for industrial purposes such as logging or mining. At Roosevelt's urging, the government began a program of conservation, which called for more efficient use of natural resources and the protection of forests. During his tenure he added 150 million acres of new forest and created the U.S. Forest Service. By doubling the number of national parks, Roosevelt did much to create the system of parks we still have today.

Reform for African Americans

After the Civil War, African Americans were no longer slaves, but they were still denied an equal opportunity to take part in American life. A system of legal segregation developed in much of the country and was declared legal by the Supreme Court in the

1896 case *Plessy vs. Ferguson*. As a result, blacks in some parts of the United States had to use separate bathrooms and attend separate schools.

Booker T. Washington (1856–1915), a former slave, believed that education was the key to a better life for African Americans. In 1881, Washington helped establish the Tuskegee Institute in Alabama. Under Washington's leadership, Tuskegee Institute grew to become an important center for black education. It prepared blacks to become teachers and skilled tradesmen.

After Washington invited George Washington Carver to join the faculty, Tuskegee Institute also taught modern farming techniques. An important African-American scientist and inventor, Carver was born into slavery near the beginning of the Civil War. Through his determination, he managed to earn a degree in *botany*, the study of plants. Because he believed education is ". . . the key to unlock the golden door of freedom," Carver went to Alabama to teach botany and modern farming techniques to other blacks. He developed hundreds of products that could be made from the peanut and the sweet potato, including plastics, dyes, medicines, flour, powdered milk, and fertilizer. At lunchtime you might enjoy one of Carver's most successful inventions—peanut butter.

Booker T. Washington told blacks that, before they could expect to win social and political equality, they must first raise their economic status. In a

Booker T. Washington.

speech he gave in Atlanta in 1895, Washington asked blacks to be patient and work hard. He told them to help one another: "Cast down your bucket where you are." He also cautioned African Americans against placing too much emphasis on political agitation or civil rights protests: "The wisest among my race understand that the agitation of questions of social equality is the extremest folly."

Not true, said W. E. B. DuBois [dew-BOYZ]. While Booker T. Washington asked for quiet patience on the part of African Americans, DuBois (1868–1963) urged them to insist loudly upon the equal rights promised to them in the Fourteenth Amendment. DuBois said, "We claim for ourselves every single right that belongs to a free-born American, political, civil and social; and until we get these rights we will never cease to protest and assail the ears of America." His ideas appeared in his 1903 collection of essays entitled *The Souls of Black Folk*.

In 1905, DuBois and other well-educated blacks met at Niagara Falls, Canada, to form a civil rights group called the Niagara Movement. In 1910, members of the Niagara Movement joined with white reformers to create the National Association for the Advancement of Colored People, better known as the NAACP. As the first editor of the NAACP journal, DuBois promised to ". . . set forth those facts and arguments which show the danger of race prejudice." The NAACP has been a leading organization in the fight for racial equality ever since.

The Campaign Against Lynching

As African Americans demanded their rights, some whites responded with hatred and violence. One of the most abominable practices was lynching—hanging blacks suspected of wrongdoing without waiting for a trial. Lynching was a kind of vigilante justice, used by whites to keep blacks "in their places."

In Memphis, a newspaper editor named Ida B. Wells (1862–1931) wrote powerful protests against lynching. Wells was born in 1862, the child of Mississippi slaves. She moved to Memphis and became a teacher and the co-owner of a black newspaper called *The Free Speech and Headlight.* After a friend was lynched, she began writing articles about the outrages of mob rule and lynching. She also urged local blacks to move to the West.

Because of Wells's crusade, the office of her newspaper was bombed. She moved to Chicago, where she continued to write and speak against lynching. She helped DuBois establish the NAACP and continued to campaign for equal rights for blacks until her death in 1931. "One had better die fighting against injustice," she once said, "than die like a dog or a rat in a trap."

Members of the NAACP picket against lynching in Washington, D.C., 1934.

Women's Rights

In the 1800s, women had few rights. Women could not vote, and most states had laws limiting a woman's right to own property. Most colleges were closed to women, as were most professions. In the previous book of this series, you may have read about the 1848 meeting at Seneca Falls, New York, in which Lucretia Mott, Elizabeth Cady Stanton, and others demanded equality for women. They wrote a Declaration of Principles along the lines of the Declaration of Independence: "We hold these truths to be self-evident: that all men and women are created equal."

In the years following Seneca Falls, Stanton joined forces with another determined advocate for women's rights, Susan B. Anthony (1820–1906). Together Stanton and Anthony helped found the National Woman Suffrage Association. *Suffrage* means the right to vote. Throughout the late 1800s, Stanton and Anthony gave speeches and organized petitions to gather support for a constitutional amendment to give women the right to vote.

In 1872, Anthony cast a vote in the presidential election. Because women were not allowed to vote, she was arrested and fined $100. At her trial, she told the displeased judge that her purpose was "to educate all women to do precisely as I have done, rebel against your man-made, unjust, unconstitutional forms of law." She never paid the fine.

Anthony sometimes wore *bloomers*—baggy pants—to show that she believed women should not always have to wear dresses. She also campaigned for equal educational rights and property rights for women.

The woman's suffrage movement was strongly opposed by many politicians, church groups, and a fair number of more traditional women. But the demand for women's rights grew stronger as America entered the twentieth century. Finally, in 1920, the Nineteenth Amendment was added to the Constitution. It says: "The right of citizens of the United States to vote shall not be denied or abridged by the United States or by any State on account of sex." In 1979, Susan B. Anthony became the first woman depicted on U.S. currency, with the minting of the Anthony one-dollar coins.

A woman suffrage headquarters
in Cleveland, 1912.

III.

Visual Arts

Introduction

This chapter presents a whirlwind history of art, beginning with the great creations of the ancient Greeks and Romans and stretching forward in time, through the Medieval and Renaissance periods. It introduces a few examples of baroque, rococo, and neoclassical Art and concludes with some treatment of romantic and realistic art. The material in this chapter overlaps in interesting ways with materials in other chapters of this book, including the brief history of classical music given in the music chapter and the discussions of the ancient world and romanticism in the history chapter.

Because of space limitations, we have only been able to reproduce a few pictures from each period. Parents and teachers can build on the treatment offered here by exposing children to additional art books and pictures, taking them to art museums, and showing them buildings with interesting architectural features. Although books are delightful and informative, there is no substitute for the experience of seeing works of art in person. Many museums make this experience possible for all by offering free admission once a week.

Children should experience art not only as spectators but also as creators. They should have frequent opportunities to draw, paint, cut, paste, mold with clay, and take photographs. They can imitate styles and artists they have encountered and, eventually, develop a style of their own.

CLASSICAL ART

Greece and Rome

Some of the earliest artistic masterpieces were produced more than 2,000 years ago in ancient Greece and Rome. Art created by the ancient Greeks and Romans is called *classical art*.

The ancient Greeks led the way, creating many wonderful works of art, including pottery, paintings, sculptures, and buildings. Unfortunately, most ancient Greek art has been lost. We know Greek art from a few surviving pieces, some written descriptions, and a collection of Roman copies.

Greek Architecture

The ancient Greeks considered balance and proportion to be important qualities of art. Greek buildings are often rectangular, carefully balanced, and symmetrical: you can divide the buildings in half so that each half is a mirror image of the other.

When the ancient Greeks built important buildings, they followed one of three classical orders. The Doric order was the oldest and plainest, the Ionic order was more elegant, and the Corinthian order was the most elaborate.

The Greeks developed specific rules for each order. For example, they set down guidelines about the height and width of the columns in relation to the other parts of the building. Every part of the building had to be exactly in proportion to all the other parts.

The Parthenon, in Athens, is a magnificent example of balance and

DORIC   IONIC   CORINTHIAN

proportion in Greek architecture. This temple is built in the Doric style and dedicated to the city's patron goddess, Athena Parthenos. It was built in the time of Pericles, on the Acropolis, the highest point in Athens.

This reconstruction shows how the Parthenon and other buildings on the acropolis of Athens looked in ancient times. The Parthenon is the highest building.

The Pantheon

Rome rose to power after the Golden Age of ancient Greece. The Romans were enthusiastic admirers of Greek art and created copies of many Greek works. You can see the Greek influence on Roman architecture if you look at the picture of the Pantheon on the next page.

The Pantheon was built from A.D. 125 to 128, during the reign of the emperor Hadrian. It was intended to honor the Roman gods; in fact, the word "pantheon" means "all the gods."

All the proportions inside the Pantheon are in perfect balance. The diameter of the dome at its widest point is 143 feet, which is exactly equal to the height from the floor to the oculus, or opening, at the top of the dome.

While it is a fine example of the classical emphasis on balance and proportion, the Pantheon also includes some elements that are new. For example, the building includes a number of arches. The Romans learned about arches from the Egyptians and perfected the use of the arch in architecture.

The builders who built the Pantheon also used a building material unknown to the Greeks—concrete. Concrete is a strong, inexpensive material made of powdered lime, sand, and small rocks or bits of broken pottery mixed with water. Concrete can be poured and molded. This meant that the Romans were no longer limited to building structures with right angles. Notice how many curves, circles, and arches there are in the Pantheon.

This painting by the 18th-century Italian artist Giovanni Paolo Panini shows the interior of the Pantheon, with its dome and oculus.

Ideal Figures

The ancient Greeks and Romans also created beautiful sculptures. They were especially good at creating sculptures that capture the beauty and symmetry of the human body. Again, the artists worked out rules to ensure that the sculptures would be beautiful and well proportioned. One artist determined that the length of a human body in a sculpture should be equal to eight times the length of the head.

Myron's Discobolus.

Apollo Belvedere.

The Greek sculptor Myron created the statue called *Discobolus* (*Discus Thrower*) around 450 B.C. The discus was one of the competitions in the original Olympics. Myron's statue shows the athlete competing in the nude, as the ancient Greeks did during the Olympics. The athlete is balancing carefully, twisting, and preparing to throw the heavy discus. Myron's original was a bronze sculpture, but it has vanished, and today we have only marble copies made by the Romans.

The statue *Apollo Belvedere* is another Roman copy of a Greek original. It shows the same appreciation for beauty and proportion as Myron's *Discus Thrower*; but in this case the subject is not a human being but the god Apollo.

GOTHIC ART

The Gothic Cathedral

Although the Roman emperors initially persecuted Christians, they eventually converted to the new religion. After the Roman Empire fell, the Catholic Church, with its headquarters in Rome, emerged as the most important cultural force in Western Europe. Gothic art, which began appearing in France in the 12th century, was an expression of the ideas and values of the medieval church.

When we think of Gothic art, we think of great stone cathedrals, filled with colored light from large, stained glass windows. The architects who designed these cathedrals were inspired by Christianity. Their goal was to build a heavenly house of God on Earth, filled with divine light. This holy place would lift and illuminate the human spirit and unite it with God. Floor plans were often in the shape of a cross, and the designers used pointed arches and vaults to achieve soaring vertical interior spaces and guide the eyes upward, toward heaven.

On the outside of these cathedrals, you can see towering spires, decorative gargoyle waterspouts, and massive flying buttresses that help support the tall stone walls.

Cathedral of Notre Dame,
Paris, France.

THE RENAISSANCE

Renaissance Sculpture

Not everybody liked Gothic art. In fact, the humanist scholars of the Renaissance hated it. It was actually these Renaissance scholars who coined the term *Gothic*. For them, *Gothic* was a scornful, disapproving term: the Goths were one of several invading peoples who helped bring down the Roman Empire. As far as the humanists were concerned, the Goths were barbarians, and Gothic art was barbarian art. What the artists and scholars of the Renaissance wanted instead was a return to the kind of art created in ancient Greece and Rome. Indeed, we speak of this age as a *renaissance*, or rebirth, precisely because interest in the classical world was reborn during this period.

Renaissance sculptors like Michelangelo (1475–1564) were deeply influenced by classical sculptures. They labored to create new works inspired by classical models. Michelangelo's statue *David* is an example. According to the Hebrew Bible, the Israelite David killed the giant Goliath with a slingshot. In Michelangelo's statue, *David* faces his mighty opponent nude, holding a sling over his left shoulder and a stone in his right hand. Like Myron's *Discus Thrower*, Michelangelo's *David* is poised in the moments before action, gathering energy and determination. Like the *Apollo Belvedere*, he is strong and graceful. The influence of classical models is clear.

Michelangelo, *David*.

Renaissance Painting

Renaissance painters also depicted classical subjects in their work. In *The School of Athens*, the painter Raphael (1483–1520) depicted an imaginary gathering of great thinkers. The Greek philosopher Plato and his student Aristotle are in the center of the picture. Each carries a book he has written. Plato points skyward, which reveals his focus on abstract ideals and the forms. Aristotle gestures toward Earth, an indication of his trust in the real world as a source of knowledge. Socrates stands with his back to the center at left, engaging in dialogue with his disciples, including Alcibiades (al-suh-BYE-uh-deez), a general who led the Athenian troops during the Peloponnesian War. (He is wearing a helmet and armor.) Also present are the geographer Ptolemy (on the far right, holding a globe) and the mathematician Euclid (also on the far right, bending down with his compass to draw on a slate). All these ancient figures are harmoniously arranged, like actors on a stage.

Raphael, *School of Athens.*

But not every figure in Raphael's picture was born a thousand years earlier. The solitary figure in the foreground, left of center, sitting and leaning on a block of marble, is Michelangelo, who was painting the frescoes in the Sistine Chapel while Raphael was creating *School of Athens*. Raphael also included a self-portrait. He is the figure looking out at us in the black hat second from the far right (just behind Ptolemy).

By picturing himself and his contemporaries in the company of ancient scholars and philosophers, Raphael made an important statement. He made it clear that he believed he and his fellow Renaissance artists were carrying on the great educational, artistic, and philosophical traditions of the ancient world. Perhaps no picture tells us more about the spirit and outlook of the Renaissance artist than this one.

Raphael's *School of Athens* is a special kind of painting called a *fresco*. A *fresco* is made with water-based paints applied to either wet or dry plaster on a wall. This particular fresco was painted on a wall in the Vatican in Rome. It is a very large work—19 feet tall and 27 feet wide!

Perspective

Although Renaissance artists drew inspiration from classical models, they did more than just rediscover old ideas and techniques. Filippo Brunelleschi [broo-null-ESS-key] devised a revolutionary system of *linear perspective* about 1420. This was a mathematical system that allowed painters to create a convincing, seemingly three-dimensional space on a two-dimensional surface, such as a wall or a board.

Raphael's *School of Athens* is one of many Renaissance paintings that use perspective. If you look again at the picture, you will see a series of arches, each one of which seems to be behind the previous arch. These successive arches give the painting the illusion of depth, even though it is painted on a flat wall. Essentially, the painter has used the technical art of linear perspective to trick our eyes into seeing depth where there is only a flat surface.

BAROQUE ART

El Greco

El Greco (1541–1614) was an important painter of the late Renaissance. El Greco, meaning the Greek, was born on the Greek island of Crete in 1541. He spent many years in Italy, studying the works of the great Italian painters of the Renaissance, including Raphael and Michelangelo, but he later settled in Spain.

One of El Greco's best-known works is a landscape painting of his adopted hometown, Toledo. Rather than picturing Toledo as it really looked, El Greco used dramatic contrast of light and dark to evoke an emotional response in the viewer. Bonelike walls, bridges, and buildings collide with and intersect the swelling hill. The sky seems to be about to split open with thunder and lightning. The viewer senses, with some anxiety, that something dramatic is about to happen.

El Greco, *View of Toledo.*

Caravaggio and the Baroque

Some of the aspects we have seen in El Greco's *View of Toledo* became characteristics of the style of art known as *baroque*. Baroque art is characterized by the dramatic use of light and shade (also known as *chiaroscuro*), turbulent compositions, and vivid emotional expression. Baroque painters often try to create an emotion in the viewer. Compared with the classicism of the Renaissance, baroque art must have seemed contorted or grotesque at first.

You can see many of these features in the Italian painter Caravaggio's *The Calling of St. Matthew*. The painting illustrates the moment in the Bible where Jesus selects Matthew, who would become one of his most devoted followers. Jesus stands on the right and points at Matthew. Matthew (with the beard) points at the man next to him, as if to say, "Do you mean me? Or him?" The unusual lighting suggests that something very dramatic and significant is happening.

Caravaggio, *The Calling of St. Matthew.*

Rembrandt

Rembrandt van Rijn (1606–1669) was one of the greatest painters of all time. Throughout his life he painted self-portraits, so we have many images of him at different ages done in varying styles. This one, painted in 1659, was done when Rembrandt was fifty-three and living in Amsterdam. It shows some aspects of baroque style.

Rembrandt makes use of light and shade: against the dark background and clothing, the lighter flesh tones of Rembrandt's face stand out dramatically. His clasped hands catch light that falls across his left shoulder. He looks directly out at us with a somber, penetrating gaze. The painter has not idealized his own features. Instead, he reveals his wrinkled and sagging flesh. His expression is riveting and seems calculated to cause a sympathetic response in the viewer.

Rembrandt van Rijn, *Self-Portrait*, 1659.

ROCOCO ART

The Pleasures of Life

The rococo period is usually said to have lasted from about 1750 to 1800. Rococo art is characterized by its decorative look, achieved by the use of delicate pastel colors. The subject matter is often playful and lighthearted. Many rococo paintings depict scenes from the lives of European aristocrats during the years before the French Revolution.

In 1767, Jean-Honoré Fragonard created a charming scene of flirtation and fantasy in *The Swing*. The central figure is a young woman, lit by a ray of sunshine, riding on a swing. She wears a voluminous creamy pink dress and a hat. She has just lost one of her dainty slippers, which can be seen flying through the air. Behind her, in the shadows of a huge leafy tree, a man pushes the swing. Opposite him a young man reclines in flowering bushes, with hat in hand, and reaches toward the object of his affection. On the left, a statue of the love god, Cupid, stands with a finger to his lips, perhaps indicating that he will keep this romantic meeting a secret.

Jean Honoré Fragonard,
The Swing.

Below is another example of the rococo style. This painting is by the French artist Jean-Antoine Watteau (1684–1721). It shows French aristocrats playing music and relaxing. Both the picture itself and the title—*The Pleasures of Life*—are good examples of the rococo spirit.

Jean-Antoine Watteau, *The Pleasures of Life.*

NEOCLASSICAL ART

Classical Forms

In the late 18th and early 19th centuries, many artists began to turn away from the expressive drama of the baroque and the lighthearted gaiety of the rococo styles. The Enlightenment, with its emphasis on reason, helped bring about a new style of art, which was later called *neoclassical*. Like the artists of the Renaissance, neoclassical artists revived classical forms and subjects and emphasized balanced, clearly articulated forms. They believed in the high moral purpose of art: the public could—and should—be educated and improved by the visual arts.

Jacques-Louis David

Jacques-Louis David (1748–1825) was commissioned by King Louis XVI to create a series of pictures that would teach the French people good citizenship and improve morality. In 1784, David [dah-VEED] began work on *The Oath of the Horatii*, which shows a scene from the early history of ancient Rome.

Jacques-Louis David, *The Oath of the Horatii*.

The three Roman Horatii brothers (on the left) are shown swearing an oath to their father, who holds their swords in the center of the picture. The brothers are swearing to defend Rome against the city of Alba, even though two of them have relatives in Alba. The men are consciously choosing loyalty to their city-state over loyalty to relatives, putting national loyalty above personal connections. Their father approves, but the women in the family (on the right) tearfully lament the decision. David presents this ancient historical moment as an inspiring example of the nobility and courage of these heroic patriots, who were willing to sacrifice their lives and family obligations for Rome.

David also painted a well-known picture of the death of Socrates. David shows the philosopher just before his death, after the great philosopher has refused to escape. Socrates is reaching for the cup of poisonous hemlock. His followers are devastated, almost swooning. Only Plato, sitting next to the bed, seems to be in control of himself. Again, David has chosen a classical subject with a view to inspiring people with a love for noble actions.

Later in life, David became sympathetic to ideals of the French Revolution and painted some of the leaders of the French Revolution in a neoclassical style.

Jacques-Louis David, *The Death of Socrates.*

ROMANTIC ART

Imagination and Emotion

The romantic movement in art began in the late 1700s and lasted until the mid-1800s. Like many other movements in art, it was partly a reaction against the style and ideas of the previous era. Romantic painters reacted against the orderliness of neoclassical art. They drew heavily on the imagination and were attracted to exotic and romantic subjects—nature scenes, high peaks, revolutions, bullfights. They also favored a bolder, more expressive, and highly emotional style.

Goya

Francisco Goya (1746–1828) was a Spanish painter who worked in many different styles. Some of his early works are painted in a rococo style, but some of his later works are more romantic.

Like many Spaniards, Goya loved bullfighting. He painted several paintings of bullfights. The one shown below was done about 1824. Goya presents a dramatically lit bullring in which a picador on horseback prepares to weaken the bull by stabbing him with a lance.

Other bullfighters cluster around and wounded animals lie on the ground.

In creating this painting, Goya used a heavily loaded brush, a rag, and even his bare fingers to apply the paint. The result is an exciting, dramatic scene, full of energy and anticipation.

Francisco Goya,
Bullfight.

Delacroix

Earlier in this book, you read about the French Revolution and Napoleon. France continued to be politically turbulent even after Napoleon was sent into exile. In 1830, another revolution broke out in France, during which members of the French middle class drove the king from the throne. The French painter Eugène Delacroix [dell-uh-KWAH] watched the Revolution of 1830 unfold from the windows of his studio in Paris and commemorated the event with the picture *Liberty Leading the People*.

Eugène Delacroix, *Liberty Leading the People*.

As in David's *Oath of the Horatii*, Delacroix (1798–1863) presents a dramatic moment of heartfelt patriotism. But in this romantic picture, we sense the immediacy, messiness, and chaos of the events. Unlike David's picture, this image is not idealized. The central female figure symbolizes Liberty. She waves the tricolor flag of France and carries a rifle with a bayonet. A boy with pistols in both hands and a top-hatted member of the middle class are among her many followers. The glowing colors and emotional style convey the romantic passion for revolution and freedom.

Friedrich

One of the most important subjects in romantic art and literature is nature. You may have read about the romantic fascination with nature in the history chapter of this book and in the poems by Wordsworth and Byron (pages 5–7). You can see the same fascination in this painting by the German painter Caspar David Friedrich [FREE-drick] (1774–1840).

In *Chalk Cliffs on Rügen*, created in 1818–1819, three figures perch on the edge of a white cliff, looking out over the Baltic Sea. The woman in red points down over the edge. The man in the middle has removed his hat in order to crawl up to the edge and gaze down. The third man—leaning against the tree on the right—seems to be absorbed in thought.

Caspar David Friedrich,
Chalk Cliffs on Rügen.

REALISM

The Realists

Many of the paintings we have seen so far depict great figures from history, like the Israelite warrior David or the Greek philosopher Socrates; great moments in history, like the French Revolution of 1830; or exotic figures, like bullfighters. However, beginning in the middle of the 19th century, many painters began to question the traditional emphasis on historically important, idealized, and exotic subjects. These painters chose to focus instead on everyday scenes and the lives of ordinary people. They did not believe that art had to be uplifting, edifying, or even beautiful. They thought it only had to be realistic. That is why these painters are called realists.

Jean Millet, *The Gleaners.*

European Realism

In *The Gleaners*, painted in 1857, the French painter Jean Millet [mih-LAY] shows three women gleaning—picking up stray bits of grain left behind after the harvest. Hours of this work might yield enough grain to make a loaf of bread. Because the women's faces are not visible, they are not seen as individuals but serve as representatives of a class of poor rural workers. Millet (1814–1875) uses muted, glowing colors to portray this realistic scene.

Gustave Courbet [cour-BAY] was another French realist painter (1819–1877). He chose poor, ordinary people as subjects. In *The Stone Breakers*, painted in 1849, we see an old man breaking up stones, assisted by a younger helper. Like Millet's gleaners, these workers do not face the viewer. We sense that the life of a laborer is hard—and not likely to improve. Courbet has used few colors and dramatic lighting. The dark rise behind the figures contrasts with their light clothing and the white stones.

Gustave Courbet, *The Stone Breakers.*

American Realism

Realism became popular in the United States as well. One of the great American realists was Thomas Eakins (1844–1916). In 1875, Eakins painted *The Gross Clinic*. The painting shows Dr. Samuel Gross, a Philadelphia doctor, teaching a class on surgery. Gross stands next to the patient, with a scalpel in his bloodied hand. His assistants cluster around him, while a clerk takes notes on the procedure. The patient's mother is on the left, covering her eyes. Barely visible in the background are the faces of students observing the operation.

Although Eakins intended to show the value of science, critics were offended by the graphic nature of this realistic painting. They complained that the subject was "inappropriate," and the work was rejected by the 1876 Philadelphia Centennial art exhibition.

Thomas Eakins,
The Gross Clinic.

Henry Ossawa Tanner (1859–1937) was an African-American artist who studied with Thomas Eakins. *The Banjo Lesson*, painted in 1893, shows an elderly man teaching a young boy to play the banjo. They are in a softly lit kitchen interior, with pots and pans on the wood floor and a partly covered table with dishes and a pitcher in the background. The two are absorbed in the activity. They share a warm, familial relationship. At a time when comic stereotypes about African Americans were common, Tanner intended to show the serious and compassionate side of everyday African-American life.

Henry O. Tanner,
The Banjo Lesson.

One of the most famous American realist painters was Winslow Homer (1836–1910). During the American Civil War, Homer was a pictorial reporter, sketching and painting the lives of soldiers. Later in life, he lived on the coast of Maine, where in 1895 he painted *Northeaster*. A *northeaster*—also known as a *nor'easter*—is a storm along the Atlantic coast. In this realistic seascape, we see the wind-driven waves breaking on a diagonal slab of dark rock. Homer has incorporated some of the colors of the water with complementary crimsons in the rocks for a rich, unified scene.

Winslow Homer, *Northeaster.*

IV.

Music

Introduction

This chapter introduces some vocabulary, symbols, and concepts that will help children understand and appreciate music. The first section, on the elements of music, builds on what students should already know about musical notation from earlier books in this series. Musical notation is covered in more detail and chords and scales are introduced. The value and instructive potential of this section will be greatly enhanced if children are able to play notes, scales, and chords on a keyboard instrument. A piano, an organ, or an electronic keyboard would do the trick.

The second section, on classical music, introduces children to composers of the baroque, classical, and romantic periods. Children are introduced to the life stories and greatest musical creations of great musical masters, including Bach, Handel, Beethoven, and Mozart. The value and delightfulness of this chapter will be greatly increased if children have an opportunity to listen to the classical selections described. To facilitate such listening, the Core Knowledge Foundation has assembled CD collections of the works discussed here. These are available for purchase on our website:

www.coreknowledge.org.

In music, as in art, students benefit from creating and participating every bit as much as they benefit from formal study. Singing, playing instruments, active listening, following musical notation, dancing, and moving to music all help sharpen a child's sense of how music works. We encourage you to share good music with children by playing and singing songs, attending concerts, listening to the radio, and playing audio recordings.

ELEMENTS OF MUSIC

Musical Notation

One way to introduce music is to contrast it with art. Whereas we appreciate art with our eyes, we appreciate music with our ears. Whereas works of art occupy a certain space, and artists arrange figures within this space, works of music occupy a certain period of time, and composers and songwriters arrange notes and sounds within this period of time.

Because music happens in time, people have developed a system of recording what should happen at each moment in a particular song or musical composition. Songwriters and composers use a special kind of writing called *notation* to set down their music. Singers and players can read this notation to sing or play the piece over and over again.

When played or sung, musical sounds are called *pitches*; when these pitches are written down, we call them *notes*. A piece of music that includes notation for all the voices or instruments in a piece is called a *score*.

Staffs and Clefs

Musical notes are written on a set of five parallel lines called a *staff* (plural: *staves*). Notes can be placed on lines or between them. High notes are placed higher on the staff than low notes. Players or singers read the notes from left to right, just as you read words on the page.

The notes in a score are divided into smaller sections, called *measures*, which are marked by *bar lines*. A double bar line marks the end of a piece. Here are four measures of music:

Sometimes you will see two staves, one on top of another, like this:

The symbol at the beginning of the top staff is the *treble clef*, also called the G *clef*. The symbol on the bottom staff is the *bass clef*, also called the F *clef*. Each clef lets music readers know the names of the notes written on the lines and spaces for that clef. The treble clef is used to record notes for voices and instruments that generally sing or play higher pitches, and bass clef for those that sing or play lower pitches.

The piano and other keyboard instruments use both clefs; generally the musician plays the treble with the right hand and the bass with the left. When both clefs are present, as they are on the previous page, the arrangement is called a *grand staff*.

Sometimes a composer may want to use a note that's a little higher or lower than the lines on the staff. In such cases small lines called *ledger lines* can be added above or below the staff as needed.

Notes and Rests

This chart shows some common musical notes and rests:

Whole note	o	Whole rest	▬
Half note	𝅗𝅥	Half rest	▬
Quarter note	♩	Quarter rest	𝄽
Eighth note	♪	Eighth rest	𝄾

Each note on this chart lasts half as long as the note above it. A quarter note lasts half as long as a half note, and an eighth note lasts half as long as a quarter note. What lasts half as long as an eighth note? A sixteenth note. Here's a sixteenth note:

♬

Notes are composed of a *head*, which centers the note on the staff line or space; an upward or downward line called a *stem*; and, in the case of eighth or sixteenth notes, a *flag*. Often, eighth and sixteenth notes are grouped by omitting the flags and connecting the stems with a *beam*. Eighth notes are connected with a single beam, sixteenth notes with a double beam.

In the music below, the first measure contains eight eighth notes; the second contains eight sixteenth notes, two eighth notes, and a quarter note.

If a composer wants the musicians or singers to hold a note a little longer, he can put a *dot* to the right of the note head. The dot increases the note's value by half. So a dotted quarter note lasts 50 percent longer than an undotted quarter note.

When a pitch needs to be held past a bar line, the initial note can be *tied* to another of the same pitch name, on the same line or space on the staff. The curved line connecting the notes is called a *tie*. The values of the notes connected by the tie are simply added together.

Sharps and Flats

The pitches on a staff are identified with the first seven letters of the alphabet.

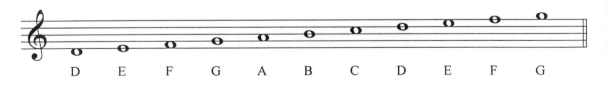

D E F G A B C D E F G

A is one note higher than G, and F is one note lower. However, it is also possible to play or sing notes that fall between A and G, or between G and F. If a composer raised a G by one *half step* (from one key on the piano to the very next one to the right, regardless of color), he or she would write a *sharp* sign (♯) in front of the note head, and the new note would be called G-sharp. If the composer lowered a note by one half step (from one key on the piano to the very next one to the left, regardless of color), he or she would put a *flat sign* (♭) in front of the note head, and the resulting note would be called G-flat.

Here is a series of notes, some of which are marked with the sharp sign:

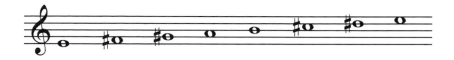

A musician reading this will play C♯ instead of C, D♯ instead of D, F♯ instead of F, G♯ instead of G.

Now suppose the composer wanted to tell the musicians to play *every* C, D, F, and G in the entire piece as sharps? In that case, the composer would insert a *key signature* after (to the right of) the clef sign. Here is the same series of notes as the one shown above, but shown with a key signature:

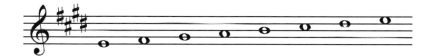

The sharp signs on the lines and spaces for C, D, F, and G tell the musicians to make every note on those lines and spaces a half step higher. Writing a key signature is easier than going through a long piece of music and adding a sharp sign to every note that needs one. You can also write a key signature with flat signs; this tells the musicians to make the notes on those lines and spaces a half step lower.

If there is a particular note that the composer does not want to be played or sung as a sharp or flat, the composer can place a *natural* sign (♮) next to the note to cancel the effect of the key signature for that note.

The Beat

The underlying pulse, or heartbeat, in a piece of music is called the *beat*. Beats are usually organized and felt as groups of twos or threes. Twos can often be combined into groups of four, and threes into groups of six. When beats are organized or grouped in this way, the composer lets the musicians know by putting a *meter signature* (also called a *time signature*) at the beginning of the piece near the clef sign.

A meter signature consists of two stacked numerals that look somewhat like a fraction. The lower number lets the players know what note value will function as the basic beat. The upper number lets players know how many of that kind of note (or the equivalent) may appear in each measure. For example, a 3/4 time signature means that the basic unit will be a quarter note, and there will be three quarter notes, or the equivalent, per measure.

The most common meter signature is 4/4, which is also known as *common time*. When the meter signature is 2/4 or 3/4, the quarter note is still the unit of beat, but each measure has two or three beats. A 6/8 meter means that eighth notes are grouped into measures of six beats. Here's a song in 6/8 time that you probably know.

Scales

A *scale* is a progression of notes moving from low to high or high to low, according to a specific pattern of intervals. You can play a simple scale on a piano by successively pressing the eight keys labeled in gray in the picture below: C, D, E, F, G, A, B, and C. Notice how this scale begins and ends with C. However the second C is one octave higher in pitch than the first C.

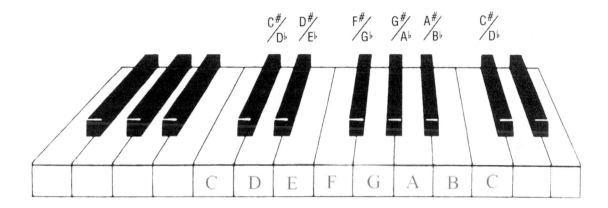

Although the piano keys are labeled in the picture, for best results, try to play the notes on a real piano or electronic keyboard. As you play these notes, comprising the C major scale, you may wish to sing along, using the syllables traditionally used to sing scales: do, re, mi, fa, sol, la, ti, do.

Notice that there are also black keys on the piano, keys you did not play when you played the C major scale. The picture above shows that the black key between C and D can be called either C♯ or D♭. Remember: C♯ is a half step higher than C, and D♭ is a half step lower than D. This explains why each black key has two names. C♯ is the same pitch as D♭ on a piano; musicians call two such tones *enharmonic*.

The distance from any key on a piano keyboard to the next black or white key is one half step. For example, the distance between G and G♭ is one half step. Two half steps equal a whole step. The interval between C and D, for example, is a whole step.

Notice that there are some white keys that do not have black keys between them. This happens between E and F and also between B and C. So the C major scale described above is made up of the following series of seven steps linking eight notes: whole step (C to D), whole step (D to E), half step (E to F), whole step (F to G), whole step (G to A), whole step (A to B), and a half step (B to C).

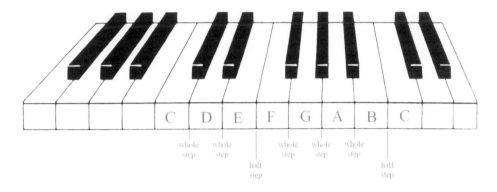

All major scales are made up of this same series of steps: 2 whole steps, a half step, 3 whole steps, and a final half step.

You can construct a major scale by starting on any black or white key and following the pattern just given. If you start on G and follow the pattern, you would play G, A, B, C, D, E, F♯ (also known as G♭), and then G again. The picture below shows the steps.

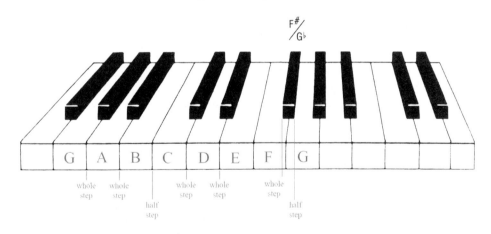

The first five notes in the scale are pretty easily understood:

Whole step	G to A
Whole step	A to B
Half step	B to C
Whole step	C to D
Whole step	D to E

On first glance, you might think that the next move would be from E to F. But notice that there is no black key between E and F, so in fact this is only a *half* step. The pattern calls for a *whole* step. You have to add another half step, to F♯/G♭, in order to follow the pattern. Then the last move is a half step from F♯/D♭ to G.

Because musicians follow this pattern and end up with an F♯ in the G major scale, the key signature for G major consists of one sharp sign placed at the start of the music on the F line, like this:

Other groupings of sharps or flats are used for other key signatures. See if you can figure out the steps and the key signature for E major using the keyboards on page 204.

Chords

You can create harmony by playing or singing two or more pitches at the same time. When you play several notes at a time, you play a *chord*. Most harmony is built on chords of three or four notes. Three-note chords are called *triads*. The three most common chords in a major key are the 1, 4, and 5 chords, which are built on the first, fourth, and fifth tones of a scale. These three triads alone (often written in Roman numerals as I, IV, and V) provide the basis for the melodies of hundreds of folk, popular, and sacred songs, as well as many classical pieces. Folk, jazz, and classical musicians are so familiar with these three chords that they often are able to play them and the melodies above them completely by ear—that is, by listening alone, without reading sheet music.

In the key of C, you would play the I triad by simultaneously playing the first, third, and fifth tones of the scale—the keys labeled 1, 3, and 5 in the illustration below.

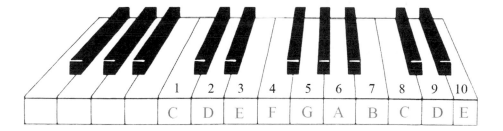

To play the IV triad in the key of C, it's the fourth, sixth and eighth tones, and for the V triad it is the fifth, seventh, and ninth tones. Try these on a keyboard if you can.

The I, IV, and V chords—also called *tonic, subdominant,* and *dominant* chords—are major chords and usually follow one another in melodies in one of several predictable patterns called *chord progressions.* The most common chord progression is I, IV, V, I; the tonic triad (I) is the home-base chord. Another historically important progression in American music is I, IV, I, V, IV, I. This progression is the foundation for the kind of music we call the blues. Again, you can try some simple chord progressions on a keyboard if you have one.

In addition to these major chords, music also includes *minor chords.* For example, in the key of C, one important minor chord is A, C, E—the sixth, eighth, and tenth tones of the scale; this is called the A minor triad.

The minor triads sound different because there is one half step fewer between the lower and middle notes of the chord. For example, in the chord highlighted above, the 6 key (A) is only *three* half steps from the 8 key (C). If you had played a major chord, such as the one consisting of the keys numbered 1, 3, and 5, there would have been *four* half steps from the first key (C) to the second (E).

Musicians often say that major triads sound happy and minor triads sound sad.

Famous violinist Fritz Kreisler.

CLASSICAL MUSIC

The Western Musical Tradition

Now that we have reviewed some basic information about written music, let's learn a little about some composers from the past and the music they created.

The history of Western music is often divided into periods. If you don't already know about Medieval and Renaissance music, you can learn about them in the earlier books in this series. In this book, we will learn about music from three later periods known as the baroque, the classical, and the romantic periods.

Music scholars tell us that the baroque period lasted from about 1600 to 1750, the classical period from about 1750 to 1825, and the romantic period from about 1800 to 1900. The names and dates were not agreed upon until many years later, after people had time to listen to older music and reflect on it, but they are widely accepted today.

If you can, try to borrow recordings of the music discussed below, so you can hear how it sounds. Your local library may have recordings.

The Baroque Period

During the baroque period, music tended to be elaborate and ornate. Baroque music often features *polyphony*, or the interplay of many sounds and voices. During the baroque period, an Italian composer named Gabrieli wrote a piece of music that featured a small, rather quiet group of instruments in contrast to a larger and louder group. He wrote the Italian terms *piano* (soft) and *forte* (loud) in the score for his piece. Because later composers often studied in Italy, these and other Italian words eventually came to be used to indicate *dynamics* (volume) and *tempo* (speed). To this day, you will find Italian words in printed music, even when the words to be sung are in English. Here are some Italian words and abbreviations that composers use to tell musicians when to play louder and when to play softer. The abbreviations are listed from quietest to loudest:

pp (*pianissimo*) very soft
p (*piano*) soft
mp (*mezzo piano*) medium soft
mf (*mezzo forte*) medium loud
f (*forte*) loud
ff (*fortissimo*) very loud

Bach

The greatest composer of the baroque period was Johann Sebastian Bach (1685–1750). Bach—the name rhymes with rock—was a Lutheran church musician who lived in Germany. He played the organ for church services, composed music for the choir, and taught in the church schools.

Almost every Sunday, Bach had to write new music for church services. One kind of music he produced is known as a *cantata*. In Bach's time, a church cantata typically involved vocal soloists, a small choir, and an organ or other instruments.

One of Bach's best-known cantatas is number 80, which is based on a hymn written by Martin Luther, the father of the Reformation. Luther's hymn is called "A Mighty Fortress Is Our God"—"Ein' feste Burg ist unser Gott" in German. This hymn has been called the battle hymn of the Reformation.

Bach's cantata captures the passionate spirit of Luther. It contains eight movements for various combinations of voices and instruments. In the first movement, the chorus sings together. In the next three movements we hear a soprano and bass taking turns singing solo. Then there is another chorus. Movements 6 and 7 feature alto and tenor soloists, and the piece ends with another chorus.

Johann Sebastian Bach.

Remember: voices are classified by their *range* (how high or low they can sing) and also by their *timbre* (the special quality of sound each has).

Soprano: highest female voice

Mezzo-soprano: middle soprano; a voice that is slightly lower and darker in quality than a soprano

Alto: lowest female voice

Tenor: highest male voice

Baritone: mid-range male voice; between tenor and bass

Bass: Lowest male voice

A characteristic of Bach's cantata, and of baroque music generally, is *counterpoint*. Counterpoint is the art of combining different melodies and bits of music in such a way that they sound good and complement one another. Throughout Bach's Cantata No. 80, various voices or instruments play the main "Mighty Fortress" melody, imitating each other closely while also weaving in new but harmonically related melodies.

Ein' fe - - - - - ste Burg ist un - ser Gott,

Ein' fe - - - - - ste Burg ist un - ser Gott.

Outstanding examples of counterpoint can also be found in Bach's works for keyboard instruments. The piano as we know it was perfected toward the end of Bach's life. When Bach wrote music for keyboard instruments, he focused on older instruments, including the organ, harpsichord, and clavichord. The organ makes notes by pushing air through pipes, the harpsichord by plucking strings, and the clavichord by striking strings with a piece of metal.

In The Well-Tempered Clavier, Bach set out to compose polyphonic keyboard pieces in each of the 12 major and 12 minor keys. Because *clavier* simply means keyboard, the 48 pieces in these books may be played on almost any keyboard instrument. Each piece includes a *prelude* (an introductory piece) and a *fugue*. A fugue is a piece of music in which one or more melodies are imitated throughout the composition, usually following a standard pattern.

Bach also wrote music for secular (non-church) events. For one nobleman, the Margrave of Brandenburg, Bach wrote six instrumental concertos which came to be called the Brandenburg Concertos. These works have a three-movement format that became popular with other European composers. The first movement is generally fast (*allegro*), the second, more leisurely (*andante*), and the third fast again.

More Italian Words

These Italian words tell musicians how fast to go in a movement or section.

grave (very, very slow)
largo (very slow)
adagio (slow)
andante (moderate; "walking")
moderato (medium)
allegro (fast)
presto (very fast)
prestissimo (as fast as you can go)

Handel

George Frideric Handel [HAHN-dull] (1685–1759) was another German composer of the baroque period. Whereas Bach worked mostly for the church, Handel worked mostly for various noblemen. His most important *patron* (or supporter) was George, the Elector of Hanover, a German nobleman who eventually became King George I of England.

Handel wrote one his most famous instrumental pieces, the Water Music, for King George I. While the king and his court floated down the Thames River in London on the royal barge, Handel led musicians playing on another barge. As you might expect, Water Music has a very grand and noble sound to it. It is often performed at weddings and other ceremonial occasions.

George Frideric Handel.

Handel was also famous for his oratorios. An *oratorio* uses music and singing to tell a story from the Bible. Oratorio might be described as a cross between a cantata and an opera. An oratorio is religious like a cantata, but it is not always written to be performed in a church and is usually longer than a cantata, with more players and singers. An oratorio features a chorus and solo singers, and it tells a story, like an opera, but there are no stage decorations and no acting—just a lot of singing.

For his oratorios, Handel used a chorus of voices, a small orchestra, and an organ. Handel's oratorios were very popular in England. The most famous one—Messiah—is still performed today. The subject is Jesus, whom Christians believe to be the messiah, or savior. Handel's Messiah includes individual solos for soprano, alto, tenor, and bass, as well as powerful choruses. The best-known chorus is the "Hallelujah Chorus." It is said that when King George II of England (the son of Handel's patron) first heard this chorus, he was overcome with emotion and rose to his feet. Since he was the king, everybody else stood up, too. That is why, even today, audiences at performances of Handel's Messiah stand up during the "Hallelujah Chorus."

The Classical Period

The classical period (circa 1750–1825) got its name because many composers of this period were interested in stories from the classical days of Greek and Roman civilization. These composers also reacted against certain tendencies in baroque music. They wanted to use the elements of music (tempo, form, dynamics, and timbre) in a formal, restrained, and usually unemotional way.

In baroque music, each movement of a piece tends to have a single dominant character. Musicians of the classical period began to experiment with changes of melody, rhythm, and dynamics *within* a movement. Rather than writing music that remained in one mood, at one volume, and at one speed throughout a movement, composers wrote instrumental music instructing players to add expression by *gradually* increasing or decreasing the volume, by *gradually* slowing down or speeding up the tempo, or by playing the notes in a smooth, flowing way or in a more abrupt and distinct fashion. Again, there are Italian terms for all of these ways of playing or singing:

ritardando (gradually slowing down)
accelerando (gradually getting faster)
crescendo (gradually increasing volume)
decrescendo (gradually increasing volume)
legato (a smoothly flowing progression of notes)
staccato (crisp, distinct notes)

Harmony was simple in the classical period. Composers used the basic I, IV, and V chords in many compositions. Other chords might also be included, but they were generally less important.

Haydn

One of the most eminent composers of the classical period was Franz Joseph Haydn (1732–1809). Haydn [HIE-den] was born into a poor Austrian family. He had little formal musical training. He learned music by singing in a choir, taught himself counterpoint by reading a book on his own, and picked up a few lessons in music theory whenever he could.

Haydn spent much of his life working for the Esterhazy family, wealthy and powerful patrons of music and the arts. This family kept a 25-piece orchestra, keyboard instruments, and a small choir at Haydn's disposal. Haydn supervised the musicians and put on regular concerts for the family for nearly 30 years.

Franz Joseph Haydn.

During his lifetime, Haydn created 108 symphonies, 68 string quartets, 47 piano sonatas, 20 operas, and 6 oratorios.

Haydn was distinguished not only for the amount of music he produced, but also for his variety. He wrote symphonies to be performed by large orchestras in vast concert halls and also chamber music that could be performed by a few musicians in a sitting room. Haydn was particularly successful at writing chamber music for a *string quartet* —a group of four musicians, each playing a string instrument (usually a viola, a cello, and two violins).

A string quartet.

Perhaps the best-known of Haydn's string quartets is Opus 76, No. 3, in C Major, known as the "Emperor." This quartet has four movements in a format that became quite standard in the classical period. The first and last movements are in sonata form, the second movement is a theme and variations, and the third a minuet and trio.

A *sonata* is a multi-part instrumental work that became popular in the classical period as part of the reaction against the single themes and unified moods of the baroque style. A sonata generally has three main sections: the *exposition*, in which two or more themes are stated; the *development*, in which these themes are developed and elaborated upon; and the *recapitulation*, in which the music returns to the themes in their original form.

In the Emperor quartet, two contrasting musical themes are set forth in the exposition. After the listener has been exposed to these themes, Haydn develops them by using them together in various expressive ways in the development. Toward the end, the two melodies are replayed again in the recapitulation.

Sonata Form

Sonatas generally have three sections, each of which has its own distinctive character and themes.

	Exposition	→	Development	→	Recapitulation
Sections:					
Themes:	Main themes		Main themes varied		Main themes return
Character:	Stable		Unstable, unpredictable		Return to stability

Mozart

Probably the most famous composer of the classical period was Wolfgang Amadeus Mozart (1756–1792). Mozart [MOTE-sart] was a child prodigy, who was shown off by his musician father to nobility all over Europe. He published four violin sonatas when he was only eight years old!

As an adult, Mozart composed very quickly; the musical ideas were always at the tip of his pen, ready to be recorded on the staff. Although he did not live long, he composed a staggering amount of beautiful music.

Like Haydn before him, Mozart was a master of the symphony. Indeed, he helped make the symphony a popular form during the classical period. One of the best-known classical symphonies is Mozart's

Mozart performing for aristocrats in Vienna, Austria.

Symphony No. 40 in G Minor, K. 550. Like other classical works, Mozart's fortieth symphony contains four movements and uses sonata form in several of its movements. At this point in his life, Mozart was working within the established patterns of composing but also seeing if he could subtly break rules and give the listeners a treat in each piece. For example, Mozart used the basic chords commonly used by classical composers, but he used them in different orders and used novel combinations of instruments to play them.

Mozart was a superb organist and harpsichordist. He also wrote for a newer keyboard instrument, the *pianoforte*, so called because it could be played either softly (piano) or loudly (forte), depending on how hard the player pressed the keys. Today, we call this instrument the piano.

Mozart wrote a number of concertos for the piano. A *concerto* is a multi-movement musical work in which a solo instrument is accompanied by an orchestra. One of the best-known of Mozart's piano concertos is Concerto No. 21, K. 467. Its three movements follow a fast-slow-fast plan. In two of the three movements, there is a cadenza. A *cadenza* is a section in a concerto where the orchestra stops playing in order to give the soloist a chance to play alone and show off his or her abilities.

Beethoven

Ludwig van Beethoven [LOOD-vig vahn BATE-hove-en] (1770–1827) is one of the best-known composers in music history. Nearly everyone has heard about him, and most people recognize at least one or two pieces of his music, even if they cannot name them.

One reason that Beethoven is so important is that his life and music were like a bridge between the classical and romantic periods. He started out writing music in the classical style, more or less in the tradition of Mozart and Haydn. Beethoven actually played for Mozart when he was young, and he studied musical composition with Haydn. Haydn predicted: "Beethoven will one day be considered one of Europe's greatest composers, and I shall be proud to be called his teacher."

Beethoven did become a great composer, but he also developed a style very different from the style perfected by Haydn and Mozart. When he was twenty-eight, Beethoven began to lose his hearing. Eventually he went completely deaf. As Beethoven's hearing deteriorated, his music changed. He left behind some of the restraint associated with the classical period, and his music began to reflect more emotion. His later works are full of dramatic emotions and drastic changes of dynamics.

Ludwig van Beethoven.

One of his most famous works, the Moonlight Sonata, was written just as Beethoven's style began to evolve from the classical style toward what we now call romantic. The sonata was given its nickname by a music critic who thought the haunting melody in C-sharp minor reminded him of moonlight on ocean waves. The first movement of the piece is calm, but the third movement is fast and stormy—so stormy that Beethoven sometimes broke pianos while playing it. Beethoven's tempo marking for the final movement of the Moonlight Sonata is *presto agitato*, which means "fast and agitated."

Beethoven wrote only nine symphonies, but they are considered to be some of the greatest symphonies ever written. You may be familiar with his Symphony No. 5 in C Minor, with its famous opening, containing three quick G's and a long E-flat:

Another famous Beethoven symphony is his Symphony No. 3 in E Flat Major, known as the "Eroica." Some scholars consider this symphony the beginning of the romantic movement in music. Beethoven planned to dedicate the symphony to Napoleon, whom he admired and whom he expected to create a government that did not give all power to a king or emperor. However, when Napoleon had himself crowned emperor, Beethoven became so furious that he tore up the page on which he had written the dedication.

Beethoven's final symphony, Symphony no. 9 in D Minor, is another powerful piece. This was the first symphony to use a solo voice and a chorus. It premiered in 1824, with a completely deaf Beethoven conducting the orchestra!

Although the whole Ninth Symphony is wonderful, the fourth and final movement is particularly well known. This movement features a contest between calm melodies and furiously loud outbursts. For a while, the negative and noisy drown out the quiet and restful. Soon though, the confusion is overcome by joy as the bass soloist sings, "O brothers, let us have no more of these sad tones. Let us rejoice together!" These lines are taken from a poem, "Ode to Joy," by the German romantic poet Schiller. Beethoven's tremendous finale broke most of the rules of form that had been followed during the classical period and influenced romantic composers of the next generation.

The Romantic Period

Like the romantic period in art history, the romantic period in music history is characterized by a reaction against classical ideas—a shift away from balance, reason, and restraint and toward imagination, emotion, and fantasy. This period began around the time of the French Revolution. If you have read the history chapter of this book, you know how the French Revolution and the rise and fall of Napoleon disrupted the old order in Europe and encouraged revolt against political authority and social conventions. You also know about the romantic ideas of Jean-Jacques Rousseau, who wrote about the beauties of nature and the noble savage. If you have read the poetry section, you know how romantic poets like Byron and Wordsworth celebrated nature and made their inner emotional lives the subject of their poetry. If you have looked at the paintings in the visual arts chapter, you have seen expressions of romanticism in painting, in the bold, expressive paintings of Goya, Delacroix, and Friedrich. Romanticism in music is closely linked to romanticism in these other fields, while also growing out of the musical traditions you have been reading about.

Schubert

Franz Schubert (1797–1828) was one of the first great romantic musicians. Schubert was born in Austria during the French Revolution. As a young boy he sang (soprano) in the church choir and learned to play the piano, violin, and viola. Eventually he became a member of the Vienna Boys' Choir, which is still famous today.

As an adult, Schubert was famous as a songwriter. The songs he wrote were called *lieder*, or *art songs*, and they became very popular during the romantic period. Schubert would take a poem and set it to music. He could do this as well as anybody who ever lived. Schubert wrote 8 songs in one day, 140 in a single year, and more than 600 in his lifetime.

Schubert's song "Gretchen at the Spinning Wheel" ("*Gretchen am Spinnrade*" in German) was based on a poem by the German poet Goethe [GUH-tuh]. In Schubert's day, wool was spun into thread or yarn by women and young girls operating spinning wheels. The women pumped a foot pedal up and down to keep the wheel spinning. Schubert's song helps us see Gretchen spinning at her wheel. As she spins, she thinks of being courted by a man she does not love. Her wheel stops when she imagines his unwelcome kiss, but it resumes when she returns to

Franz Schubert.

work. Schumann captures the sound of the spinning wheel with a series of rapid, rolling notes played by the pianist's right hand and the thump-thump of the foot pedal with a heavy rhythm played by the left hand.

Another well-known Schubert song is called "The Trout" (*Die Forelle.*) In this song Schubert uses the piano to imitate the water flowing in the stream where the trout lives and to tell the story of the fish's adventures.

Schubert's short life came to an end in 1828. He was buried in Vienna, in precisely the location he had requested—beside Beethoven.

Schumann

Robert Schumann (1810–1856) was a romantic composer whose personal life was closely intertwined with his musical life. While studying piano with a teacher named Friedrich Wieck, Schumann fell in love with Wieck's teenage daughter, Clara, who was also a talented musician. Unfortunately, Mr. Wieck did not want the two to marry. He recognized that Schumann had talent, but he questioned whether the young man had the determination and drive he would need to succeed.

Eventually, Schumann and Clara Wieck did get married. Clara Schumann became a mother of eight children, a distinguished concert pianist, a talented composer of her own music, and the inspiration for many of her husband's compositions. Schumann himself became a noted composer and music critic. He wrote songs like Schubert, but he also wrote symphonies, concertos, and chamber music.

One of Schumann's best-known longer pieces is his Piano Concerto in A Minor, written in 1845. The three movements of this concerto follow the fast-slow-fast pattern with the middle movement marked *intermezzo: andantino grazioso*. That is, Schumann thought of this middle movement as a special kind of *interlude*, a piece of music that moves the listener from one movement or section to another. When the piece was first performed in 1846, it was Schumann's beloved wife Clara who played it.

Robert Schumann.

Chopin

Frédéric Chopin [SHOW-pan] (1810–1849) was a child prodigy who left Poland at age twenty for the musical life of Paris and never returned. In Paris he became a celebrated concert pianist, adored by his fans, and especially by young women.

Schubert had played the piano well. Schumann played even better. But Chopin was the best—he was a true *virtuoso*, a master of the highest order.

In addition to his piano playing, Chopin was also famous for his long-term romantic friendship with Aurore Dudevant, a female writer who used a male pen name—George Sand—to get her novels published.

Even though Chopin left Poland, his native

Frederic Chopin.

land remained close to his heart. Some of his solo piano pieces were based on dances from his homeland, such as the lively *mazurka* and the stately *polonaise*. Another famous piano piece is his "Minute Waltz." A waltz is a German dance for couples.

Chopin also taught the piano, and he composed special practice pieces called *etudes* in order to challenge his pupils to learn new techniques. *Etude* is a French word that means "a study." Pupils learning to play an etude are studying a new way of playing their instrument. One of Chopin's most popular etudes is his Etude in C Minor, also known as the "Revolutionary Etude." This etude has a rapid, even rhythm that reminds many listeners of marching soldiers.

A final famous selection by Chopin is sometimes called "The Funeral March." This march is really the third movement of his Piano Sonata No. 2. Other pieces of music have come to symbolize victory or joy; Chopin's march has come to symbolize death.

V.

Mathematics

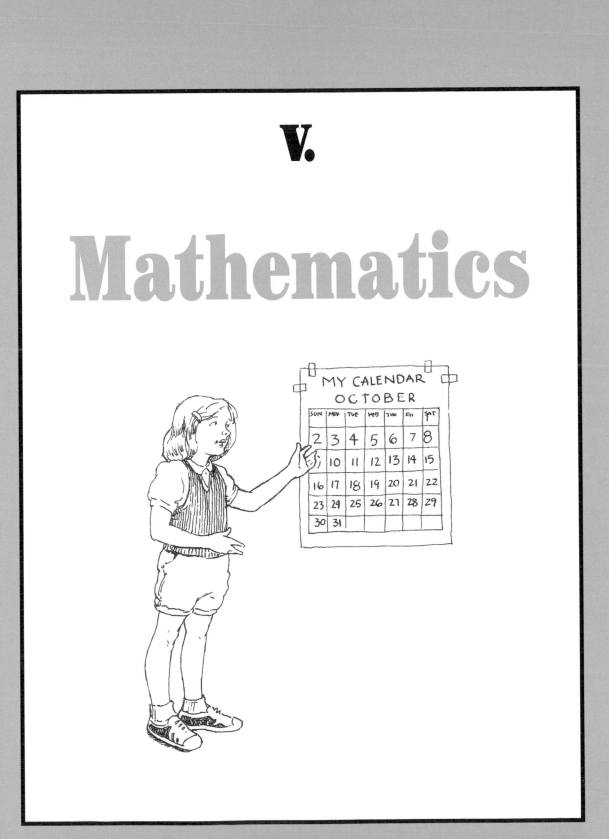

Introduction

This chapter offers a brief overview of sixth-grade math. It assumes that students have mastered basic number sense and measurement, computational techniques for whole numbers, and elementary geometry. Students who have not mastered these topics may need to consult the earlier volumes in this series.

Students reading this book will extend their computational and measuring skills, deepen their understanding of probability and statistics, and move into some basic pre-algebra. In geometry, they will study congruence and similarity, work with angles and triangles, and find areas of polygons and circles.

Please note that the brief outline presented here *does not constitute a complete math program,* since it does not include the many practice problems students need to do to achieve mastery. To achieve mastery in math, children need to be shown concepts and then given plenty of opportunities for practice — not mindless, repetitive practice but thoughtful practice, with a variety of problems. While it is important to work toward the development of higher-order problem-solving skills, such skills depend on a sound grasp of basic facts and an automatic mastery of fundamental operations. Since practice is the secret to mastery, practice is a prerequisite for more advanced problem solving. The best math programs offer many opportunities for practice and incremental review.

Some well-meaning people fear that practice in mathematics constitutes joyless, soul-killing drudgery for children. In fact, it is *anxiety* that kills the joy in mathematics, not practice. One way of overcoming anxiety is by practicing until the procedures become so easy and automatic that anxiety evaporates.

One effective method of practice is to have a student talk out loud while doing problems, explaining steps along the way. In this way, the student's mental process and misunderstandings become clear to you and problems can be addressed as they occur.

NUMBERS AND NUMBER SENSE

Trillions

In our number system, a numeral is made up of groups of numbers called periods. Each period contains three columns — a hundreds, tens, and ones column — and each is separated from the next period with a comma. Here's a number that fills five periods:

$$163,321,987,654,322$$

You read this number as one hundred sixty-three trillion, three hundred twenty-one billion, nine hundred eighty-seven million, six hundred fifty-four thousand, three hundred twenty-two. Remember: as you move to the left, each numeral has a value ten times greater than the same numeral would have in the previous place: the 2 in the tens place stands for a value ten times larger than the 2 in the ones place, and the 3 in the trillions place stands for a value ten times larger than the 3 in the hundred billions place. That is how our *base-ten* number system, also known as the *decimal* system, works.

Try writing the following words as a number, with commas separating the periods. One hundred seven trillion, four hundred thirty-one billion, seventeen thousand, forty-five.

Instead of writing the ending zeros in large numbers, we often use a shortened word form. 586,000,000,000,000 can be written "586 trillion." 2,998,810,000,000 can be written as "2 trillion, 998 billion, 810 million." You can also use decimals to write these abbreviations. Remember that places to the right of the decimal point represent values smaller than 1: tenths, hundredths, etc. So, 3,700,000 can be written 3.7 million because 700,000 is 7 tenths of a million.

Integers

Here is a number line.

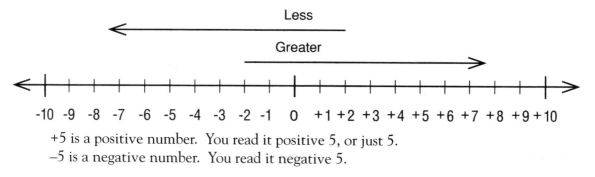

+5 is a positive number. You read it positive 5, or just 5.
−5 is a negative number. You read it negative 5.

Numbers to the left of 0 on the number line are negative, numbers to the right of 0 are positive. The number 0 is neither positive nor negative. You can write positive numbers with or without a + sign: +2 = 2 (positive two = two) +3 = 3.

All of the numbers identified on the number line above are integers. The word *integer* means whole. The positive integers are the numbers +1, +2, +3, and so on. The negative integers are the numbers –1, –2, –3, and so on. 2.5 is not an integer, because it is not a whole number. The set of numbers called integers is made up of the negative integers, zero, and the positive integers.

We use integers all the time in everyday life. For example, we use integers to count items and to report the temperature. If the temperature is +70 degrees Fahrenheit, you probably don't need a coat. If it is –10 degrees F, you may not want to go outside! Or think about football. You might indicate an eight-yard gain as +8 and a five-yard loss as –5. Integers are used in hockey, too. Each player on a pro hockey team has a statistic called the plus/minus value. A +5 value means the team has outscored opponents by 5 goals while this player was on the ice. A –4 value means the team has been outscored by 4 goals while this player was on the ice.

Opposites

Numbers that are the same distance from zero in opposite directions are called opposites. –3 and +3 are opposites; +4.5 and –4.5 are opposites; zero is its own opposite: +0 = –0 = 0.

To find the opposite of a number, change its sign: the opposite of –100 is +100; the opposite of +100 is –100.

Look what happens when you take the opposite of an integer twice.

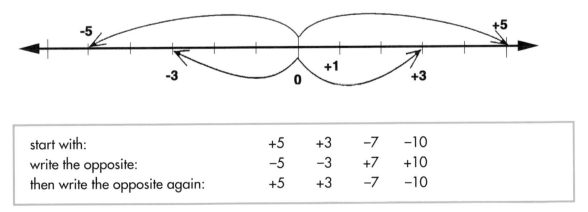

start with:	+5	+3	–7	–10
write the opposite:	–5	–3	+7	+10
then write the opposite again:	+5	+3	–7	–10

Changing the sign of an integer twice gives you the integer you started with.

Prime and Composite Numbers

A *factor*, or *divisor*, divides a number without leaving a remainder. Positive integers that have exactly two factors are called *prime* numbers. Another way of saying this is — a prime number is an integer greater than 1 that is divisible only by 1 and the number itself. The number 5 is a prime number. Its only factors are 1 and 5. Two other primes are 23 and 47. The only even number that is prime is 2. Can you think why none of the other even numbers are prime?

Positive integers that have more than two distinct factors are called *composite* numbers. One example is 4, which has factors of 1, 2, and 4. Another example is 27, which has factors of 1, 3, 9, and 27.

The positive integer 1 is neither prime nor composite since it only has one factor — the number 1 itself.

Which of the following numbers are prime: 5, 8, 17, 19, 21?

Comparing Numbers

The symbol > means "is greater than." You can write "12 is greater than 5" like this — 12 > 5.

The symbol < means "is less than." You can write "6 is less than 8" like this: 6 < 8. You already know that the symbol = means "is equal to." 4 + 2 = 6. The symbol ≠ means "is not equal to." You can write 6 ≠ 8 or 2 ≠ 10.

When you order numbers from least to greatest, or greatest to least, you can use the symbols < or >.

For example, integers that are farther to the right on the number line are greater. So, +5 > +2 and –2 > –5. Integers that are farther to the left on the number line are less. –7 < –4 and 4 < 7.

Two facts to remember:

➤ A positive integer is always greater than a negative integer (1 > –100).
➤ The farther to the left a negative integer is from zero, the smaller its value is (–300 < – 3).

You can think about the number line in the same way when you order fractions or decimals. Look at the following examples:

From least to greatest: $-2.5 < -2 < 2 < 2.1 < 2.15 < 2.152$

From greatest to least: $35.67 > 3.56 > -35.07 > -306.7$

From least to greatest: $-\dfrac{1}{2} < -\dfrac{3}{8} < \dfrac{1}{2} 1\dfrac{3}{4} < 1\dfrac{15}{16} < 2\dfrac{1}{2}$

From greatest to least: $2.5 > 2.23 > 2\dfrac{1}{5} > 1\dfrac{3}{5} > -1.8 > -2\dfrac{1}{2}$

Rounding

Remember: to round a decimal number, identify the place value where you want to round, and then look at the digit in the place directly to the right. If that digit is 5 or larger you round up; if the digit is 4 or smaller, you round down.

For example, if you want to round 3,675 to the nearest thousand, you will focus on the digit to the right of 3, or the digit 6, to determine if 3,675 is closer to 3,000 or 4,000. The 6 in the hundreds place tells you that this number is closer to 4,000, since 3,500 would be exactly halfway in between 3,000 and 4,000 and 3,600 is larger than that.

Using 3,675 again, if you were rounding to tens, you would look at the digit 5 in the ones place to determine if 3,675 is closer to 3,670 or 3,680. When the digit is a 5, exactly in the middle between the two values, the most common convention is to round up to the next higher place. So, 3,675 rounded to tens would be 3,680. In fact, 3,675 is just as close to 3,670 as to 3,680, so in this case the decision to round up is somewhat arbitrary. However, this convention reflects the fact that there are often more digits to the right of the 5 in question and any value in those decimal places, no matter how small, will tip the scale up. For example, if the number to be rounded were 3,675.96, then the number would indeed be closer to 3,680 than 3,670.

Suppose you wanted to round a really big number, such as 435,268,773, to the nearest million? No problem—just do the same thing as before. Since the 5 is in the millions place, look at the 2 to the right to determine if 435,268,773 is closer to 435 million or 436 million. Since 268,773 is less than halfway between these two values, 435,268,773 would round to 435,000,000, or 435 million. What about rounding 435,268,773 to the nearest ten million?

Estimation

When you estimate the answer to a problem, you can round in different ways. How you round will determine how close to the actual answer your estimate is.

To estimate the sum of 12,422 + 36,367, you can round the addends to the nearest ten thousand, thousand, hundred, or even ten.

Rounded to ten thousands:	Rounded to thousands:	Rounded to hundreds:	Actual sum:
10,000	12,000	12,400	12,422
+ 40,000	+ 36,000	+ 36,400	+ 36,367
50,000	48,000	48,800	48,789

The smaller the place value you use to round, the more precise your estimate will be, but the less of an *estimate* it will be.

Often it is helpful to figure out whether your estimate is greater or less than the actual answer. Another useful device is to *compensate*. When adding or multiplying, you can compensate by rounding one number up and the other down. The larger number obtained by rounding up will tend to compensate for the smaller number obtained by rounding down. When subtracting or dividing, you can compensate by making both numbers smaller or both numbers larger. When you are working with decimal fractions or mixed numbers, you often estimate by rounding numbers to the nearest whole number.

		Estimate			Estimate
763	→	800	364.232	→	364
× 218	→	× 200	× 8.427		× 8
		160,000		→	2,912

Since the numbers were rounded in different directions, it is hard to tell whether the actual product will be greater or less than 160,000. However, the estimate is actually *better* because 763 was rounded up and 218 was rounded down. The actual product is 166,334, which is only a little greater than 160,000.

Since both numbers were rounded down, you know that the actual product is greater than 2,912. The actual product is 3069.383064, which is greater than 2,912.

In this case, a slightly more accurate estimate could be obtained (with less mental work) by figuring 400 × 8 = 3200.

Suppose you are finding the difference between two fractions. Once again, rounding allows you to estimate:

$$18\frac{5}{8} - 12\frac{2}{5} \rightarrow 19 - 12 = 7$$

When $18\frac{5}{8}$ is rounded up and $12\frac{2}{5}$ is rounded down, the difference between them becomes greater. The actual difference is $6\frac{9}{40}$ which is less than 7. In this case you could get a better estimate by compensating. Round both numbers down: $18 - 12 = 6$, which is closer to the correct answer.

Greatest Common Factor

The *factors* or *divisors* of 12 are {1, 2, 3, 4, 6, 12}, and the factors of 16 are {1, 2, 4, 8, 16}. The *common factors* or *common divisors* of 12 and 16 are {1, 2, 4}. The *greatest common factor* or *greatest common divisor* of 12 and 16 is {4}. The term *greatest common factor* is often abbreviated GCF. Sometimes you will also see the term GCD, for *greatest common divisor*. One way to find the GCF of two or more numbers is to think of all of the factors of each number, then compare to find the common factors, and choose the greatest of the common factors.

You can use the idea of GCF when you are simplifying fractions. A fraction is in *lowest terms*, or is *simplified*, when its numerator and denominator have no common factor greater than 1. You can write an equivalent fraction in lowest terms by dividing both the numerator and denominator of a fraction by their GCF.

For example, if you were asked to put $\frac{12}{16}$ in lowest terms, you would find the GCF of 12 and 16, which is 4. So, divide both numerator and denominator by 4.

$$\frac{12}{16} \div \frac{4}{4} = \frac{3}{4}$$

Notice that what you are really doing is dividing the fraction by another fraction equivalent to 1, so your answer will represent the same amount as the original fraction.

Because the numerator and denominator get smaller when you put a fraction in lowest terms, people often say you "reduce" a fraction to lowest terms, but don't be misled by the word *reduce*—the value of the fraction is not getting smaller!

Least Common Multiple

Remember that {3, 6, 9, 12, 15, ...} is the set of *multiples* of 3, because you can multiply 3 by a whole number greater than 0 to get these multiples. {2, 4, 6, 8, 10, 12, ...} is the set of multiples of 2. The *common multiples* of 2 and 3 are {6, 12, 18, 24, ...}. The *least common multiple* of 2 and 3 is {6}. Least common multiple is abbreviated LCM.

You can use the LCM to find the least common denominator (LCD) of a fraction. So, if you wanted to find the LCD for $\frac{3}{4}$ and $\frac{1}{6}$, you can find the LCM for 4 and 6. The multiples of 4 are {4, 8, 12, 16, ...} and the multiples of 6 are {6, 12, 18, 24, ...}, so the LCM for 4 and 6 is 12. Therefore, the LCD for $\frac{3}{4}$ and $\frac{1}{6}$ is also 12.

Exponents

An *exponent*, or *power*, indicates how many times a number is used as a factor in multiplication. For example, $3^4 = 3 \times 3 \times 3 \times 3$. In other words, 3 is used as a factor 4 times. You read 3^4 as "three to the fourth power." The number that is being used as a factor is called the *base*. The raised number is the exponent, or power. In 3^4, 3 is the base and 4 is the exponent or power.

Below are some examples of how you read and evaluate expressions with exponents.

- 5^2 is read "five squared" (or "five to the second power"). The second power is called "squared" because you can represent n^2 as the area of a square. For example, a square that has a side length of 5 would have an area expressed as follows:

$$5^2 = 5 \times 5 = 25$$

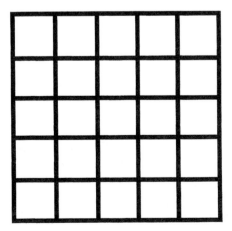

- 4^3 is read "four cubed" (or "four to the third power"). The third power is called "cubed" because you can represent n^3 as the volume of a cube. For example, a cube that has a side length of 4 would have a volume expressed as follows:

$$4^3 = (4) \times (4) \times (4) = 16(4) = 64$$

- n^5 is read "n to the fifth power."

$$n^5 = n \times n \times n \times n \times n$$

- 2^n is read "2 to the nth power."

$$2^n = 2 \times 2 \times 2 \dots (n \text{ times})$$

Remember: the exponent tells you how many times to use the base as a factor. Now practice. What is 4^4? 3^6? 7^3?

Powers of 10

Powers of 10 refers to placing various exponents on a base of 10. The powers of 10 are very important in working with place value because our decimal system is based on powers of 10.

Consider the following list of numbers: 10, 100, 1,000, 10,000, etc. It is the number of zeros following the 1 in each number that tells you what power of ten it is. Since 10,000 has 4 zeros, it is 10^4 ($10 \times 10 \times 10 \times 10 = 10,000$). In the same way, the exponent in a power of 10 tells you the number of zeros the number has when it is multiplied out: 10^6 has *six* zeros. 10^6 equals 1,000,000 or one million.

Can you guess what 10^0 equals? $10^0 = 1$, which has no zeros after the 1.

Multiplying Decimals by 10, 100, 1000

When you multiply any decimal number by 10, you move its decimal point one place to the right. You make the place value of each digit ten times as large.

$$10 \times 2.345 = 23.45 \qquad 0.026 \times 10 = 0.26$$

Notice that when you are multiplying a whole number like 6 by 10, moving the decimal point one place to the right is the same as adding one zero.

$$10 \times 6.0 = 60 \qquad 10 \times 6 = 60$$

When you multiply a number by 1,000, you move its decimal point 3 places to the right. You make the place value of each digit 1,000 times as large.

$$1,000 \times 2.345 = 2345 \qquad 0.026 \times 1,000 = 26$$

Practice multiplying many decimal numbers by powers of 10, observing how the decimal point moves in each problem.

Also practice doing problems like these, in which you must decide either the power of 10 that was used or the number being multiplied by the power of 10:

What power of 10 times 43.82 is equal to 438.2?
What power of 10 times 0.008 is equal to 8?
10^2 times what number is equal to 32.56?

Expanded Notation

Remember that you can write a number like 365,807 in *expanded form* or *expanded notation*. In expanded notation:

$$365,807 = (3 \times 100,000) + (6 \times 10,000) + (5 \times 1,000) + (8 \times 100) + (7 \times 1)$$

You can also write a number in expanded notation using exponents:

$$365,807 = (3 \times 10^5) + (6 \times 10^4) + (5 \times 10^3) + (8 \times 10^2) + (7 \times 10^0)$$

Write numbers in expanded notation with exponents often, so you get used to this form.

Check out two more examples.

1) $1,086,520 = (1 \times 1,000,000) + (8 \times 10,000) + (6 \times 1,000) + (5 \times 100) + (2 \times 10)$
   $ = (1 \times 10^6) + (8 \times 10^4) + (6 \times 10^3) + (5 \times 10^2) + (2 \times 10^1)$

2) $(8 \times 10^4) + (9 \times 10^3) + (4 \times 10^2) + (6 \times 10^1) + (3 \times 10^0) = 89,463$

Square Roots

You have learned that $2^2 = 2 \times 2 = 4$ and $12^2 = 12 \times 12 = 144$ and that $n^2 = n \times n$. Squaring is an operation that you can perform on a number. Just like other operations, squaring has an inverse, or opposite, operation—finding the *square root* of a number. The symbol for square root is $\sqrt{}$. Remember that inverse operations undo one another. So, if you square a number, then take the square root of the result, you should be back where you started, and that's exactly what happens.

$$4^2 = 4 \times 4 = 16 \qquad \text{and} \qquad \sqrt{16} = 4$$

COMPUTATION

Inverse Operations: Addition and Subtraction

Remember that addition and subtraction are inverse operations. That is why you can write a related subtraction fact from an addition fact, or a related addition fact from a subtraction fact. For example, here are three different ways of writing the same information.

$$8 + 7 = 15 \quad \text{and} \quad 8 = 15 - 7 \quad \text{and} \quad 7 = 15 - 8$$

You can use addition and subtraction as inverse operations to solve equations.

To solve the equation:	$n + 43 = 74$
rewrite it as a subtraction problem:	$n = 74 - 43$
subtract 43 from 74:	$n = 31$

You can check the solution $n = 31$ by putting 31 into the original equation, in place of n.

$31 + 43 = 74$
$74 = 74$, so the answer $n = 31$ checks.

Check out another example of using addition and subtraction as inverse operations to solve an equation:

To solve the equation:	$a - 6 = 8$
rewrite it as an addition problem:	$a = 8 + 6$
add 8 and 6:	$a = 14$

You can check the solution $a = 14$ by putting 14 into the original equation, in place of a.

$14 - 6 = 8$
$8 = 8$, so the answer $a = 14$ checks

Even though you probably have been using properties of addition since you were much younger, you now should learn the names for some of the rules about addition. These rules are called *properties* of addition because they are always true about the operation of addition, whether you're using integers, fractions, or decimals.

1) The *Commutative Property of Addition* says that addends can be added in any order without changing the sum. For example,

$$5 + 3 = 8, \text{ and}$$
$$3 + 5 = 8, \text{ or}$$
$$5 + 3 = 3 + 5$$

2) The *Associative Property of Addition* says that addends can be grouped in any way without changing the sum. For example,

$$(2 + 6) + 3 = 8 + 3 = 11, \text{ and}$$
$$2 + (6 + 3) = 2 + 9 = 11, \text{ or}$$
$$(2 + 6) + 3 = 2 + (6 + 3)$$

Note: Neither the commutative property nor the associative property works with subtraction. Look at this example (or non-example) for the commutative property, and then try one yourself for the associative property.

$$5 - 3 = 2, \text{ and}$$
$$3 - 5 = -2, \text{ so}$$
$$5 - 3 \neq 3 - 5, \text{ since } 2 \neq -2$$

Adding Positive and Negative Numbers

You need to understand a little bit about the *absolute value* of a number in order to fully understand addition of positive and negative numbers. The absolute value of a number is the distance the number is from zero on the number line. Since distances are always positive, absolute values are always positive. The symbol for the absolute value of 6 is $|6|$. From the definition above, you can see that each of the following would be true:

$$|6| = 6 \qquad\qquad |-6| = 6$$
$$|-10.2| = 10.2 \qquad\qquad |10.2| = 10.2$$
$$\left|\frac{1}{2}\right| = \frac{1}{2} \qquad\qquad \left|-\frac{1}{2}\right| = \frac{1}{2}$$

In each case, the positive value of the number is the same distance from zero on the number line as the negative value of the number.

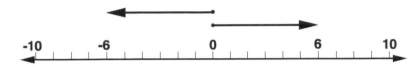

Now that you understand absolute value, you will be better able to understand how to add integers, fractions, and decimals. Carefully study the following true equations, which involve addition of integers, and see if you can figure out a set of rules for adding positive and negative numbers. You can picture these problems as movements along a number line:

$$-6 + -2 = -8 \qquad 7 + 3 = 10$$
$$-6 + 2 = -4 \qquad 7 + -3 = 4$$
$$10 + -10 = 0 \qquad -7 + 3 = -4$$

If you came up with the following rules for adding integers, you're right on target:

Rules for Adding Positive and Negative Numbers

- ➤ The sum of two positive numbers is positive.
- ➤ The sum of two negative numbers is negative.
- ➤ The sum of a negative number and a positive number is the difference in the absolute values of the two numbers, with the sign of the answer being the sign of the number with the larger absolute value.
- ➤ The sum of a number and its opposite is zero.

The same rules apply for fractions.

Reminders for Adding Fractions

- ➤ Fractions must have a common denominator before you can add. The least common denominator is the least common multiple of the denominators.
- ➤ Once you have determined a common denominator, multiply your original fraction(s) by a value of 1 that will create an equivalent fraction using the common denominator.
- ➤ Then add numerators, place the result over the common denominator, and simplify your answer, if needed.

Look at these problems, reviewing what you know about adding fractions and applying what you have learned about adding positive and negative fractions:

$$7\frac{1}{4} + 3\frac{1}{2} = 7\frac{1}{4} + 3\frac{2}{4} = 10\frac{3}{4} \qquad -\frac{3}{5} + \frac{10}{5} = 1\frac{2}{5} \qquad -\frac{3}{4} + \frac{1}{8} = -\frac{6}{8} + \frac{1}{8} = -\frac{5}{8}$$

Reminders for Adding Decimal Fractions

➤ To add decimal fractions, first line up the numbers by the decimal point; that is, line up like place values (tenths with tenths, hundreds with hundreds, and so on...)
➤ Once you have lined up the numbers, add and bring the decimal straight down into the answer.

Check out these problems to see how this works with adding positive and negative decimal numbers:

−6.5 + −2 can be written:

$$\begin{array}{r} -6.5 \\ + \ \underline{-2.0} \\ -8.5 \end{array}$$

3.25 + (−3.257) can be written:

$$\begin{array}{r} -3.257 \\ + \ \underline{3.250} \\ -0.007 \end{array}$$

Subtracting Positive and Negative Numbers

Remember that addition and subtraction are inverse operations, so you might expect that the rules for subtracting positive and negative numbers might have some relationship with the rules for adding. Carefully study the following true equations, which involve subtraction of integers, and see if you can figure out a set of rules for subtracting positive and negative numbers. You may find this a little more challenging than you did for addition, but look closely and compare these equations with the same addition equations above:

$$-6 - (-2) = -4 \qquad 7 - 3 = 4$$
$$-6 - 2 = -8 \qquad 7 - (-3) = 10$$
$$10 - (-10) = 20 \qquad -7 - 3 = -10$$

Subtraction is defined in terms of addition in the following way:

Definition of Subtraction

For all real numbers a and b:

$$a - b = a + (-b)$$

In other words, subtracting a number is the same as adding its opposite.

So, each problem above can be changed to "addition of the opposite" of the second number:

$$-6 - (-2) = -4 \text{ can be written as } -6 + 2 = -4.$$
$$-6 - 2 = -8 \text{ can be written as } -6 + (-2) = -8.$$
$$7 - (-3) = 10 \text{ can be written as } 7 + 3 = 10.$$

In other words, once you have rewritten your subtraction problem as an "addition of the opposite" problem, you can use the rules for addition of positive and negative numbers that you already learned!

Once again, the same process of subtraction is used for fractions.

Reminders for Subtracting Fractions and Decimal Fractions

The same reminders apply to subtracting fractions and decimal fractions as for adding them. Just remember that you are subtracting!

Remember that each subtraction problem can be changed to "addition of the opposite" of the second number. Therefore,

➢ $-\dfrac{3}{5} - 2$ can be written as $-\dfrac{3}{5} + (-2) = -2\dfrac{3}{5}$

➢ $3.25 - (-3.257)$ can be written as $3.25 + 3.257$ or like this:

$$
\begin{array}{r}
3.25 \\
+\ 3.257 \\
\hline
6.507
\end{array}
$$

Inverse Operations: Multiplication and Division

Remember that multiplication and division are also inverse operations. That is why you can write a related division fact from a multiplication fact, or a related multiplication fact from a division fact. For example, here are three different ways of writing the same information.

$$8 \times 7 = 56 \quad \text{or} \quad 8 = 56 \div 7 \quad \text{or} \quad 7 = 56 \div 8$$

You can use multiplication and division as inverse operations to solve equations.

To solve the equation,	$43 \times n = 215$	or	$43n = 215$
rewrite it as a division problem:	$n = 215 \div 43$		$n = 215 \div 43$
divide 215 by 43.	$n = 5$		$n = 5$

You can check the solution
$n = 5$ by putting 5 into the $43 \times 5 = 215$
original equation, in place of n. $215 = 215$, so the answer $n = 5$ checks.

Here's another example of using multiplication and division as inverse operations to solve an equation:

To solve the equation: $\dfrac{a}{6} = 8$

rewrite it as a multiplication problem: $a = 8 \times 6$
multiply 8 and 6: $a = 48$

You can check the solution $a = 48$

by putting 48 into the original $\dfrac{48}{6} = 8$

equation, in place of a.

                                        $8 = 8$, so the answer $a = 48$ checks.

Like addition, multiplication is commutative and associative.

1) The *Commutative Property of Multiplication*
   Factors can be multiplied in any order without changing the product. For example,

$$10 \times 6 = 60, \text{ and}$$
$$6 \times 10 = 60, \text{ or}$$
$$10 \times 6 = 6 \times 10$$

2) The *Associative Property of Multiplication*
Factors can be grouped in any way without changing the product. For example,

$$(4 \times 5) \times 2 = 20 \times 2 = 40, \text{ and}$$
$$4 \times (5 \times 2) = 4 \times 10 = 40, \text{ and}$$
$$(4 \times 5) \times 2 = 4 \times (5 \times 2)$$

Note: Neither the commutative property nor the associative property works with division. Look at this example (or non-example) for the commutative property, and then try to think up one for the associative property.

$$6 \div 3 = 2, \text{ and}$$
$$3 \div 6 = \frac{1}{2}, \text{ so}$$
$$6 \div 3 \neq 3 \div 6, \text{ since } 2 \neq \frac{1}{2}$$

There is another very useful property of multiplication, which also involves addition or subtraction, called the Distributive Property.

3) The *Distributive Property*
When you multiply a sum by a number:
1) you can add, and then multiply,
2) or you can multiply each addend by the number, and then add.

You get the same result either way.

For example:

$$4 \times (3 + 9) = 4 \times 12 = 48, \text{ or}$$
$$4 \times (3 + 9) = (4 \times 3) + (4 \times 9) = 12 + 36 = 48$$

Without making any calculations, the distributive property tells us that:

$$4 \times (3 + 9) = (4 \times 3) + (4 \times 9)$$

The distributive property also applies when you multiply a difference by a number. For example:

$$4 \times (3 - 9) = 4 \times -6 = -24, \text{ or}$$

$$4 \times (3 - 9) = (4 \times 3) - (4 \times 9) = 12 - 36 = -24$$

Again, without making any calculations, the distributive property tells us that:

$$4 \times (3 - 9) = (4 \times 3) - (4 \times 9)$$

The distributive property can be a big help when doing mental multiplication. For example, suppose that you are to multiply 67 by 8. Using the distributive property, you may be able to do this problem in your head:

$$67 \times 8 = (60 + 7) \times 8 = (60 \times 8) + (7 \times 8)$$
$$= 480 + 56$$
$$= 536$$

You could also use the distributive property with subtraction to think of multiplying 67 by 8 this way:

$$(70 - 3) \times 8 = (70 \times 8) - (3 \times 8)$$
$$= 560 - 24$$
$$= 536$$

Multiplying and Dividing Multi-digit Whole Numbers

Before jumping into multiplying and dividing positive and negative integers, fractions, and decimals, review the algorithms for multiplying and dividing whole numbers. *Algorithm* is a fancy name for a process with several steps, such as the one you use when you multiply or divide two numbers.

The distributive property is "built into" the usual algorithms for multiplication and division. For example, returning to the example given above, 67×8, we can modify the usual algorithm only slightly to see exactly the same calculations occur:

$$
\begin{array}{r}
67 \\
\times\ 8 \\
\hline
56 \\
480 \\
\hline
536
\end{array}
$$

What the algorithm tells us to do is multiply 8 times 7 (56), then multiply 8 times 60 (480), and then add the two figures to get the product (536).

One of the most important things to remember when you multiply and divide numbers is the idea of place value. For example, consider the problem 326×47.

You can think of 326 in expanded form as $300 + 20 + 6$, and you can think of 47 as $40 + 7$. So, suppose you recorded the multiplication of 326 by 47 as shown on the left below. Compare the results on the left with the way you typically write this problem using the short form, shown to the right:

$$
\begin{array}{rl}
3\,0\,0 + 2\,0 + 6 & \\
\times \quad\quad 4\,0 + 7 & \\
\hline
4\,2 & (= 7 \times 6) \\
1\,4\,0 & (= 7 \times 20) \\
2\,1\,0\,0 & (= 7 \times 300) \\
2\,4\,0 & (= 40 \times 6) \\
8\,0\,0 & (= 40 \times 20) \\
\underline{1\,2\,0\,0\,0} & (= 40 \times 300) \\
1\,5\,3\,2\,2 & (= 47 \times 326)
\end{array}
\qquad
\begin{array}{rl}
3\,2\,6 & \\
\times\,4\,7 & \\
\hline
2\,2\,8\,2 & (= 42 + 140 + 2100) \\
\underline{1\,3\,0\,4\,0} & (= 240 + 800 + 12000) \\
1\,5\,3\,2\,2 & (= 326 \times 47)
\end{array}
$$

Note: Even though the shorter form requires less writing, you may find that the longer form may be easier for you to understand and use. It shows very clearly what is happening when you multiply two multi-digit numbers.

If using a calculator is appropriate for the situation, you would key in:

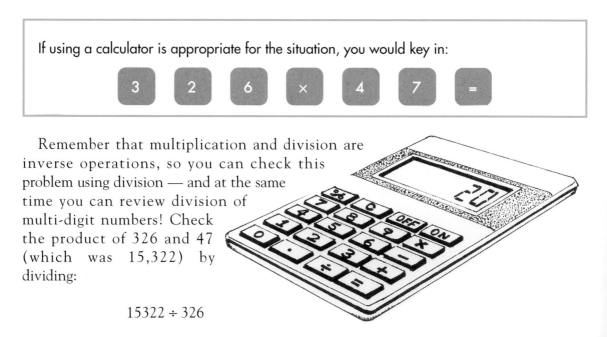

Remember that multiplication and division are inverse operations, so you can check this problem using division — and at the same time you can review division of multi-digit numbers! Check the product of 326 and 47 (which was 15,322) by dividing:

$15322 \div 326$

Working this problem requires the *long division algorithm*. Follow the steps shown below:

Step 1. Round 326 to 300 and think $326\overline{)1532}$. Since $5 \times 300 = 1500$, which is almost too big, 5 times the "rounded out" 26 will certainly "push it over." So try 4.

$$
\begin{array}{r}
4 \\
326\overline{)15322} \\
\underline{1304} \\
228
\end{array}
$$

Check: Is 228 < 326? Yes, so press on...

Step 2. Bring down the 2 ones. Think $300\overline{)2282}$ Since $7 \times 300 = 2100$, try 7.

$$
\begin{array}{r}
47 \\
326\overline{)15322} \\
\underline{1304} \\
2282 \\
\underline{2282} \\
0
\end{array}
$$

Check: Is 0 < 326? Yes, so the quotient is 47, and there is no remainder.

This quotient of our division problem also tells us that the product you got in the earlier multiplication problem ($326 \times 47 = 15322$) is correct.

If using a calculator is appropriate for the situation, you would key in:

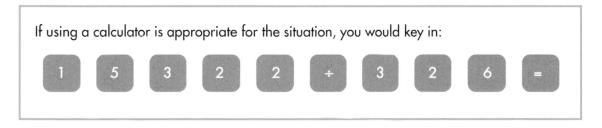

Practice using a calculator to solve multiplication and division problems, but also practice using just paper and pencil.

Multiplying and Dividing Positive and Negative Numbers

Study the following true equations, which involve multiplication and division of integers, and see if you can figure out a set of rules for multiplying and dividing positive and negative numbers.

$$-6 \times -2 = 12 \qquad 12 \div 3 = 4 \qquad -12 \times -3 = 36$$
$$-6 \div 2 = -3 \qquad 12 \times -3 = -36 \qquad -12 \div -3 = 4$$
$$10 \times -10 = -100 \qquad -12 \div 3 = -4 \qquad -8 \times 8 = -64$$

If you came up with the following rules for multiplying and dividing integers, you're right on target:

Rules for Multiplying and Dividing Positive and Negative Numbers

➤ The product or quotient of two positive numbers is positive.
➤ The product or quotient of two negative numbers is positive.
➤ The product or quotient of a negative number and a positive number is negative.

Multiplying and Dividing Positive and Negative Fractions

The same rules apply for all real numbers, including fractions. Look at an example of a situation in which you multiply two fractions:

Gabe came home and found half of an angel food cake left.
He ate $\frac{2}{3}$ of what was left. How much of the *whole cake* did Gabe eat?

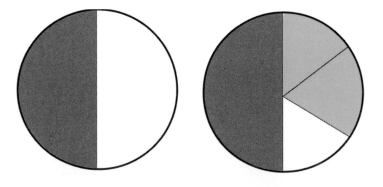

You can see from the picture that Gabe ate $\frac{2}{6}$ or $\frac{1}{3}$ of the whole cake. To find $\frac{2}{3}$ of a given amount, you multiply $\frac{2}{3}$ by that amount.

$$\frac{2}{3} \times \frac{1}{2} = \frac{2}{6} = \frac{1}{3} \text{ or } \frac{2}{3} \times \frac{1}{2} = \frac{\overset{1}{\cancel{2}}}{3} \times \frac{1}{\underset{1}{\cancel{2}}} = \frac{1}{3}$$

Reminders for Multiplying Fractions

➤ You *do not* need a common denominator when multiplying fractions.
➤ Convert any whole numbers or mixed numbers to improper fractions.
➤ Try to simplify any combination of a numerator and denominator in the original problem by dividing out all of their common factors.
➤ Then multiply numerators, multiply denominators, and simplify your answer, if needed.

Look at these problems, reviewing what you know about multiplying fractions and applying what you have learned about multiplying positive and negative fractions:

1) $-\dfrac{3}{5} \times 2 = -\dfrac{3}{5} \times \dfrac{2}{1} = -\dfrac{6}{5} = -1\dfrac{1}{5}$

2) $-\dfrac{3}{4} \times \dfrac{6}{11} = -\dfrac{3}{\underset{2}{\cancel{4}}} \times \dfrac{\overset{3}{\cancel{6}}}{11} = -\dfrac{9}{22}$

3) $-1\dfrac{7}{8} \times -2\dfrac{4}{5} = -\dfrac{15}{8} \times -\dfrac{14}{5} = \dfrac{\overset{3}{\cancel{15}}}{\underset{4}{\cancel{8}}} \times \dfrac{\overset{7}{\cancel{14}}}{\underset{1}{\cancel{5}}} = \dfrac{21}{4} = 5\dfrac{1}{4}$

Remember that multiplication and division are inverse operations, so you might expect that the rules for dividing fractions have some relationship with the rules for multiplying. Carefully study the following true equations, which involve division of fractions, and see if you can figure out a set of rules for dividing fractional numbers. You may find this a bit challenging, but look closely and compare these equations with the same multiplication equations above:

1) $\quad -\dfrac{3}{5} \div 2 = -\dfrac{3}{5} \div \dfrac{2}{1} = -\dfrac{3}{5} \times \dfrac{1}{2} = \dfrac{3}{10}$

2) $\quad -\dfrac{3}{4} \div \dfrac{6}{11} = -\dfrac{3}{4} \times \dfrac{11}{6} = -\dfrac{\overset{1}{\cancel{3}}}{5} \times \dfrac{11}{\underset{2}{\cancel{6}}} = -\dfrac{11}{8} = -1\dfrac{3}{8}$

3) $\quad -1\dfrac{7}{8} \div -2\dfrac{4}{5} = -\dfrac{15}{8} \div -\dfrac{14}{5} = -\dfrac{15}{8} \times -\dfrac{5}{14} = \dfrac{75}{112}$

Did it seem like the second number flipped? That's close! Division is defined in terms of multiplication, using the *reciprocal* of the divisor. For example, dividing by 2 is equivalent to multiplying by $\frac{1}{2}$.

Remember that the product of a number and its reciprocal is always 1.

Definition of Division

For all real numbers a and b, $b \neq 0$:
$$a \div b = a \times \dfrac{1}{b}$$

Here is an example of a situation in which you would divide by a fraction:
Chef Showoff wants to know how many cheese and broccoli pies he can make with 2 heads of broccoli, if each pie calls for $\frac{2}{3}$ of a head of broccoli.

Solution:
Chef Showoff needs to find how many $\frac{2}{3}$s there are in 2. He needs to *divide* 2 by $\frac{2}{3}$.
Rule: To divide by a fraction, multiply by its reciprocal.

$$2 \div \dfrac{2}{3} = 2 \times \dfrac{3}{2} = \dfrac{2}{1} \times \dfrac{3}{2} = \dfrac{6}{2} = \dfrac{3}{1} = 3$$

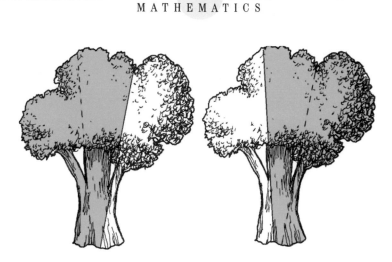

From the picture you can see that the answer is correct: there are 3 two-thirds in 2. Therefore, Chef Showoff can make 3 broccoli and cheese pies with 2 heads of broccoli. So, each problem above can be changed to "multiplication by the reciprocal" of the divisor.

In other words, once you have rewritten your division problem as a "multiplication by the reciprocal" problem, you can use the rules for multiplication of positive and negative numbers that you already learned!

Multiplying and Dividing Positive and Negative Decimals

Reminders for Multiplying Decimal Fractions

- You *do not* need to line up decimal place values when multiplying decimal fractions.
- Multiply as usual, without using the decimals.
- Once you have a solution, count the number of decimal places in each factor and add to find the number of decimal places in the answer. For example, there are 3 decimal places in 6.213 and 1 decimal place in 14.2, so there are 3 + 1 = 4 decimal places in the product of 6.213 and 14.2.

Check out these problems, to see how this works with multiplying positive and negative decimal numbers:

−6.213 × −14.2 can be written:

$$
\begin{array}{r}
-6.1\,2\,3 \\
\times\ 1\,4.2 \\
\hline
1\,2\,2\,4\,6 \\
2\,4\,4\,9\,2\,0 \\
6\,1\,2\,3\,0\,0 \\
\hline
8\,6.9\,4\,6\,6
\end{array}
$$

There are 3 decimal places in the first factor and 1 in the second factor, so there are 4 decimal places in the product.

3.25 × −5.4 can be written:

$$
\begin{array}{r}
3.2\,5 \\
\times\ -5.4 \\
\hline
1\,3\,0\,0 \\
1\,6\,2\,5\,0 \\
\hline
-1\,7.5\,5\,0
\end{array}
$$

There are 2 decimal places in the first factor and 1 in the second factor, so there are 3 decimal places in the product. (You can rewrite the answer in the equivalent form −17.55.)

−12.24 × 52 can be written:

$$
\begin{array}{r}
-1\,2.2\,4 \\
\times\ 5\,2 \\
\hline
2\,4\,4\,8 \\
6\,1\,2\,0\,0 \\
\hline
-6\,3\,6.4\,8
\end{array}
$$

There are 2 decimal places in the first factor and 0 in the second factor, so there are 2 decimal places in the product.

Remember that multiplication and division are inverse operations, so you can check these problems using division.

Reminders for Dividing Decimal Fractions

➤ Write the division problem, taking note of what power of 10 needs to be multiplied by both the dividend and the divisor to convert the divisor into a whole number. (If the divisor is already a whole number, just skip the next point and begin at the third arrow below.)
➤ Multiply both the dividend and the divisor by that power of 10.
➤ Write the decimal point in the space for the quotient directly above where the decimal point is in the new dividend.
➤ Divide as usual, disregarding the sign at this point.
➤ Once you have the quotient, determine the appropriate sign, using the Rules for Dividing Positive and Negative Numbers.

Check out the product of 3.25 and −5.4 (which was −17.550) by dividing:

$$-17.550 \div 3.25$$

Working this problem requires the long division algorithm. Follow the steps shown below:

Step 1.

Another way to write:

$$-17.550 \div 3.25 \text{ is } \frac{-17.550}{3.25}$$

Convert the divisor to a whole number by multiplying both dividend and divisor by 100, in this case:

$$\frac{-17.550}{3.25} \times \frac{100}{100} = \frac{-1755.0}{325}$$

So, the equivalent problem you will solve is:

$$325\overline{)-1755.}$$

Step 2.

Disregard the sign of the answer until you have divided, but bring the decimal straight up from its location in the dividend into the same location in the quotient.

$$325\overline{)-1755.}$$

Divide. Round 325 to 300 and think

$$300\overline{)-1755}$$

Since $5 \times 300 = 1500$, try 5.

$$\begin{array}{r} 5 \\ 325\overline{)-1755.0} \\ \underline{1625} \\ 130 \end{array}$$

Check: Is $130 < 325$? Yes, so press on ...

Step 3.

Bring down the 0 tenths and divide.

Think: $300\overline{)1300}$

Since $4 \times 300 = 1200$, try 4.

$$\begin{array}{r} 5.4 \\ 325\overline{)-1755.0} \\ \underline{1625} \\ 1300 \\ \underline{1300} \\ 0 \end{array}$$

Check: Is $0 < 325$? Yes, so the quotient is -5.4, since a negative number is being divided by a positive number, and there is no remainder.

This quotient also serves as a check for our earlier multiplication problem. Since $-1755 \div 325 = -5.4$, we know that $325 \times -5.4 = 1755.0$, and $3.25 \times -5.4 = -17.55$.

Estimation: Products and Quotients

When you estimate a product or a quotient, you can use rounding to help. How you round will determine how *precise* — or close to the actual answer — your estimate is. You have already seen some examples of estimating products. (See pages 226–7.) But what about estimating quotients?

Estimate

$$218\overline{)763} \quad \rightarrow \quad 200\overline{)800}^{\,4}$$

The actual quotient is 3.5, which is less than 4.

Estimate

$$6.3\overline{)43.26} \quad \rightarrow \quad 6\overline{)43.00}^{\,7.17}$$

The actual quotient is 6.87, to the nearest hundredth, which is less than 7.17.

As with subtraction, more accurate estimates can often be made by compensating, or rounding both the dividend and the divisor up or down together. In the first case, rounding 763 up to 800 would suggest rounding 218 up as well — but not too far. Choosing a number that's easy to work with is also key; in this case, 250 works well because 800/250 = (800/250) × (4/4) = 3200/1000 = 3.2, which is a better estimate than 4. However, the trade-off is that we knew 4 was too big, but we wouldn't know, without further checking, that 3.2 is too small.

In the second example, rounding 6.3 down to 6 would indicate rounding 43.267 down as well. How much? Make it easy, 42! Then $\frac{42}{6} = 7$ is the estimate.

Suppose you are finding the product or quotient of two fractions. Once again, rounding allows you to estimate

Estimate

$$18\frac{5}{8} \times 2\frac{2}{8} \quad \rightarrow \quad 19 \times 2 = 38$$

Since the numbers were rounded in different directions, it is hard to tell whether the actual product is greater or less than 38.

The actual product is $44\frac{7}{10}$, which is quite a bit greater than 38.

Estimate

$$14\frac{3}{8} \div 2\frac{2}{5} \quad \rightarrow \quad 14 \div 2 = 7$$

Rounding both numbers down yields an estimate of 7. The actual quotient is $5\frac{95}{96}$.

Note: If you rounded $2\frac{2}{5}$ up to

$2\frac{1}{2}$ and $14\frac{3}{8}$ up to the next integer, 15,

you would get $15 \div 2\frac{1}{2}$

$= 15 \div \frac{5}{2}$

$= 15 \times \frac{2}{5} = \frac{30}{5} = 6$, which is a very good

estimate.

Estimation: Multiplying and Dividing by Numbers Close to 1

When you are multiplying or dividing by a number close to 1, estimate in advance whether your answer will be greater or less than the number you are multiplying.

1) When you multiply a *positive* number by a number greater than 1, you make the number larger.

$$85 \times 1.2 > 85 \qquad 85 \times 1.2 = 102$$

(Keep in mind that 1.2 could be written as $1\frac{2}{10}$ or $1\frac{1}{5}$.)

2) When you multiply a *positive* number by a number between 0 and 1, you make the number smaller.

$$85 \times 0.8 < 85 \qquad 85 \times 0.8 = 68$$

(This is the same as multiplying by $\frac{8}{10}$ or $\frac{4}{5}$.)

3) When you divide a *positive* number by a number greater than 1, you make the number smaller.

$$85 \div 1.2 < 85 \qquad 85 \div 1.2 \text{ is } 70.8 \text{ (to the nearest tenth)}$$

4) When you divide a *positive* number by a number *between* 0 and 1 (not 0 or 1), you make the number larger. (Remember that division by 0 is undefined!)

$$85 \div 0.8 > 85 \qquad 85 \div 0.8 = 106.25$$

Take a few minutes with a calculator and see what happens if you change the word *positive* in each rule above to *negative*.

Word Problems with Multiple Steps

Knowing how to calculate with integers, fractions, and decimals will allow you to solve many types of practical problems. Here are several examples:

1) Joe had 2 friends over to watch the game last week. Each of the guys, including Joe, ate $2\frac{1}{2}$ subs and $\frac{2}{3}$ of a large bag of chips and drank 32 ounces of soda. Joe plans to invite 5 friends over this week. He knows that he and 4 of the friends will eat the same amount as last week's group, but he's pretty sure that his 5th buddy will eat $1\frac{1}{2}$ times as much as any of the other guys. How many subs, bags of chips, and ounces of soda should Joe buy for himself and his friends this week?

Solution: (Hint: Once you calculate the amounts, think before you write your final answers!)

	Joe & 4 friends	5th friend

Subs:

$$2\frac{1}{2} \times 5$$

$$= \frac{5}{2} \times \frac{5}{1}$$

$$= \frac{25}{2} = 12\frac{1}{2} \text{ subs}$$

$$2\frac{1}{2} \times 1\frac{1}{2}$$

$$= \frac{5}{2} \times \frac{3}{2}$$

$$= \frac{15}{4} = 3\frac{3}{4} \text{ subs}$$

$$2\frac{1}{2} = 12\frac{2}{4}$$

$$+ \frac{3}{4} = \frac{3}{4}$$

$$\frac{5}{4} = 16\frac{1}{4} \text{ subs}$$

Chips:

$$\frac{2}{3} \times 5$$

$$= \frac{2}{3} \times \frac{5}{1}$$

$$= \frac{10}{3} = 3\frac{1}{3} \text{ bags}$$

$$\frac{2}{3} \times 1\frac{1}{2}$$

$$= \frac{2}{3} \times \frac{3}{2}$$

$$= \frac{\overset{1}{\cancel{2}}}{\underset{1}{\cancel{3}}} \times \frac{\overset{1}{\cancel{3}}}{\underset{1}{\cancel{2}}} = 1 \text{ bag}$$

$$3\frac{1}{3} + 1 = 4\frac{1}{3} \text{ bags of chips}$$

Soda: $32 \times 5 = 160$ oz

$$\times 1\frac{1}{2}$$

$$= \frac{32}{1} \times \frac{3}{2}$$

$$= \frac{\overset{16}{\cancel{32}}}{1} \times \frac{\overset{1}{\cancel{3}}}{\underset{1}{\cancel{2}}} = 48 \text{ oz}$$

$$160 + 48 = 208 \text{ oz}$$

So, Joe should buy 17 subs (so that he'll have at least $16\frac{1}{4}$), 5 bags of chips (so he'll have at least $4\frac{1}{3}$ bags), and 208 oz of soda (in however many cans or bottles are needed).

2) Larry and Carol watched the rise and fall of one of their stocks during one business week. The results are represented in the following problem, where the negatives show the stock going down in value and the positives show the stock rising in value:

$$-3.25 + 5.125 + 1.5 - 2.375 - 0.25$$

First, figure out the change in their stock over the week without using a calculator, then check with a calculator.

Solution: (Hint: Use the commutative, associative, and distributive properties to arrange the problem into the difference between the sum of all the positive values and the sum of all the negative values.)

$$-3.25 + 5.125 + 1.5 - 2.375 - 0.25$$
$$= 5.125 + 1.5 - 3.25 - 2.375 - 0.25$$
$$= (5.125 + 1.5) - (3.25 + 2.375 + 0.25)$$
$$= 6.625 - 5.875$$
$$= 0.75$$

So, Larry and Carol's stock went up 0.75 points that week.

3) Yolanda's grocery receipt showed the following:

2 @ 3.49 (2 items at $3.49 each)
6 @ 6.00
9 @ 1.99
− 4 @ 1.99

The last entry shows that the cashier had rung up 9 @ 1.99 incorrectly and it should have been 5 @ 1.99. The problem can be represented as follows:

$$2 \times 3.49 + 6^2 + 9 \times 1.99 - 4 \times 1.99$$

First, use *order of operations* to figure out Yolanda's correct total at this point, then use a calculator to check your results.

(*Hint:* You can remember the order of operations by the first letters in the words of the following saying, "Pretty Please, My Dear Aunt Sally": Parentheses, Powers, Multiplication and Division, Addition and Subtraction. Note that with multiplication and division, if there is more than one of these operations in the expression, take them as they come in the problem from left to right. If division comes first and then multiplication, that's fine—do the division first. The same applies to addition and subtraction.

Solution:

$2 \times 3.49 + 6^2 + 9 \times 1.99 - 4 \times 1.99$	Original problem
$2 \times 3.49 + 36 + 9 \times 1.99 - 4 \times 1.99$	Since there are no Parentheses, the Power (or exponent) is computed first.
$6.98 + 36 + 9 \times 1.99 - 4 \times 1.99$	Multiplication and Division, as they
$6.98 + 36 + \ 17.91 \ - 4 \times 1.99$	appear in the problem from left to right,
$6.98 + 36 + \ 17.91 \ - 7.96$	are next.
$42.98 \ + \ 17.91 - 7.96$	Addition and Subtraction, as they appear
$60.89 \qquad - 7.96$	in the problem from left to right, are last.
52.93	

So Yolanda's correct total is $52.93.

RATIO, PROPORTION, AND PERCENT

Ratios and Proportions

A *ratio* compares one number to another. A *proportion* is an equation stating that two ratios are equal to each other.

$$\frac{7}{10} = \frac{21}{30} \text{ is a proportion.}$$

You read this proportion as follows: "7 is to 10 as 21 is to 30." You know the ratios are equal, because $\frac{7}{10}$ multiplied by $\frac{3}{3}$ equals $\frac{21}{30}$. Since multiplying by $\frac{3}{3}$ is the same as multiplying by 1, you know that $\frac{7}{10} = \frac{21}{30}$.

A kind of problem that you should be able to solve is a proportion that contains a variable, such as:

$$\frac{n}{20} = \frac{5}{8}$$

A useful way to solve this kind of problem is to *cross multiply*. Multiply the numerator of the left ratio by the denominator of the right ratio and set this equal to the product of the numerator of the right ratio and the denominator of the left ratio, as shown below:

Step 1: Solve for n in the proportion:

$$\frac{n}{20} = \frac{5}{8}$$
$$n \times 8 = 20 \times 5$$
$$8n = 100$$
$$\frac{\cancel{8}}{\cancel{8}}n = \frac{100}{8}$$
$$n = 12.5$$

Step 2: Check by substituting 12.5 for the value of n in the original proportion, and cross multiply to see if the proportion is true:

$$\frac{n}{20} = \frac{5}{8}$$
$$\frac{12.5}{20} = \frac{5}{8}$$
$$12.5 \times 8 = 20 \times 5$$
$$100 = 100$$

So, the value $n = 12.5$ checks.

The two products you get when you cross multiply are called *cross products*.

> Equal ratios have equal cross products.

But why is this true? What you are really doing when you find the cross products is finding the numerators of the two ratios, if they were expressed with a common denominator. The common denominator is not necessarily the least common denominator, but it will be the product of the two denominators shown in the proportion. Using the example given above, look at how this works:

You already know that $\dfrac{12.5}{20} = \dfrac{5}{8}$. But suppose you didn't.

To compare the two ratios, you can use a common denominator. Even though it's not the lowest common denominator, one possible common denominator is the product of the current denominators: $20 \times 8 = 160$.

So, convert each ratio into an equivalent ratio with denominator 160:

$$\frac{12.5}{20} \times \frac{8}{8} = \frac{100}{160} \qquad \frac{5}{8} \times \frac{20}{20} = \frac{100}{160}$$

When you closely inspect the *products in the numerators* (12.5×8 on the left and 5×20 on the right), you can see that those are the *cross products*! So, cross multiplication works and is a shortcut to having to find the common denominator to create equivalent fractions.

Solving Word Problems Using Ratios and Proportions

Proportions can help you solve word problems. Check out the following problem:

Joe wants to make a pie crust for a slightly larger than normal pie pan. His recipe calls for 7 T of butter and 5 oz of flour. If Joe decides to make slightly more pie crust by using 6 oz of flour instead of 5 oz, how many tablespoons of butter should he use, to keep the proportion of butter to flour the same?

To solve this problem, you write a proportion, thinking: "7 T of butter is to 5 oz of flour as n T of butter is to 6 oz of flour" or

$$\frac{7}{5} = \frac{n}{6} \quad \frac{\text{(T of butter)}}{\text{(oz of flour)}}$$

Cross multiply to solve for n.

$$7 \times 6 = 5 \times n$$
$$42 = 5n$$
$$\frac{42}{5} = \frac{\cancel{5}}{\cancel{5}} n$$
$$8.4 = n$$

Joe should use 8.4 T of butter for 6 oz of flour. Because 8.4 is very close to 8.5, he might use $8\frac{1}{2}$ T of butter or just slightly less.

Using Proportions with Scale Drawings

Maps are good examples of scale drawings. Below is a table of distances: the distances on a map compared to the actual distances.

Map distance	1 cm	1.2 cm	2 cm	2.6 cm	3.2 cm	?
Actual distance	50 km	60 km	100 km	130 km	?	260 km
		Scale: 1 cm = 50 km				

Figure out the actual distance that is represented by 3.2 cm on the map. You can write a proportion using the scale of 1 cm = 50 km. Think: 1 cm is to 50 km as 3.2 cm is to n km.

$$\begin{array}{l} \text{map distance in cm} \rightarrow \\ \text{actual distance in km} \rightarrow \end{array} \quad \frac{1}{50} = \frac{3.2}{n}$$
$$n = 50 \times 3.2$$
$$n = 160$$

So, 3.2 cm on the map represents 160 km of actual distance.

You can also use a proportion to find what the map distance would be, given the actual distance. What map distance would represent 260 km of actual distance?

$$\begin{array}{r} \text{map distance in cm} \rightarrow \\ \text{actual distance in km} \rightarrow \end{array} \quad \frac{1}{50} = \frac{d}{260}$$

$$260 = 50d$$

$$5.2 = d$$

So, 260 km of actual distance would be represented by 5.2 cm on the map.

Fractions, Decimals, and Percents

Fractions, decimals, and percents are often used interchangeably. For example, you might say $\frac{1}{4}$ of Jim's marbles are green or 0.25 of Jim's marbles are green or 25% of Jim's marbles are green ($\frac{1}{4}$ = 0.25 = 25%). Since you are thinking about a part of a whole, you could also say that $\frac{3}{4}$ of Jim's marbles are not green or 0.75 of Jim's marbles are not green or 75% of Jim's marbles are not green. ($\frac{3}{4}$ = 0.75 = 75%).

Suppose 10% of Andrea's marbles are blue. Practice writing six statements like the statements above about this fact.

You should memorize the percent equivalents for common fractions: $\frac{1}{4}$ is 25%, $\frac{1}{2}$ is 50%, $\frac{1}{10}$ is 10%, etc.

But, what if you don't know the percent or decimal for the fraction? How can you find it? Remember that a percent is a ratio of a number to 100. For example, 5% = $\frac{5}{100}$.

Percents are always in hundredths.

To write a fraction as a percent, you can sometimes easily write an equivalent fraction with a denominator of 100.

$$\frac{2}{5} = \frac{40}{100} = 40\%$$

But sometimes it's not that easy. So, in general, use the following method to write a fraction as a percent:

Step 1: Write the fraction as a decimal by dividing its numerator by its denominator.

Step 2: Write the decimal as a percent by multiplying the quotient by 100.

For example, you would write $\frac{5}{8}$ as a percent in the following way:

$$\begin{array}{r} 0.625 \\ \textit{Step 1:} \quad 8\overline{)5.000} \end{array} \qquad \textit{Step 2:}\ 0.625 = 62.5\%$$

Remember: to write a decimal as a percent, you multiply the decimal by 100, or move its decimal point two places to the right.

The decimal for $\frac{5}{8}$ is a *terminating decimal*, meaning that the decimal "stops" (in the thousandths place for $\frac{5}{8}$). When the fraction cannot be written as a terminating decimal, we usually round the percent to a convenient place. Look for example at changing $\frac{5}{11}$ to a percent:

$$\begin{array}{r} 0.4545 \\ 11\overline{)5.0000} \end{array}$$

Since the digits 45 will continue to repeat forever, you can write the resulting *repeating decimal* as $0.\overline{45}$. To change $0.\overline{45}$ to a percent, move the decimal two places to the right, still showing the repeating decimal places.

So, $\frac{5}{11} = 0.\overline{45}$, or 45.45% to the nearest hundredth of a percent, or 45.5% to the nearest tenth of a percent.

Sometimes it is more convenient to write a fraction that results in a repeating decimal, as a mixed number percent. For example, $\frac{1}{3}$ may be written as a mixed number percent by this method:

1) Divide its numerator by its denominator and find the quotient to the hundredths place.
2) Then, write the remainder as a fraction.
3) Finally, write this quotient as a percent.

In doing so, the fraction $\frac{1}{3}$ can be written exactly as $33\frac{1}{3}\%$, since $\frac{1}{3}$ of 100 is $33\frac{1}{3}$.

Here is a conversion of $\frac{5}{6}$ to a mixed number percent.

$$\frac{5}{6} = 6\overline{\smash{)}5.00}^{\displaystyle 0.83\frac{1}{3}}$$

$$\begin{array}{r} 0.83\frac{1}{3} \\ 6\overline{)5.00} \\ \underline{4.8} \\ 20 \\ \underline{18} \\ 2 \end{array}$$

$$.83\frac{1}{3} = 83\frac{1}{3}\%$$

To write a percent as a decimal or fraction, remember that a percent is *always in hundredths*. Therefore, 35 percent is the same as 35 hundredths, and 8 percent is the same as 8 hundredths.

$$35\% = 0.35 = \frac{35}{100} = \frac{7}{20} \qquad\qquad 8\% = 0.08 = \frac{8}{100} = \frac{2}{25}$$

A quick way to write a percent as a decimal is to divide by 100:

$35\% = 0.35$ and $2\% = 0.02$ (Move the decimal point two places to the left.)

To write a decimal as a percent, think of the decimal in terms of hundredths. Then you can write it as a percent. For example, 7 tenths (0.7) is the same as 70 hundredths (0.70), which is the same as 70%.

A quick way to write a decimal as a percent is to multiply the decimal by 100. This method works because percents are already in hundredths.

$0.7 = 70\%$ and $0.04 = 4\%$ (Move the decimal point two places to the right.)

Be sure you can complete a table like this one, writing a number as a fraction, a decimal, or a percent.

Fraction	Decimal	Percent
$\frac{1}{5}$	___	___
___	0.1	___
___	___	65%
___	0.5	___

Percents Greater Than 100% and Less Than 1%

Just as there can be fractions greater than 1, there can be percents greater than 100%. For example, a retail store may pay a certain amount for a piece of clothing but mark up the price 150% to 450% for selling the item. That is how the store makes its money. So, if the store bought a blouse for $5.00, they might mark it up 350% to $22.50. How does that work?

A whole equals 100%, so 1 = 100%, 1.5 = 150%, 2 = 200%, 2.5 = 250%, and so on. In general, to write a whole number or a decimal as a percent, move its decimal point two places to the right, and add the percent sign. Remember $a \times 1 = a$ for all real numbers a. Therefore, since 100% = 1, you do not change the actual value of a number when you multiply it by 100%. A markup of 350% means multiplying the original price by 3.5 and then adding the product to the original price: 5.00 × 3.5 = 17.50. $5.00 (original price) plus $17.50 (markup) equals $22.50.

To write a percent as a decimal, divide by 100 — or move its decimal point two places to the left — and eliminate the percent sign:

$137.2\% = 1.372$ and $3,600\% = 36.00 = 36.$

To write a mixed number as a percent, work with the whole number part and fractional part separately:

$$2\frac{3}{5} = 2 + \frac{3}{5} = 200\% + 60\% = 260\%.$$

You can also write a percent greater than 100% as a mixed number:

$$375\% = 300\% + 75\% = 3 + \frac{3}{4} = 3\frac{3}{4}.$$

Percents can also be smaller than 1%. You may be familiar with milk that contains $\frac{1}{2}\%$ fat. You can think of this value as a fractional percent. It's actually a fraction of a fraction, since percent means *hundredths*.

So you have $\dfrac{\frac{1}{2}}{100}$.

Since that may look strange to you, you can write $\frac{1}{2}\%$ as a decimal and a fraction in the following way:

$$\frac{1}{2}\% = 0.5\% = 0.005 = \frac{5}{1000} = \frac{1}{200}.$$

Percent Problems

In a percent problem, there are three possible values, any one of which may be unknown: the *whole* (sometimes called the *base*), the *part*, and the *percent*. You can set up a percent problem as a proportion, like this:

$$\frac{Part}{Whole} = \frac{Percent}{100}$$

Try this problem: There are 525 students in a school. 44% of them are boys. How many students are boys? In this problem, you know the whole (525) and the percent (44). You need to figure out the part (how many are boys).

You can solve this problem by setting up a proportion using the formula above:

$$\frac{Part}{Whole} = \frac{Percent}{100}$$

Fill in the numbers you already know; let the letter x stand for the unknown part:

$$\frac{x}{525} = \frac{44}{100}$$

Next, cross multiply:

$$100 \times x = 525 \times 44$$

$$100x = 23100$$

Then divide both sides of the equation by 100:

$$x = 231$$

So, 44% of 525 is 231.
The school has 231 boys.

Suppose that 21 students in a class of 40 are African Americans. What percent does that represent? In this case, you know the whole (40) and the part (21) but not the percent.

You can solve this problem using the same formula:

$$\frac{Part}{Whole} = \frac{Percent}{100}$$

Fill in the numbers you already know;
let the letter p stand for the unknown percent

$$\frac{21}{40} = \frac{p}{100}$$

Next, cross multiply:

$$40 \times p = 21 \times 100$$

$$40p = 2100$$

Finally, divide both sides of the equation by 40:

$$p = \frac{2100}{40}$$

$$p = 52.5$$

So 52.5% of the students are African American.

The Munster family has to pay 5.6% of last year's taxable income for state income tax. If the Munsters paid $1,237.60 in state income tax last year, what was the family's taxable income? In this case, you know the part (the $1,237.60 in taxes paid) and the percent (5.6%). You need to find the base, or the whole.

Begin with the formula:

$$\frac{Part}{Whole} = \frac{Percent}{100}$$

Fill in the numbers you already know.
Let the letter i stand for the unknown total taxable income.

$$\frac{1237.60}{i} = \frac{5.6}{100}$$

Cross multiply:

$$5.6 \times i = 1237.60 \times 100$$

$$5.6i = 123,760$$

Divide both sides of the equation by 5.6

$$i = \frac{123760}{5.6}$$
$$i = 22,111$$

So the Munsters' taxable income was $22,100.

Percent of Increase or Decrease

We often *increase* an amount by a certain percent, for example, when we are working with sales tax or a meal tax. To increase an amount by a certain percent, *multiply* the amount by the *percent of increase*, and then *add* this increase to the original amount. Here's an example:

In the city of Grand Elk the meal tax is 6%. What will be the tax on a meal at a restaurant in Grand Elk if the pretax bill is $22.65? What will be the total bill?

Solution:
Remember that 6% of $22.65 means .06 × 22.65

$$6\% = 0.06 = \frac{6}{100}$$

So you could calculate using a decimal:

$$0.06 \times 22.65 = 1.359$$

Or you could calculate using a fraction:

$$\frac{6}{100} \times 22.65 = \frac{135.9}{100} = 1.359$$

Since 1.359 rounds to 1.36, the tax on the meal would be $1.36.
Add the pretax meal cost to the tax to get the total bill:

$$\$22.65 + \$1.36 = \$24.01$$

Therefore the total cost of the meal is $24.01. (But that doesn't include the tip for the waiter!)

There are also many examples of everyday situations where we *decrease* an amount by a certain percent. For example, we may see an item on sale and want to find the new price after the discount. To decrease an amount by a certain percent, *multiply* the amount by the *percent of decrease*, and then *subtract* this decrease from the original amount. Here's an example:

During a sale at the department store, all jeans that cost less than $20 are discounted by 35%. All jeans costing $20 or more are discounted by 45%. Natalie likes one pair of jeans originally marked $18 and another marked $21. What is the discounted price of each pair of jeans?

Solution:

1) Price of $18 jeans, discounted by 35% = 0.35:

$$\text{Discount price} = \$18 - (\$18)(0.35)$$
$$= \$18 - \$6.30$$
$$= \$11.70$$

So, the $18 jeans are now $11.70.

2) Price of $21 jeans, discounted by 45% = 0.45:

$$\text{Discount price} = \$21 - (\frac{45}{100})(21)$$
$$= \$21 - \frac{\$945}{100}$$
$$= \$21 - \$9.45$$
$$= \$11.55$$

So, the $21 jeans are now $11.55.

Notice that at the discounted prices the jeans originally marked $21 are now cheaper than the ones that were originally marked $18!

MEASUREMENT

Prefixes in the Metric System

Learning the prefixes used in the metric system will help you find the equivalences among different metric units, even those that are not often used in this country.

kilo-	hecto-	deka-	basic unit	deci-	centi-	milli-
thousand	hundred	ten	one	tenth	hundredth	thousandth
1000	100	10	1	0.1	0.01	0.001

The basic unit of *length* in the metric system is the *meter*, abbreviated m. You can find how many meters are in each of the other units of length by using the *meanings* of the prefixes.

kilometer	hectometer	dekameter	meter	decimeter	centimeter	millimeter
km	hm	dam	m	dm	cm	mm
thousand	hundred	ten	one	tenth	hundredth	thousandth
1000 m	100 m	10 m	1 m	0.1 m	0.01 m	0.001 m

You can work in the same way with the metric units of capacity and mass. The basic unit of *capacity* in the metric system is the *liter*, abbreviated l, and the basic unit of *mass* in the metric system is the *gram*, abbreviated g. For example, a kiloliter (kl) is 1,000 liters or 1 cubic meter, roughly the size of a teacher's desk, and a milligram (mg) is 0.001 g — think of the mass of a flea.

Conversions Within the Metric System

In the metric system converting from one unit to another is generally quite easy, as it simply involves moving the decimal point. 1,566 mm = 156.6 cm = 15.66 dm = 1.566 m. What would 3.45 meters equal in centimeters? Millimeters? (Hint: Use the first chart above to help you determine how many places and which way to move the decimal from the basic unit of *meters*.)

In the metric system, as with any other system, area is measured in square units and volume is measured in cubic units. So, the area of a rectangle or circle, for example, may be given in m^2 or cm^2 or km^2, whereas the volume of a prism or sphere, for example, may be given in m^3 or cm^3 or km^3 or dm^3 (also known as liters).

U.S. Customary Units

Some of the more common customary units used in the United States for *length* are the inch, foot, yard, and mile. For *capacity*, we use cups, pints, quarts, and gallons. For *weight*, we use ounces, pounds, and tons. When doing arithmetic with customary units, you sometimes need to use the equivalences among the different units.

For example, you can calculate 6 × 2 ft = 12 ft easily. However, to calculate 6 × 2 ft 7 in, you need to regroup inches as feet, using the conversion 12 in = 1 ft.

Step 1:
You can begin by writing the problem vertically:

2ft 7in
×   6
———

Step 2:
You can then separately multiply the feet and the inches:

2ft   7in
×   6
———
12ft 42in

Step 3:
Convert 42 in to feet and inches by dividing 42 by 12 in per ft:

42 ÷ 12 = 3 ft 6 in

Step 4:
Combine the 3 ft 6 in with the 12 ft you already have to get the final result:

15 ft 6 in

So, 6 × 2 ft 7 in = 15 ft 6 in.

What would be 5 × 3 ft 5 in? How about 8 × 2 ft 9 in?

To find the difference between 7 gal 1 qt and 4 gal 3 qt, you need to regroup gallons as quarts, using the conversion: 1 gal = 4 qt.

Step 1:
You can begin by writing the problem vertically:

7 gal   1 qt
−4 gal   3 qt
———

Step 2:
You can then regroup and convert 7 gal 1 qt to 6 gal 5 qt:

6 gal   5 qt
−4 gal   3 qt
———

Step 3:
Find the difference:

6 gal   5 qt
−4 gal   3 qt
———
2 gal   2 qt

So, 7 gal 1 qt − 4 gal 3 qt = 2 gal 2 qt.

Units of Time as Fractions and Decimals

Time is commonly measured in seconds, minutes, hours, days, months, and years. When time is measured in hours, sometimes mixed numbers or decimals are used. For example, to translate $3\frac{1}{3}$ hours into hours and minutes, simply multiply 60 minutes by the fractional part of one hour ($\frac{1}{3}$).

$$\frac{1}{3} \times 60 = 20 \qquad \text{Since } \frac{1}{3}\text{ h} = 20 \text{ min} \qquad 3\frac{1}{3}\text{ h} = 3\text{ h } 20 \text{ min}$$

To translate 3 hours 48 minutes into fraction or decimal hours, write the mixed number $3\frac{48}{60}$ h, simplify, and convert to its decimal form.

$$3\frac{48}{60} = 3\frac{4}{5} = 3.8$$

So, 3 hours 48 minutes is $3\frac{4}{5}$ or 3.8 h.

In similar fashion, you can translate 0.3 h to minutes, by calculating 0.3 of 60 minutes.

$$0.3 \times 60 = 18 \qquad \text{So, } 0.3 \text{ h} = 18 \text{ min.}$$

Elapsed Time

Time constantly moves along, and we are often interested in how much time has passed or how long something will last. Such computations result in *elapsed time*. Consider the following everyday problem:

Ari's plane is to take off at 4:38 P.M. and arrive at his destination at 7:15 P.M. the same evening. Assuming the plane is on schedule, how much time will it take from takeoff until Ari arrives at his final destination?

Solution:

Just as with other units of measure, you may need to use some conversion facts (such as 60 min = 1 h) to regroup:

Step 1:
Begin by writing the subtraction problem vertically in hours and minutes:

$$\begin{array}{r} 7\,h \quad 15\ min \\ -4\,h \quad 38\ min \\ \hline \end{array}$$

Step 2:
You can then regroup and convert 7 h 15 min to 6 h 75 min:

$$\begin{array}{r} 6\,h \quad 75\ min \\ -4\,h \quad 38\ min \\ \hline \end{array}$$

Step 3:
Find the difference:

$$\begin{array}{r} 6\,h \quad 75\ min \\ -4\,h \quad 38\ min \\ \hline 2\,h \quad 37\ min \end{array}$$

So, from takeoff until Ari arrives at his final destination will be 2 h 37 min.

Occasionally elapsed time may involve several conversions. Consider this situation: Rosa is paid by the hour. She was curious how many full (24-hour) days she worked, and found that she clocked total hours amounting to 1 d 18 h 45 min of work for her first week and 2 d 15 h 50 min for her second week. Rosa is to report her time in hours to the nearest half-hour, but she still wants to know how many full days she worked. Help Rosa satisfy her curiosity about full days, but also find out what she should report to the nearest half hour for these two weeks.

Solution:

Step 1:
Write the addition problem vertically:

$$\begin{array}{r} 1\,d \quad 18\,h \quad 45\ min \\ -2\,d \quad 15\,h \quad 50\ min \\ \hline \end{array}$$

Step 2:
You can add each of the units:

$$\begin{array}{r} 1\,d \quad 18\,h \quad 45\ min \\ -2\,d \quad 15\,h \quad 50\ min \\ \hline 2\,d \quad 33\,h \quad 95\ min \end{array}$$

Step 3:
Convert the solution, using: 60 min = 1 h and 24 h = 1 d.

$$\begin{array}{r} 3\,d \quad 33\,h \quad 95\ min \\ = 3\,d \quad 34\,h \quad 35\ min \\ = 4\,d \quad 10\,h \quad 35\ min \end{array}$$

So, Rosa worked 4 days 10 hours 35 minutes.
(To the nearest half hour, Rosa worked 4 days $10\frac{1}{2}$ hours)

Since Rosa worked for 4 full days, she would compute:

$4 \times 24 = 96$ h, and then add the additional $10\frac{1}{2}$ h.
$96 + 10\frac{1}{2} = 106\frac{1}{2}$.

She would have to ignore the extra 5 minutes she worked or, if allowed, carry it over to the next pay period.

So, Rosa should report $106\frac{1}{2}$ h of work.

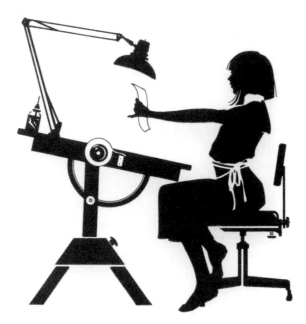

GEOMETRY

Parallel and Perpendicular Lines

Parallel lines are defined as two lines in the same plane that do not intersect. The symbol ‖ means "is parallel to." In the following diagram, $\overleftrightarrow{ZC} \parallel \overleftrightarrow{TS}$, or $\overrightarrow{ZC} \parallel \overrightarrow{TS}$.

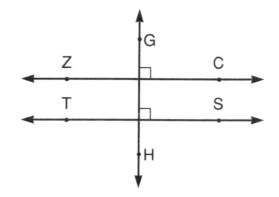

The symbol ⊥ means "is perpendicular to." In the same diagram above, $\overleftrightarrow{ZC} \perp \overleftrightarrow{GH}$ or $\overleftrightarrow{ZC}$ is perpendicular to $\overleftrightarrow{GH}$, and also $\overleftrightarrow{TS} \perp \overleftrightarrow{GH}$.

If two lines are parallel, any line in the plane that is perpendicular to one is also perpendicular to the other.

If $\overleftrightarrow{AB} \parallel \overleftrightarrow{CD}$ and $\overleftrightarrow{AB} \perp \overleftrightarrow{TS}$ then $\overleftrightarrow{CD} \perp \overleftrightarrow{TS}$.

Two lines perpendicular to the same line are parallel.

If $\overleftrightarrow{AB} \perp \overleftrightarrow{TS}$ and $\overleftrightarrow{CD} \perp \overleftrightarrow{TS}$ then $\overleftrightarrow{AB} \parallel \overleftrightarrow{CD}$.

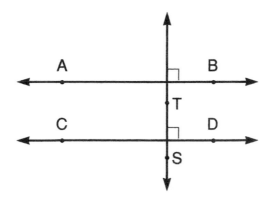

Lines, Rays, Segments

A *line* goes on forever in both directions. A *ray* has one endpoint and goes on forever in only one direction. A *segment* has two endpoints and includes all points between them.

When two segments have the same length, we say that they are *congruent*. The symbol ≅ means "is congruent to." Because $\overline{BA}$ and $\overline{CD}$, on the previous page, have the same length, $\overline{BA} \cong \overline{CD}$.

Angles

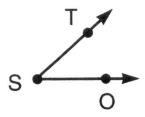

The two rays that form an *angle* are called the *sides* of the angle. You can name an angle by three points, putting the *vertex*, which is the common endpoint of the two rays, in the middle. You can also name an angle by its vertex alone, *if no other angle has the same vertex*. So, this angle could be named: ∠*TSO* or ∠*OST* or ∠*S*.

We usually measure an angle in *degrees*. Two angles that have the same measure are congruent.

So, m∠*QRS*=m∠*ABC* reads: "the measure of angle *QRS* equals the measure of angle *ABC*," and if m∠*QRS*=m∠*ABC* then ∠*QRS* ≅ ∠*ABC*.

Classifying Angles

There are four classifications of angles based on the number of degrees that the angle measures. An *acute angle* has a measure greater than 0° and less than 90°. A *right angle* has a measure of exactly 90°. An *obtuse angle* has a measure greater than 90° and less than 180°. A *straight angle* has a measure of exactly 180°. You can see all four kinds of angles in the illustration below. ∠*BAC* is an acute angle. ∠*BAE* is a right angle. ∠*BAG* is an obtuse angle. And ∠*BAH* is a straight angle. What kind of angle is ∠*HAE*? ∠*HAG*? ∠*CAD*?

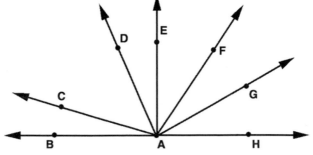

Angle Bisectors

A ray that divides an angle into two congruent angles is called a *bisector*.

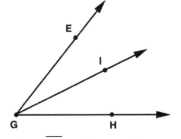

∠EGI ≅ ∠HGI, therefore $\overline{GI}$ is the angle bisector of ∠EGH.

The Angles of a Triangle

The sum of the measures of the angles of a triangle is 180°. Therefore, if you know the measure of any two angles of a triangle, you can always find the measure of the third.

You know that:

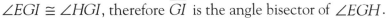

x + 65° + 35° = 180°
x = 180° − 65° − 35°
x = 115° − 35°
x = 80°

Kinds of Triangles

We classify triangles according to the lengths of their sides.

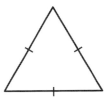 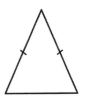 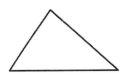

Equilateral triangle:
Three sides of
equal length

Isosceles triangle:
Two sides of
equal length

Scalene triangle:
No sides of
equal length

We also classify triangles according to their angles.

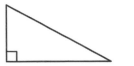

Right triangle:
one right angle

Obtuse triangle:
one obtuse angle

Acute triangle:
three acute angles

Can a triangle have more than one obtuse angle? One right angle? Why or why not?

Similar Figures

Figures that have exactly the same size and shape are *congruent*. We show this using the symbol ≅.

Figures that have the same shape, but not necessarily the same size, are *similar*. We show this using the symbol ~. If two triangles, for example, have the exact same shape but are different sizes, you would write $\triangle ABC \sim \triangle SQW$ to say that triangle ABC is similar to triangle SQW. Similar polygons have congruent angles.

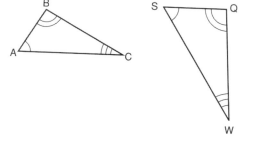

Notice that you list vertices of similar polygons so that you can read off the congruent angles:

$$\angle A \cong \angle S, \angle B \cong \angle Q, \angle C \cong \angle W$$

Proportional Polygons

You can enlarge or reduce a polygon and create a similar polygon by multiplying the length of each side by the same factor. For example, you can enlarge triangle ABC, with sides of 3 cm, 5 cm, and 6 cm, by multiplying the length of each side by 2. This will give you triangle A′B′C′ with side lengths 6 cm, 10 cm, and 12 cm. The two triangles will be similar.

These similar triangles show the following property of similar polygons:

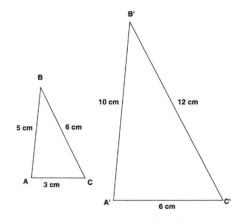

The lengths of corresponding sides of similar polygons are proportional.

In other words, the lengths of corresponding sides of similar polygons form equal ratios. For example:

$$\frac{\text{Lengths of sides of triangle } ABC \text{ (in cm)}}{\text{Lengths of sides of triangle } DEF \text{ (in cm)}} = \frac{3}{6} = \frac{5}{10} = \frac{6}{12}$$

You can use this property of similar triangles (or other polygons) to find the length of a missing side. Set up a proportion that describes the relationships between the corresponding sides of the two figures. If $\triangle HIJ \sim \triangle KRS$, in the diagram below, then x is to 5 m as 24 m is to 7 m.

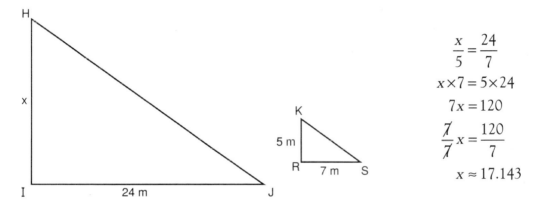

$$\frac{x}{5} = \frac{24}{7}$$
$$x \times 7 = 5 \times 24$$
$$7x = 120$$
$$\frac{7}{7}x = \frac{120}{7}$$
$$x \approx 17.143$$

The symbol $\approx$ means "is approximately equal to." The missing side is about 17.143 m (rounded to the nearest thousandth of a meter) or about 17 m (rounded to the nearest whole meter).

Lines of Symmetry

When a geometrical figure can be divided into two identical halves by a line, we say that it is *symmetrical*. A line that divides the figure into identical halves is called an *axis of symmetry*. Some figures have no axis of symmetry, some have one, and some have several. A circle has infinitely many; any line through the center of a circle is an axis of symmetry.

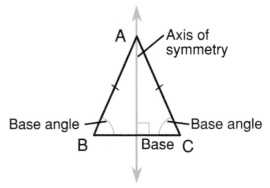

Properties of Parallelograms

A *parallelogram* is a quadrilateral (a four-sided figure) with two pairs of parallel sides. The opposite sides and opposite angles are congruent, but a parallelogram does not necessarily have any axes of symmetry.

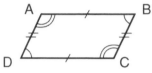

A *rhombus* is a particular kind of parallelogram with all four sides congruent. A rhombus has exactly *two* axes of symmetry that run along its diagonals.

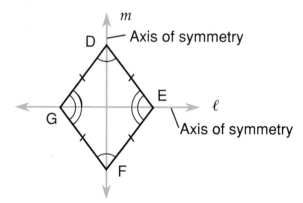

You can think of a rhombus as either isosceles triangle *DEG* reflected over line *l*, or as isosceles triangle *DGF* reflected over line *m*.

A *rectangle* is a parallelogram with four right angles. Adjacent sides (the ones next to each other) are perpendicular:

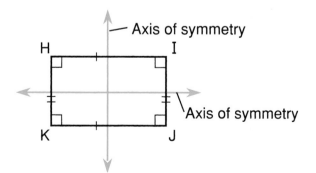

The rectangle has two axes of symmetry that run through the midpoints of the opposite sides.

Since a square is both a rectangle and a rhombus, it shares the properties of both figures and has four axes of symmetry: two along its diagonals and two that run through the midpoints of the opposite sides.

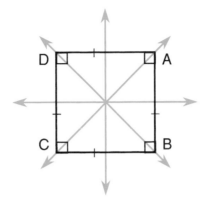

Translations, Reflections, Rotations

When two figures are congruent, we can use three kinds of rigid motions to make them occupy exactly the same place, or to *coincide*. The first kind of rigid motion is a *translation*, sometimes called a *slide*. Here's an example of a slide:

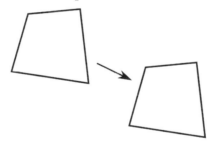

The second kind of motion is a *reflection*, sometimes called a *flip*. Here's a figure flipped across an axis:

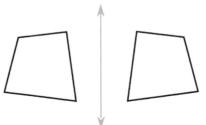

The third kind of motion is a *rotation*, or *turn*. Here's a figure rotated around a point:

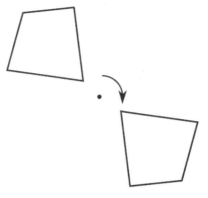

Creating a Congruent Shape Using a Reflection

A point, a line, or a figure can be reflected over a line. The line over which the figure is reflected is called the *line of reflection* or the *reflection line*.

When a polygon is reflected over a line, each point of the polygon is reflected over the line. You can reflect a polygon over a line by reflecting its vertices over the line and connecting them.

Notice that if you reflect point A over the line, you can label it A′ ("A prime"). Point A′ is said to correspond to point A. The reflection line will be the perpendicular bisector of $\overline{AA'}$. The same facts are true for points B, C, and D and their corresponding points.

The reflected polygon A′B′C′D′ will be congruent to the original polygon ABCD.

Perimeter and Area

The *perimeter* of a closed figure is the linear distance around the figure, and the *area* is the number of square units of space in the interior of the figure. Using common formulas will help you calculate the perimeter and area of shapes or find a missing dimension when you know the perimeter or area:

Area and Perimeter Formulas

Rectangle	Square	Triangle	Parallelogram
$P = 2(l+w)$	$P = 4s$	$P = s_1 + s_2 + s_3$	$P = 2(b+s)$
$A = lw$	$A = s^2$	$A = \frac{1}{2}bh$	$A = bh$

Look at the following examples, noting that the perimeter and individual dimensions are expressed in *linear units* and that area is expressed in *square units*:

1) A rectangle has a length of 12 cm and a perimeter of 32 cm. What is its area?

Solution:

To find the area of the rectangle, you first need to find its width. Use the formula for the perimeter of a rectangle and substitute the known values to find the width. Once you know the width, you can use the formula for the area of a rectangle:

Step 1: First find the width:

$P = 2(l+w)$

$32 = 2(12+w)$

$32 = 24 + 2w$

$8 = 2w$

$4 = w$

Step 2: Now, find the area:

$A = lw$

$A = 12 \times 4$

$A = 48$

So, the area of the rectangle is 48 square centimeters, or 48 cm².

2) A parallelogram has a height of 5 m and an area of 68 m². What is the length of its base?

Solution:

To find the length of the base, substitute the known values into the formula for the area of a parallelogram.

$$A = bh$$
$$68 = b \times 5$$
$$68 = 5b$$
$$13.6 = b$$

So, the base of the parallelogram is 13.6 m.

3) One of the congruent sides of an isosceles triangle is 15 cm, its height is 12 cm, and its area is 108 cm². Find its perimeter.

Solution:

To find the perimeter of the triangle, you need to find its base. Using the formula for the area of a triangle, substitute the known values to find the base. Once you know the base, you can add it to the lengths of the other two sides to find the perimeter.

First find the base:

$$A = \frac{1}{2}bh$$

$$108 = \frac{1}{2} \times b \times 12$$

$$108 = 6b$$

$$18 = b$$

Now, find the perimeter:

$$P = s_1 + s_2 + s_3$$

$$P = 15 + 15 + 18$$

$$P = 48$$

So, the perimeter of the triangle is 48 cm.

The formula for the area of a square is A = s². The area of a square with sides of 4 cm is 4^2 cm² or 16 cm². That is why we read a number to the second power such as 4^2 as "four squared": 4^2 is the area of a square with sides 4 units long.

The Volume of a Rectangular Prism

To find the volume of a rectangular prism, you first multiply the length times the width. The product gives you the area of the base of the rectangular prism. Then you multiply the area of the base by the height to find the volume of the rectangular prism. You

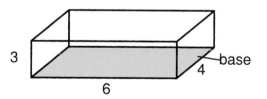

can find the volume of any prism in the same way, by multiplying the area of its base by its height. The volume of the prism shown would be (6 × 4) × 3 = 72.

Volume of Any Prism

V = area of the base × height

or

V = Bh (B = area of base)

Volume of a Rectangular Prism
V = lwh

Volume of a Cube
V = e2 (e is the length of the edge)

These formulas help you find the volume of a rectangular prism or cube, or work backward to find a missing dimension. Study the following examples:

1) If a rectangular prism has a length of 6 cm, a height equal to half its length, and a volume of 63 cm^3, what is its width?

Solution:

To find the width, substitute the known values into the formula for the volume of a rectangular prism.

$$V = lwh$$
$$63 = 6 \times w \times \frac{1}{2}(6)$$
$$63 = 6 \times w \times 3$$
$$63 = 18 \times w$$
$$3.5 = w$$

So, the width of the rectangular prism is 3.5 cm.

2) If the base of a cube has an area of 144 in^2, what is the cube's volume?

Solution:

The area of the base of a cube is an edge times an edge, or e^2. If the area is 144 in^2, then you are looking for what number times itself is 144. In other words, the length of the edge is

$$\sqrt{144} = 12.$$

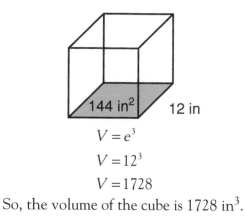

$$V = e^3$$
$$V = 12^3$$
$$V = 1728$$

So, the volume of the cube is 1728 in^3.

Notice that the cube's volume is 12^3 in^3. We usually read 12^3 as "12 cubed," since 12^3 is the volume of a cube with edges 12 units long. Notice also that each side of the cube is 1 foot long. So, you could say that the volume of the cube is 1 ft^3, which equals 1,728 in^3.

Circles

Circles have a vocabulary of their own. Here are some important key words to know:

Term:	Definition:	Diagram:
chord	A line segment joining two points on a circle.	
diameter	A chord that passes through the center of the circle.	
radius	A segment extending from the center of a circle to a point on the circle; half of a diameter. (Plural: radii)	
arc	The path of the curve on a circle from one point to another.	
circumference	The perimeter of a circle.	

Practice using a compass to construct circles with a given diameter or radius. For example, to construct a circle with a radius of 6 cm, extend the two points of your compass along a ruler a distance of 6 cm. Then place the pointy end of the compass at the center of the circle and rotate the other leg around to draw your circle.

But suppose you were asked to draw a circle with a diameter of 14 cm. Since the distance between the two points on a compass is the radius, you would have to take half of 14 to draw a circle with a radius of 7 cm.

Circumference of a Circle

The circumference, or distance around a circle, is always a little more than 3 lengths of its diameter. The actual number of diameter lengths is represented by the Greek letter π, which can be spelled *pi* and is pronounced "pie."

Pi is a constant value equal to the ratio of the circumference of a circle to its diameter. This ratio π is the same for all circles, but you cannot write its *exact* value as either a fraction or a decimal. From early in history, mathematicians from many peoples have tried to write fractions that were close approximations to π, such as

$$\frac{256}{81} \text{ (Egyptians)}, \quad \frac{25}{8} \text{ (Babylonians)}, \quad \frac{355}{113} \text{ (Chinese)}, \text{ and } \frac{22}{7} \text{ (Greeks)}.$$

Today mathematicians have used super computers to write decimal approximations of π to billions of decimal places:

$$\pi = 3.14159265358979323384626433...$$

For most calculations you can use these approximations

$$\pi \approx 3.14 \qquad \text{or} \qquad \pi \approx \frac{22}{7}$$

So, if you had pieces of string each the length of the diameter, it would take you π number of these pieces of string to go all the way around a circle or about 3.14 pieces of diameter.

Length of diameter.

Formulas for the Circumference of a Circle

$$C = \pi d \qquad C = 2\pi r$$

You know that $\pi = \frac{C}{d}$, so you can see that the first formula is just another way of saying the same thing. The second formula comes from the fact that a diameter is the same as two radii. So, the formula can be written $C = \pi d$, but typically it is written $C = 2\pi r$.

Using the value 3.14 for π, practice finding the circumference of a circle.

1) Find the circumference of a circle to the nearest tenth of a centimeter if the circle has a diameter of 13 cm.

Solution:

$$C = \pi d$$
$$C \approx 3.14(13)$$
$$C \approx 40.83$$

So, the circumference rounds to 40.8 cm to the nearest tenth of a centimeter.

2) Find the perimeter of the figure shown below:

Solution:

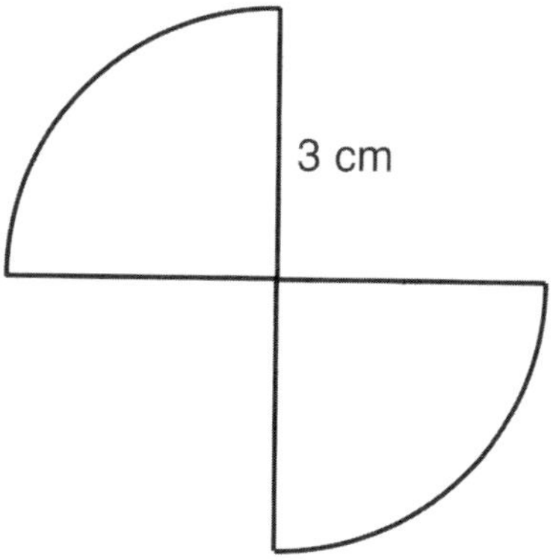

This figure is in the shape of 2 quarter circles with radius 3 cm. So the perimeter of the figure is one half the circumference of a circle with a radius of 3 cm, plus the four 3 cm straight lengths.

3 cm

$$P = \frac{1}{2}C + 4(r)$$

$$P = \frac{1}{2}(2\pi r) + 4(r)$$

$$P = (\pi r) + 4(r) \qquad \text{since } \frac{1}{2}(2) \text{ is } 1$$

$$P \approx 3.14(3) + 4(3)$$

$$P \approx 9.42 + 12$$

$$P \approx 21.42$$

So, the perimeter of the shape is about 21.42 cm.

Area of a Circle

A square with sides of length r units has an area of r^2 square units.

How many squares, with sides the length of the radius, are there inside a circle? It turns out that there are a little more than 3 such squares. In fact, there are π squares with area r^2 inside a circle, just as there are π diameters in the circumference of a circle!

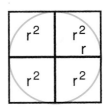

Formula for the Area of a Circle

$$A = \pi r^2$$

Check out these examples, using the area formula for a circle:

1) Find the area of a circle with a diameter of 7 cm to the nearest tenth of a cm^2.

Solution:

The radius is half of the diameter, so the radius is $7 \div 2 = 3.5$ cm. Substitute the value for the radius into the formula for the area of a circle. The work below assumes the use of a calculator, where the π key is used in the calculation. If you were working the problem without a calculator, you could use 3.14 as an approximation for π, but your answer would not be as precise.

$$A = \pi r^2$$
$$A \approx \pi (3.5)^2$$
$$A \approx \pi (12.25)$$
$$A \approx 38.485$$

So, the area of the circle is about 38.5 cm^2.

Sometimes, rather than use an approximation for π, we leave π in the answer and write the answer exactly, as in this second example:

2) Find the area of the shaded region:

Solution:
There are two circles. The area of the shaded
region is the area of the larger circle minus the area
of the smaller circle.

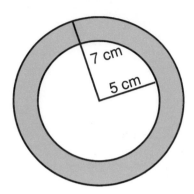

The area of the *larger* circle is:

$$A = \pi r^2$$
$$A \approx \pi(7)^2$$
$$A \approx \pi(49)$$
$$A \approx 49\pi$$

The area of the *smaller* circle is:

$$A \approx \pi r^2$$
$$A \approx \pi(5)^2$$
$$A \approx \pi(25)$$
$$A \approx 25\pi$$

The area of the *shaded region* is: $49\pi - 25\pi = 24\pi$.

So, the area of the shaded region is 24π cm^2, or roughly 75.4 cm^2.

PROBABILITY AND STATISTICS

Mean, Median, Mode, and Range

The mean, median, and mode of a set of data are called *measures of central tendency*, because in different ways they describe the "middle" of the data.

Look at a set of test scores for a class with 12 students:

$$87, 84, 92, 84, 72, 77, 59, 51, 84, 72, 99, 69$$

The *mean*, or average, of the set of scores is the sum of the scores divided by the number of scores.

$$\text{mean} = \frac{87 + 84 + 92 + 84 + 72 + 77 + 59 + 51 + 84 + 72 + 99 + 69}{12}$$

$$= \frac{930}{12} = 77.5$$

Therefore, the mean of the scores is 77.5.

The *median* of a set of numbers is the number in the middle of the set when the numbers in the set are ordered by size. When there is an even number of values in the set, the median is the average of the middle two numbers.

To find the median score in the data above, order the scores from least to greatest:

$$51, 59, 69, 72, 72, 77, 84, 84, 84, 87, 92, 99$$

The middle two numbers are 77 and 84. The median is their average.

$$\text{Median} = \frac{77+84}{2} = \frac{161}{2} = 80.5$$

So, the median score is 80.5.

The *mode* of a set of data is the number that occurs most frequently. The score 84 occurs more frequently than any other in the data of the scores, so

84 is the mode of the scores.

The *range* of a set of numbers is the difference between the greatest and the least of the numbers. The highest test score is 99, and the lowest is 51.

So, the range is 99 – 51 = 48.

Using the Mean, Median, Mode, and Range

Knowing when to use each of these measures is a very important skill. When have you seen the range used in everyday life? the mean? the mode? the median? Check out these ideas:

> Your weather forecaster will predict the high and low temperatures for each day of the week. You may be interested in the *range*, especially if the high temperature is going to be 75° while the low that night is to be 43°. That's quite a range!

> You may have a set of math test scores for the grading period, and you know that your teacher will be averaging the test scores for your final grade. You can determine what you need to get on the final test for a particular grade by using the *mean*.

> Reports of incomes or values of homes in a particular area often use the *median*. The median is not changed by one very high or very low income, as the mean would be. For example, if most of the 25 people in a company make about $40,000 per year, but the top three executives make $150,000 per year, the median would be about $40,000. The median would give you a better idea of the income of the company employees than the mean, which would be shifted upward by the top three salaries. In fact, the mean would be $53,200—much higher than the typical employee salary.

Histograms

A *histogram* is a kind of bar graph used to show how frequently certain numbers occur in a set of data. The histogram on the right shows in how many games Lyla, a forward for the Awesome Tigers, made a certain number of rebounds.

You can see right away that Lyla made 5 rebounds more often than any other number of rebounds. Therefore, 5 is the *mode* of the number of rebounds she made in each game.

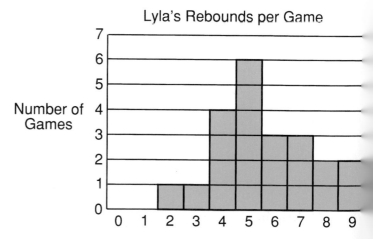

To find the mean of the number of rebounds she made in each game, you must first find the total number of rebounds she made.

# of Rebounds	×	Games	=	Total		# of Rebounds	×	Games	=	Total
2	×	1	=	2		6	×	3	=	18
3	×	1	=	3		7	×	3	=	21
4	×	4	=	16		9	×	2	=	18
5	×	6	=	30						

Total *rebounds* = 2 + 3 + 16 + 30 + 18 + 21 + 18 = 108

To find the mean you also need to find how many numbers are in the set, in this case how many games there were.

Number of *games* = 1 + 1 + 4 + 6 + 3 + 3 + 2 = 20

Mean number of rebounds = $\dfrac{108}{20}$ = 5.4

Lyla made an average of 5.4 rebounds per game. (Obviously, Lyla cannot make 0.4 rebounds, but this figure gives you the idea that she made an average of 5–6 rebounds per game.)

You can also use the histogram above to find the median and the range. See if you can work out both numbers.

Circle Graphs

A *circle graph*, or *pie chart*, is a great way to interpret how individual data relate to a larger whole. For example, look at the data on the crops at Fertile Farms this summer:

Using this graph you can answer questions like:

1) Which crop represents the greatest percentage? Which represents the smallest percentage?
2) About what percent of all the crops is soybeans? Alfalfa?
3) What percentage of the crops are corn and soybeans?

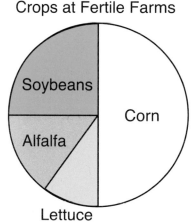

Crops at Fertile Farms

See how you did:

1) Corn represents the greatest percentage and lettuce is the smallest.

2) About 25% is soybeans; about $\dfrac{1}{6}$ or 16.7% is alfalfa.

3) Together the corn and soybeans make up about 75% of all the crops.

Sampling a Population

Sampling is a technique used in many fields to make predictions about data. Sampling is used in business, medicine, government, and scientific research. When you hear a report like, "9 out of every 10 dentists recommend Sparkling White toothpaste," that means somebody has been doing sampling. If you hear a news report that a particular candidate is likely to win an election, even though all the votes have not been counted, the prediction is almost certainly based on sampling.

Sampling is done by taking a smaller group from the entire population and using their preferences or characteristics to predict what is probably true for the entire population. For example, to find out how 4 million voters in a state might vote in an upcoming election, you might call 1,000 of them. Then you can use measures of central tendency and also ratios and proportions to make predictions about how the larger population will vote.

Sampling can be quite accurate if it is done properly. But it is not always done properly. Two very important things to remember when gathering data through sampling are:

➤ The size of the sample must be fairly large. The larger the sample, the more accurate the findings are likely to be.

➤ The sample must be truly representative of the entire population. For example, if the only dentists that were surveyed for Sparkling White toothpaste were the ones who already used only that brand for their patients, the sample would not represent the entire population of dentists.

Simple Probabilities

We write the *probability*, or the chance, that an event will happen as a ratio. Suppose you wanted to know the probability of drawing a green marble out of a jar that contains only 4 white, 3 gray, and 2 green marbles of the same size.

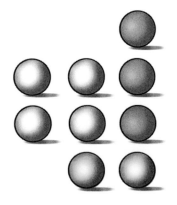

The probability of this event is the ratio of the number of outcomes that favor the event to the total number of possible outcomes:

$$P = \frac{\text{number of outcomes that favor the event}}{\text{number of possible outcomes}}$$

There are 9 marbles altogether, or 9 possible outcomes. There are 2 green marbles, or 2 favorable outcomes. So the probability of drawing a green marble is written:

$$P(\text{green}) = \frac{2}{9}.$$ We read $P(\text{green})$ as "the probability of green."

What is the probability of drawing a white or a green marble? There are 9 possible outcomes. There are 4 white and 2 green marbles, or 6 favorable outcomes:

$$P(\text{white or green}) = \frac{6}{9} = \frac{2}{3}$$

What is the probability of drawing a yellow marble? There are no yellow marbles, so there are 0 favorable outcomes.

$$P(\text{yellow}) = \frac{0}{9} = 0$$

Since there are no yellow marbles, it is impossible that a yellow marble will be drawn.

> The probability of an impossible event is 0.

What is the probability that a white or gray or green marble will be drawn? There are 4 + 3 + 2 or 9 favorable outcomes, and 9 possible outcomes.

$$P(\text{white, gray , or green}) = \frac{9}{9} = 1$$

Since all the marbles are white, gray, or green, it is certain that a white, gray, or green marble will be drawn.

> If an event is certain to occur, the probability of the event is 1.

We can represent the probability of an event occurring with a fraction, or with a number from 0 to 1, including 0 and 1. For example, if something has a "fifty-fifty" chance of happening, we would say the probability of the event is 0.5.

Illustrating Possible Outcomes Using a Tree Diagram

Sometimes when you are trying to find a probability, it is helpful to make a *tree diagram* to show all the possible outcomes.

Suppose there is a spinner with three sections of equal size: a gray section, a green section, and a white section.

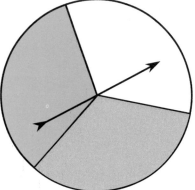

What is the probability of getting white once and green once if the spinner is spun twice?

Solution:

Make a tree diagram to show all the possible outcomes.

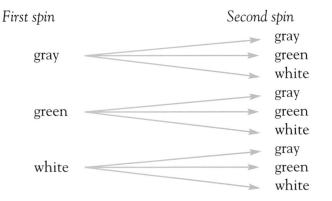

First spin	Second spin
gray	gray
	green
	white
green	gray
	green
	white
white	gray
	green
	white

The first column shows what can happen on the first spin; the second column shows what can happen on the second spin. The second column of the tree diagram shows that there are 9 possible outcomes if the spinner is spun twice. There are two outcomes of "one white and one green," so the probability of getting one white and one green is written:

$$P(\text{one white and one green}) = \frac{2}{9}$$

There are five outcomes with at least one gray, so the probability of getting gray at least once, if the spinner is spun twice, is written:

$$P(\text{at least one gray}) = \frac{5}{9}$$

Notice that the probability of getting gray twice, if the spinner is spun twice, is $\frac{1}{9}$. It is not coincidental that the probability of getting gray on each spin is 1/3, and (1/3) x (1/3) = 1/9.

Mutually Exclusive Events

When two sets of events are not overlapping in any way, they are called *disjoint sets* or sets of *mutually exclusive events*. For example, you might have two dice, one red and one green, with the numbers 1–6 on each of their 6 faces.

If you toss both dice, getting an even sum and getting an odd sum would be mutually exclusive events. You will get *either* an even sum *or* an odd sum. The red cube showing a 2 and the sum of the cubes being 2 would also be mutually exclusive.

> If A and B are mutually exclusive events, then
>
> P (A or B) = P (A) + P (B)

So, if you have events A and B where the $P(A) = \frac{2}{3}$ and $P(B) = \frac{1}{6}$, then:

$$P(A \text{ or } B) = \frac{2}{3} + \frac{1}{6} = \frac{4}{6} + \frac{1}{6} = \frac{5}{6}$$

PRE-ALGEBRA

Variables

You already know that a letter can stand for a number. A letter that stands for a number is called a *variable*. For example, instead of writing 6 + _ = 8, we can write $6 + b = 8$. In this equation, $b = 2$. We can also write $c - 4 = 10$. In the second equation, $c = 14$. We call a letter like b or c a variable because to vary means to change. These letters can stand for different numbers in different situations.

Finding what number or numbers the variable in an equation may represent is called *solving the equation*. You learned earlier that you can use inverse operations to solve equations. (See page 232.) For example, suppose you wanted to know the value of y in the following equation:

$$3y - 16 = 20$$

You want to know what number, when multiplied by 3 and then with 16 taken from the result would give you 20. You can "undo the mystery" with inverse operations. Begin with the inverse operations of addition and subtraction:

$$3y - 16 = 20$$
$$3y - 16 + 16 = 20 + 16$$
$$3y = 36$$
$$\frac{\cancel{3}}{\cancel{3}} y = \frac{36}{3}$$
$$y = 12$$

The best way to think about your result is to say that in this equation, y can be replaced with 12 and the equation will be true:

$$3y - 16 = 20$$
$$3(12) - 16 = 20$$
$$36 - 16 = 20$$
$$20 = 20$$

Sometimes, a single variable can represent lots of numbers. For example, in the following equation the variable x can represent any real number!

$$x + 3 = 3 + x$$

A less extreme example is an equation such as $x^2 = 16$. Here x can be either 4 or −4 but nothing else.

Evaluating Expressions

Variables are often used in expressions in the area of math called *algebra*. For example, the following are all variable expressions:

(1)	(2)	(3)	(4)
$a + 2b$	$\dfrac{x}{5} - 3y$	$2pq + (-5r)$	$\dfrac{3d^2 - e}{2f}$

When you know the values of the variables in these expressions, you can find the value of the entire expression. This is called *evaluating the expression*. Use the following values for the variables, and evaluate each of the expressions above:

$$a = 2 \qquad d = -2 \qquad p = -4 \qquad x = 0$$
$$b = -3.5 \qquad e = \frac{1}{2} \qquad q = 7.6 \qquad y = \frac{1}{3}$$
$$f = 1.2 \qquad r = -1$$

Solutions: (Hint: When you evaluate expressions, write your work vertically, aligning by the equal sign if possible, substituting under each variable, then simplifying):

(1)	(2)	(3)	(4)
$a + 2b$	$\dfrac{x}{5} - 3y$	$2\ p\ q\ \ + (-5r)$	$\dfrac{3d^2 - e}{2f}$
$= 2 + 2(-3.5)$	$= \dfrac{0}{5} - 3\left(\dfrac{1}{3}\right)$	$= 2(-4)(7.6) + (-5(-1))$	$= \dfrac{3(-2)^2 - \dfrac{1}{2}}{2(1.2)}$
$= 2 + (-7)$	$= 0 - 1$	$= -60.8 + 5$	$= \dfrac{3(4) - \dfrac{1}{2}}{2.4}$
$= -5$	$= -1$	$= -55.8$	$= \dfrac{11.5}{2.4} \approx 4.79$

Simplifying Expressions by Combining Like Terms

Terms are products or quotients (or single numbers or variables) that are being added or subtracted in an expression. For example, look at the expressions below and notice to the right the number of terms in each expression:

Expression:	Number of Terms
1) $12 + 5(x - 1)$	2 terms
2) $2a + 10ab - \dfrac{3b}{4} - 56$	4 terms
3) $2x + 6.2xy - 4x^2 + \sqrt{5} + 7\dfrac{1}{2} + 5xy - \dfrac{14x}{3} + 2(x - y)$	8 terms

In order to work out many algebra problems, you will need to simplify expressions by combining like terms. *Like terms* have *exactly* the same variables in their terms. Look, for example, at these expressions of like and unlike terms:

Expression:	Like terms, shown in parentheses together:
1) $18 + 5x - 2x^2 + 9 - 7x$	$(18 + 9) + (5x - 7x) - 2x^2$
2) $2x + 6.2xy - 4x^2 + 7 + 5xy + 2x^2 + 3xy$	$x + (6.2xy + 5xy + 3xy) + (-4x^2 + 2x^2) + 7$
3) $-3a + 10ab - 16a^2b^2$	None of the terms are like terms.

As you have probably figured out, *combining* like terms simply means to add or subtract the terms that are alike. So, looking at the first two examples above:

1) $18 + 5x - 2x^2 + 9 - 7x$

= $(18 + 9) + (5x - 7x) - 2x^2$

= $27 - 2x - 2x^2$

2) $2x + 6.2xy - 4x^2 + 7 + 5xy + 2x^2 + 3xy$

= $2x + (6.2xy + 5xy + 3xy) + (-4x^2 + 2x^2) + 7$

= $2x + 14.2xy - 2x^2 + 7$

Using the Distributive Property in Variable Expressions

You may recall that the Distributive Property says, for example, that:

$$4 \times (3 + 9) = (4 \times 3) + (4 \times 9) \quad or \quad 4 \times (3 - 9) = (4 \times 3) - (4 \times 9)$$

In general, the property is stated:

The Distributive Property

For real numbers a, b, and c:

$$a(b + c) = ab + ac \text{ or } a(b - c) = ab - ac$$

If you apply the distributive property to variable expressions, you multiply the term outside the parentheses by each term within the parentheses. Also, if a collection of terms has a common factor, you can divide out that factor using the distributive property.

Look at the following examples. The examples on the left apply the distributive property in the usual manner, while the examples on the right divide out a common factor.

$a(b + c) = ab + ac$ or $a(b - c) = ab - ac$ $ab + ac = a(b + c)$ or $ab - ac = a(b - c)$

1) $-4(7x + 3y) = -28x - 12y$

1) $-28x - 12y = -4(7x + 3y)$

2) $3x(2x - 5) = 6x^2 - 15x$

2) $6x^2 - 15x = 3x(2x - 5)$

3) $10(5x^2 + 2x - 3) = 50x^2 + 20x - 30$

3) $50x^2 + 20x - 30 = 10(5x^2 + 2x - 3)$

Solving Word Problems Using Variables

Most often when you encounter a word problem, you will find that there is more than one way to solve the problem. However, there are several general steps to follow to be sure that you think through the problem carefully and solve it correctly.

Key Steps for Solving Word Problems

➤ State the problem in your own words, deciding which value or values are unknown.
➤ Choose a variable or variables to represent the unknown(s), using the facts from the given problem.
➤ Draw a diagram, use a formula, create a table, or use any other strategy that will help you write an equation for the situation given in the problem.
➤ Solve the equation for the unknown value(s).
➤ Interpret your results according to the facts given in the problem by substituting the values you have found for the variables into the original equation.
➤ Write your final answer as a complete sentence.

Use these steps to help you solve the problems given below:

1) The length of a rectangle is 3 more than twice its width. If the perimeter of the rectangle is 36 cm, what are the length and the width?

Solution:

➤ I have a rectangle with a length longer than the width and a perimeter of 36 cm. The unknowns are the length and the width.
➤ I'll let w be the width, so $2w + 3$ is the length.
➤ A diagram of the rectangle would look like this:

w　　　$P = 36$ cm

$2w + 3$

Since $P = 2l + 2w$,
then $36 = 2(2w + 3) + 2w$

➤ Solving for w:

$$36 = 2(2w + 3) + 2w$$
$$36 = 4w + 6 + 2w$$
$$36 = 6w + 6$$
$$30 = 6w$$
$$5 = w$$

Since $w = 5$, then $l = 2w + 3 = 2(5) + 3 = 13$

➤ According to the facts of the problem, the length is 3 more than twice the width, so since 13 is 3 more than twice 5, the dimensions check out. Also, the formula for perimeter of a rectangle says:

$$P = 2l + 2w$$
$$36 = 2(13) + 2(5)$$
$$36 = 26 + 10$$
$$36 = 36$$

➤ So, the width of the rectangle is 5 cm and the length is 13 cm.

2) The sum of three consecutive numbers is 189. Find the three numbers.

Solution:
➤ Three consecutive numbers add up to 189.
➤ I'll let n be the smallest, so $n + 1$ is the middle number, and $n + 2$ is the largest number.
➤ Since the sum of the three numbers is 189, the equation is:

$$n + (n + 1) + (n + 2) = 189$$
$$n + n + 1 + n + 2 = 189$$
$$3n + 3 = 189$$
$$3n = 186$$
$$n = 62$$
$$n + 1 = 63$$
$$n + 2 = 64$$

➤ According to the facts of the problem, the three consecutive numbers add up to 189.

$$n + (n + 1) + (n + 2) = 189$$
$$62 + 63 + 64 = 189$$
$$189 = 189$$

➤ So, the three numbers are 62, 63, and 64.

The Coordinate Plane: Plotting and Identifying Points on the Plane

You can locate a single integer, such as 2 or –3 on a number line.

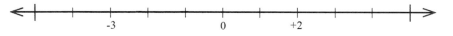

You can locate an ordered pair of integers, called *coordinates*, such as (3, 5) or (–2, 4) on a plane, called a *coordinate plane*. A coordinate plane has two lines or axes that are perpendicular to each other: the *x*-axis, which is horizontal, and the *y*-axis, which is vertical. The point where the *x*-axis and the *y*-axis meet is called the *origin*, which has a coordinate of (0, 0). Movements from the origin to the right on the *x*-axis or up on the *y*-axis are movements in the positive directions. Movements from the origin to the left on the *x*-axis or down on the *y*-axis are movements in the negative directions.

The numbers in the ordered pair are called the coordinates of the point, where the first coordinate is the horizontal distance from the origin and the second coordinate is the vertical distance from the first coordinate. So the coordinates tell where the point is in relation to the origin.

Look at the example (3, 5). The first coordinate, positive 3, gives the horizontal distance 3 to the right from the origin along the x-axis. The second coordinate, positive 5, gives the vertical distance 5 up from the x-coordinate 3, parallel to the y-axis.

Locate the point (3, 5) on the coordinate plane below, along with the points described here:

1) Plot (–3, 4): Go 3 units to the left along the x-axis, then 4 units up, parallel to the y-axis.
2) Plot (0, –2): The distance from the origin along the x-axis is 0, so go 2 units down along the y-axis.
3) Plot (–5, –4): Go 5 units left, and then 4 units down.
4) What are the coordinates of point A? Since A is 4 units right along the x-axis, then 5 units down, the coordinates are (4, –5).

Working with the Coordinate Plane

Here are some different ways you can work with the coordinate plane.

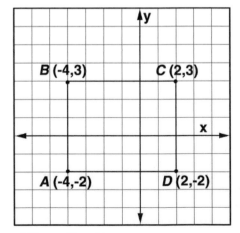

1) If ABCD is a rectangle, and you are given its coordinates as A(–4, –2), B(–4, ?), C(2, 3), and D(?, ?), you can find the missing coordinates.
Solution: Plot the points you are given, A(–4, –2) and C(2, 3). Since you know the figure is a rectangle, you can figure out what the missing coordinates must be:

The coordinates of B are (–4, 3), the coordinates of D are (2, –2).

2) Find the coordinates of the points *H, I, J, K*. Then take the opposites of each one of the *x*-coordinates of the points and make four new points *H′, I′, J′,* and *K′*. (Remember that *H′* is read "H prime.") Draw the new quadrilateral *H′I′J′K′*.

   Solution: You will find that the quadrilateral *H′I′J′K′* is the reflection of *HIJK* over the y-axis.

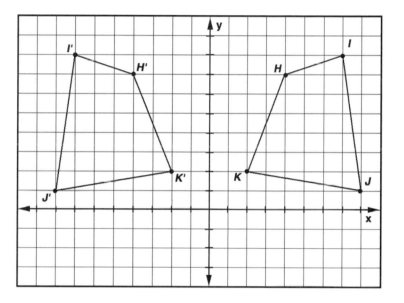

   Now, try adding 1 to the *x*-coordinate and 1 to the *y*-coordinate of the points *H, I, J,* and *K*. Is this new quadrilateral congruent to the old quadrilateral *HIJK*? If so, what rigid motion would you use to make the two quadrilaterals coincide: a translation, a reflection, or a rotation?

Graphing a Function

The table shows the function equal to y and described as "add 3 to each number *x*."

x	0	1	2	−2	−1
y = x + 3	3	4	5	1	2

You can make an ordered pair (x, y) for each column in the table. Plot these ordered pairs:

$$(0, 3), (1, 4), (2, 5), (-2, 1), \text{ and } (-1, 2).$$

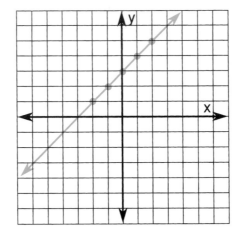

Notice that the points all lie along the green line. You can make a graph of a function such as $y = x - 4$ in the same way:

➢ Make a table of the values for x and y, starting with any values you choose for x.

➢ Plot the ordered pairs on a graph.

➢ Using a ruler or straightedge, connect the ordered pairs with a line.

VI.

Science

Introduction

This chapter outlines what sixth graders should know about science. Students will learn about plate tectonics, oceans, astronomy, energy, and the human body, especially the immune system. In addition, they will read brief biographies of some important scientists.

Parents and teachers can supplement this chapter with various science activities. Students who have studied astronomy will enjoy looking through a telescope or visiting a planetarium, and students who have studied the ocean will enjoy visits to an aquarium. There are also simple experiments students can do to see the processes described in this chapter in action. Many books collecting simple and safe science experiments are now available.

Hands-on scientific experience is so important that some educators have come to reject the very idea of teaching young children about science from books. But book learning should not be neglected altogether. It helps bring system and coherence to a young person's developing knowledge of nature and provides essential building blocks for later study. Book learning also provides knowledge not likely to be gained by simple observation: for example, books can tell us about things that are not visible to the naked eye, like tectonic plates, water vapor, and antibodies. And we should not forget that some children enjoy book learning even more than they enjoy experiments and field trips. Both kinds of experience are necessary to ensure that gaps in knowledge will not hinder later understanding.

PLATE TECTONICS

Earth's Origins

Most scientists believe that Earth, the sun, and the other planets in our solar system began to form about four and a half to five billion years ago. This diagram shows what probably happened.

Scientists believe our solar system began as a huge cloud of dust and gases that was both rotating and contracting (stage 1). Most of the material in this cloud was drawn toward the center by the force of gravity. This material eventually became the sun (stage 2). However, some of the material continued to orbit the central body in separate rings. Gradually, some of the material in these rings began to clump together. This is how the planets were formed (stage 3). Over time most of the remaining material was either drawn into one of the orbiting planets by gravity or swept out into space; and so the solar system took on its current shape (stage 4).

Scientists believe our solar system came together in stages, as shown here.

Layers of Earth

Earth is made up of four main layers: the crust, the mantle, the outer core, and the inner core.

The outermost layer, the *crust*, is cool and rocky. In most places it is between 7 and 70 kilometers thick. That's about 5 to 40 miles. The part of the crust that includes the continents is called the *continental crust*; the part that lies below the ocean is called the *oceanic crust*. On average, the continental crust is about 35–40 km (25 miles) thick, but it can be over 70 km (40 miles) thick in mountainous regions. The oceanic crust is much thinner, generally about 7 km (5 miles) thick.

The oceanic crust is made up chiefly of a dark, fairly dense rock called basalt. The continental crust includes a variety of rocks.

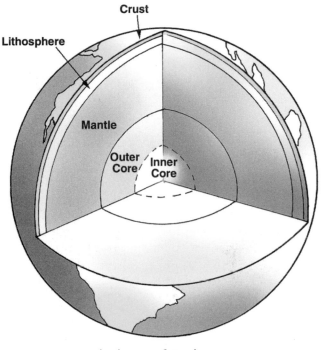

The layers of Earth.

Although the crust seems thick to those of us who live on it, it is actually very thin compared to the layers that lie beneath. If you could journey to the center of the Earth, you'd have to travel about 6,400 km (4,000 miles), through material that gets progressively hotter and denser.

The next layer below the crust is the *mantle*. The mantle is about 2,900 km (1,800 miles) thick. The inner part of the mantle is mostly solid, but, due to great heat and pressure, it can flow slowly, like warm Silly Putty. By comparison, the outermost part of the mantle is cooler and more brittle. In many ways the upper mantle behaves like the overlying crust. Together the crust and the uppermost mantle form a rigid layer of rock called the *lithosphere* (from *lithos*, Greek for stone).

Below the mantle lies the *core*. The core is almost twice as dense as the mantle. It is made up almost entirely of metals, chiefly iron and nickel. The core is made up of two distinct parts: 2,300 km (1,400 miles) of liquid outer core and 1,200 km (745 miles) of solid inner core. High temperatures in the outer core melt the iron and nickel, but the extreme pressure of the inner core squeezes them solid even as the temperature soars over 6700° Celsius (12,092° Fahrenheit)—comparable to the temperature on the surface of the sun!

Plate Tectonics

A revolution is a big change. If you've read earlier books in this series, you know about the American Revolution. Before the American Revolution, the British settlers in America were colonists, ruled by a faraway king. After the revolution, these same people were independent citizens, governed by their own elected officials.

Revolutions take place in scientific thought as well. In the 20th century, the theory of *plate tectonics* has revolutionized our understanding of our planet. Before this revolution, scientists believed the continents did not move. Nowadays, scientists believe that the continents and the whole surface of the planet Earth are in constant motion. Plate tectonics helps us understand why the continents are where they are, and where they were long ago. It also tells us how mountains are built, why volcanoes sometimes erupt, and where earthquakes are most likely to shake the land.

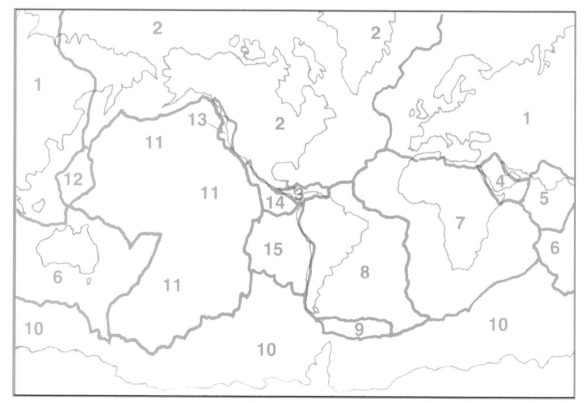

Earth's surface is made up of a number of plates. Here the plates are shown in green and the continents are outlined in gray. #1. Eurasian Plate; #2. North American Plate; #3. Caribbean Plate; #4. Arabian Plate; #5. Indian Plate; #6. Australian Plate; #7. African Plate; #8. South American Plate; #9. Scotia Plate; #10. Antarctic Plate; #11. Pacific Plate; #12. Philippine Plate; #13. Juan de Fuca Plate; #14 Cocos Plate; #15 Nazca Plate.

The theory of plate tectonics, accepted by virtually all geologists, holds that Earth's surface, or lithosphere, is composed of about a dozen major *tectonic plates*. These plates are large rigid slabs of rock that move very slowly, in part because of movements in the mantle below them. The plates move 5 to 10 centimeters (about 1–4 inches) a year, depending on their location. That may seem extremely slow; but if you remember that Earth is very old, you can see how small movements can add up over time. If a plate moves 2 inches a year, it will move more than 30 miles in a million years, and more than 300 miles in 10 million years.

Wegener's Continental Drift Theory

Many scientists have contributed to our current understanding of plate tectonics, but the person who started the revolution was the German scientist Alfred Wegener [VAY-guh-nurr] (1880–1930).

In 1912, Wegener suggested that Earth's continents might once have formed a single supercontinent, which he called *Pangaea*. (*Pan* means "all" and *gaea* means "Earth.") Wegener argued that Pangaea began to break apart into the current, smaller continents around 200 million years ago; the continents then "drifted" until they reached their present positions. Wegener's theory was known as the theory of continental drift.

PANGAEA

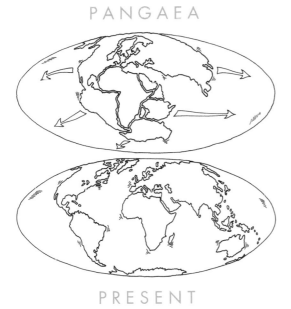

PRESENT

These two maps show how the plates that once formed the supercontinent Pangaea have shifted to reach their current locations.

German scientist Alfred Wegener, whose theory of continental drift led to the current theory of plate tectonics.

Evidence for Continental Drift

Wegener knew most people would find it hard to believe that the continents were drifting, so he worked hard to collect evidence to support his claim. He looked at the shape of the continents, rock types, distribution of fossils, and ancient climates.

Wegener pointed out that some of the continents look like they could be fitted together, like the pieces of a jigsaw puzzle. For instance, the eastern coast of South America and the western coast of Africa look like two matching pieces of a puzzle.

But Wegener went beyond looking at shapes. He also looked at geological features. He found that the geological features along the western coast of Africa corresponded quite closely with those along the eastern coast of South America. Wegener said the geological features of the two continents fit together like the two halves of a torn newspaper: "It is just as if we were to refit the torn pieces of a newspaper by matching their edges and then check whether the lines of the print run smoothly across. If they do, there is nothing left but to conclude that the pieces were in fact joined in this way."

Wegener applied the same logic to other continents. He reasoned that, if North and South America were once joined with Africa, Europe, and Asia, then there should be similar rock formations on these now separate continents. Wegener did some research and found that some rock formations were in fact similar. The Appalachian Mountains in North America were about the same age and contained the same kinds of rocks as the mountains in Scotland and those in Scandinavia. Looking at the current configuration of the continents, shown on the first map on the facing page, you would not guess that these mountains have anything in common. They look like three completely distinct mountain ranges. But Wegener argued that the geological similarities showed that these mountains once made up a single, continuous mountain range. You can see this ancient chain of mountains on Wegener's map of the "pre-drift" locations opposite.

Wegener also presented fossil evidence to support his theory. He pointed out that identical fossils can be found on continents that are now separated by vast expanses of ocean. For example, fossil remains of the *Mesosaurus*, a small crocodile-like reptile, are found on the coast of South America and also along the coast of Africa. The *Mesosaurus* is not thought to have been a good swimmer—certainly not good enough to have crossed the huge expanse of ocean that currently separates the two continents. The more likely explanation was that, during the age of the *Mesosaurus*, the two continents were connected.

Fossils of the fern *Glossopteris* provided Wegener with additional evidence for Pangaea. *Glossopteris* thrived in cool climates 200 million years ago. Fossil imprints of *Glossopteris* have been discovered in Antarctica, but also in South America, Africa, India, and Australia. *Glossopteris* fossils are found in climates that are now too warm for the fern to grow. Wegener argued that all these land masses were once joined together in a cool climate that allowed *Glossopteris* to flourish.

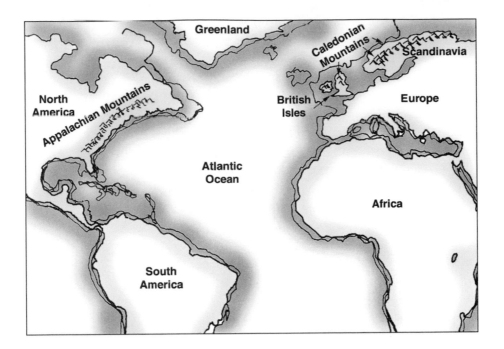

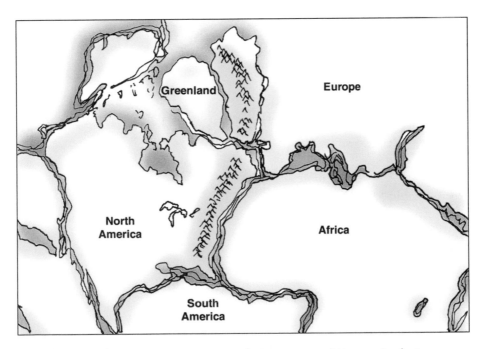

The top map shows mountains in North America and Europe in their current location. On this map the Caledonian Mountains of Scotland and Scandinavia appear to have nothing in common with the Appalachian Mountains of the eastern United States. However, the lower map, a reconstruction of Pangaea, shows that these mountains once comprised a single range.

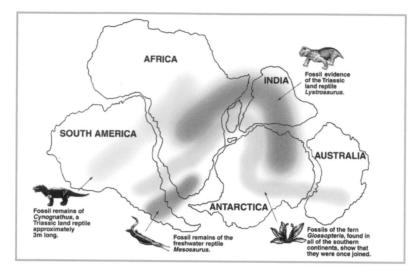

This map shows some fossil evidence for the theory of tectonic plates and Pangaea. The shaded bands represent zones where fossils of various plants and animals have been found. These bands suggest that the continents were joined many years ago when these plants and animals were alive.

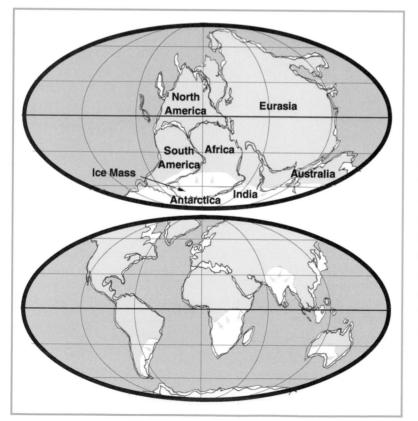

The top map shows parts of Pangaea that are believed to have been covered with glaciers. The bottom map shows the current position of the continents. You can see how several plates have drifted away from their original locations, carrying land with traces of glaciers to equatorial areas where glaciers would not now be expected.

Wegener also pointed to data about ancient climates. Rocks in South America, Africa, India, and Australia showed signs of having once been covered with glaciers. But scientists found it hard to explain how warm areas far from the poles—places like Africa and India—could have been covered with glaciers. Wegener explained this by suggesting that millions of years ago these landmasses were part of Pangaea and were closer to the South Pole. You can see the "before" and "after" situations in the two maps opposite at the bottom.

Despite all the evidence Wegener gathered, he was not able to convince many scientists that continents drift. When he died in 1930, most scientists still scoffed at his hypothesis. One of the main objections to Wegener's hypothesis was his inability to explain how continents move across the ocean floor. Wegener suggested that continents plow through the oceanic crust, much as an icebreaking ship cuts through ice. However, there was no evidence that the ocean floor was weak enough to allow the continents to plow through without breaking up the ocean floor in the process; nor could Wegener point to a force strong enough to do this.

From Continental Drift to Plate Tectonics

During the 1950s and 1960s, scientists used new technology like sonar and seismographs to study Earth. They discovered that Wegener was right about continents moving but wrong when he hypothesized that moving continents plow through a stationary ocean floor. It turns out that the lithosphere is broken up into large tectonic plates containing both oceanic and continental crust. These plates are constantly moving. The continents don't plow through the ocean floor, as Wegener thought; rather, they are carried, along with the oceanic crust, on larger plates.

Scientists believe that plates move because of convection currents in the mantle below the plates. In order to understand this, it is important to remember that the mantle, although solid, can flow slowly, like a thick fluid. Think of a pot of thick pea soup on a stove. The stove warms the bottom of the pot, heating the soup from below. The heated soup rises to the surface, spreads out, cools, and then sinks back to the bottom of the pot, where it is reheated and rises again. This type of cyclical flow is called *convection*.

Something similar is happening beneath the crust, in the mantle. Heat from deep in the Earth warms the mantle, and convection patterns in the mantle help move the plates

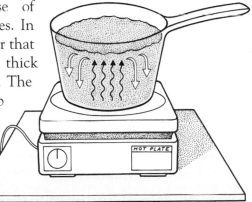

Convection causes cyclical, up-and-down motion. Warmer liquid rises, while cooler, heavier liquid sinks to the bottom of the pan.

above in the direction of the convection's flow.

Seafloor Spreading

Plates can bump into one another or spread apart. When plates spread apart, or diverge, beneath the ocean, new ocean crust is formed. This process is called *seafloor spreading*. Underwater volcanic mountain chains, called *mid-ocean ridges*, are pushed up by the hot mantle below. Mantle convection pulls the plates apart, gravity slowly pulls the ridges down, and the resulting gap fills with basalt, forming new ocean crust. Find the Mid-Atlantic Ridge on the map above. Along this underwater mountain range, new crust is being added to the plates as they move apart.

One strong piece of evidence for seafloor spreading comes from looking at the age of the rocks on the ocean floor. The illustration on the right shows that the newest rocks are the closest to the Mid-Atlantic Ridge and the older rocks are farther away. If you imagine more and more new rock welling up along the Mid-Atlantic ridge, you can see how North and South America have been driven away from Europe and Africa over many of millions of years, and how the Atlantic Ocean has grown larger during that time.

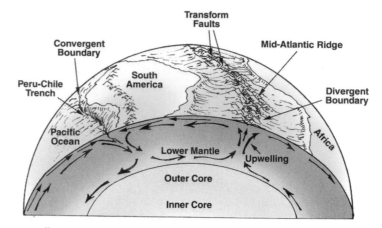

Upwelling in the mantle below the Mid-Atlantic Ridge creates new ocean crust and a divergent boundary. This causes seafloor spreading, which drives Africa and South America farther apart. Meanwhile, along the Peru-Chile Trench, a convergent boundary, rock is being thrust back down into the mantle.

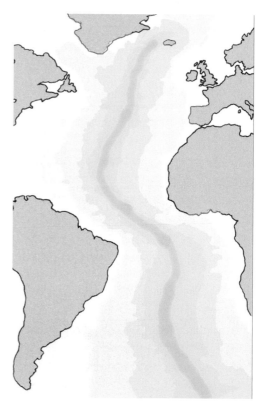

This map shows the age of the rocks on the ocean floor. The darkest colors show the newest rocks. Notice how the newest rocks are located roughly midway between the continents.

Trenches and Mountains

In other parts of Earth, plates are not moving apart but coming together. When two plates collide, crust can either be forced back down into the mantle or up to Earth's surface.

Look back at the illustration on page 314. In this picture you can see how the same convection patterns in the mantle that create a divergent boundary at the Mid-Atlantic Ridge also create a convergent boundary along the western coast of South America. A *divergent boundary* is a place where two plates are moving apart; a *convergent boundary* is a place where two plates are converging, or coming together. In this case, one of the oceanic plates (the Nazca Plate) is being forced underneath the other (the South American Plate), and driven down into the mantle. A *deep-sea trench*, or deep, underwater depression, called the Peru-Chile Trench, is formed by this convergence.

When two continental plates collide, they can also force rock upward, creating spectacular mountain ranges.

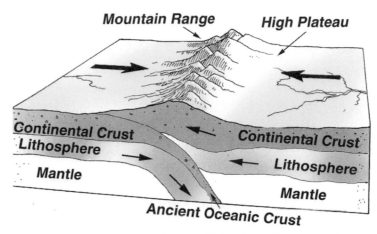

When two continental plates collide, the collision can force rock upward, creating mountain ranges.

Use the map on page 308 to locate the Eurasian Plate and the Indian Plate. These two plates are smashing into one another, forming the Himalayas.

Volcanoes

Volcanoes often occur where plates are pulling apart or coming together. Here's what many scientists think is happening: below the ocean, divergent plates are pulling apart, opening up gaps. Reduced pressure in these gaps allows some of the mantle rock to melt and come to the surface, leading to volcanic eruptions.

In other parts of the ocean, plates are colliding. When this happens, the oceanic crust of one plate may be shoved under the oceanic crust of the other. The submerging crust is heated by friction and pressure. Melted rock, called lava, may erupt from underwater

The eruption of Mount St. Helens in 1980 released huge clouds of volcanic ash into the atmosphere.

volcanoes. If the volcano is very active, it may put out enough lava to make a volcanic island. The Aleutian Islands off the west coast of Alaska were formed in this way.

Volcanoes can also erupt on land. The process is similar to what happens underwater. As an ocean plate is shoved under a continent, entire mountain chains can be formed volcanically. For example, this is how the Andes Mountains in South America were formed.

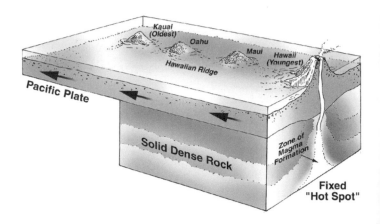

The Pacific Plate has moved over the fixed Hawaiian hot spot, creating the chain of islands we call Hawaii.

Volcanoes usually occur at plate boundaries, but some occur as a plate moves over a stationary *hot spot* in the mantle. As plates move over these hot spots, they form volcanic islands. The Hawaiian hot spot has left a long trail of volcanic islands across the Pacific Ocean floor. Some of the older volcanoes have eroded and now lie under the ocean. The Hawaiian Islands are some of the most recent formations of this hot spot. In fact, a new Hawaiian island, called Loihi, is being formed about 20 miles from the Big Island of Hawaii. This island-of-the-future is still thousands of feet below sea level. It may take thousands of years for it to rise above sea level.

Earthquakes

Earthquakes are also linked to plate movements and boundaries. Sometimes two plates slide and grind past each other. Earthquakes can occur at these "sliding" boundaries. This is what is happening along the San Andreas Fault in California, and it explains why California experiences so many earthquakes. In this case, the Pacific Plate and the North American Plate are sliding past one another.

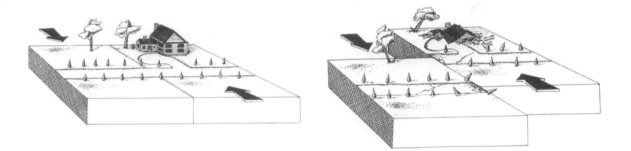

These two before-and-after pictures show what happens during an earthquake,
when there is movement along a fault line.

Although an earthquake may last only a few seconds, the forces that caused the quake may have been accumulating for years. Strain builds up along *fault lines* where plates meet. This strain can be *tension* (when plates are pulling apart), *compression* (when plates are pushing together), or *shear* (when plates are moving sideways). The strain builds and builds until a breaking point is reached and the plates shift.

When an earthquake occurs, waves of energy travel through the ground. These waves are called *seismic waves*. Seismic waves radiate outward in all directions from the *focus*—the point below Earth's surface where the earthquake originated. The point directly above the focus on the surface is called the *epicenter*.

Seismographs, instruments used to detect vibrations in the Earth, measure the amount of energy released by earthquakes. The size of the seismic waves can be measured using the Richter scale. Each unit on this scale represents a tenfold increase in wave amplitude, so an earthquake measuring 5.0 on the Richter scale is 10 times more severe than one measuring 4.0. Earthquakes measuring less than 2.0 on the Richter scale often go unnoticed, except by seismographs. An earthquake measuring 6.0 or more can have catastrophic consequences for buildings and people, especially if buildings near the epicenter have not been constructed to withstand an earthquake.

These buildings in San Francisco were damaged during a major earthquake in 1906.

OCEANS

The World Ocean

Earth is unique among the planets because of its abundance of liquid water. With over 71 percent of Earth under the ocean, there is good reason Earth is called the blue planet.

The Atlantic, Pacific, and Indian Oceans are Earth's three largest bodies of salty water, but in fact these oceans are all connected. Water flows from one to another and circulates all around the planet.

Ocean water may look like water in lakes and rivers, but there is one important difference —the amount of salt. All water, even water in lakes and rivers, contains some salt, but not nearly as much as the ocean. The salt left when you boil away a cup of ocean water is 85 percent sodium chloride, the same salt you might sprinkle onto your popcorn. Ocean water is actually a weak solution of many salts, often in minor amounts. Gases, such as oxygen and carbon dioxide, are also present, along with organic (carbon-containing) molecules. Organic molecules are produced mainly from decaying organisms. Nearly all natural elements are found in ocean water, even gold! Some of these elements, such as phosphorus, nitrogen, silica, and iron are considered nutrients essential to ocean life.

Waves and Tides

Another constant of the ocean is waves. Pretend you are standing on a cliff high above the shoreline where wave after wave tumbles onto a beach. Depending on the day, the surf might gently spill onto the beach or it might crash in a foaming rage. Either way, waves continuously wash onto the shore. Most waves are formed by wind blowing over the ocean's surface, as wind energy is transferred to wave energy. A light breeze might cause small ripples, but as wind speeds increase, so does the size of the waves. When you look at waves, it appears as if the water is moving forward with each wave, but in fact the water only moves up and down in little circles as the wave passes

A ship is tossed in large waves.

by, much as the cheer known as "the wave" travels around a stadium. People move up and down but still stay at their seats.

Scientists describe waves with a few basic terms. The top is the *crest* and the bottom is the *trough*. The distance between two wave crests is called the *wavelength*. The vertical distance from the crest to the trough is the *wave height*. As a wave enters shallow water, it slows down due to friction between the water molecules and the bottom. The wave energy propels the wave upward until its crest crashes shoreward. When a wave reaches the shore, its energy is transferred to the land, sculpting cliffs or eroding beaches.

One of the most damaging types of ocean wave is the *tsunami*. Tsunamis are often incorrectly referred to as tidal waves, although they are not caused by tides. *Tsunami* is a Japanese word meaning "harbor wave." These massive waves can devastate coastal areas. Tsunamis are usually triggered by vibrations—*seismic* waves—from volcanic eruptions

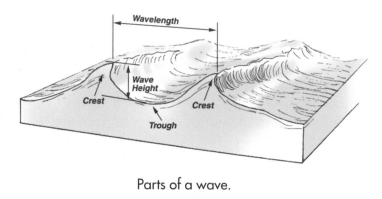

Parts of a wave.

or earthquakes, on land or underwater. When they start, tsunamis are very small but very fast. They can travel hundreds of miles across the open ocean. They become most dangerous when they reach shallow water, where they rise into a towering wall of water and release their enormous power onto the shore.

A tsunami is caused by an earthquake beneath the ocean. The large waves that result can do extensive damage to coastal settlements.

Tides rise and fall at predictable intervals. At high tide, the water in a particular place may rise so high that it covers much, or maybe all, of the beach and rocks. At low tide the water recedes, exposing large areas of the beach, and creating tide pools, ready for you to explore. In most places there are usually two daily tides.

What causes tides? The tides are caused by gravitational forces among the moon, sun, and Earth. These gravitational forces "pull" on the oceans making them rise.

The picture on the left shows a rock along the Alaska coast at low tide. The mechanism on top of the rock is a tide gauge, a device that measures sea level and tides. The picture on the right shows the same rock and tide gauge (with a visitor) several hours later, at high tide.

Ocean Circulation

Winds and waves keep the ocean's surface in constant motion. Winds blowing consistently from a particular direction create ocean surface currents. These currents are like rivers in the ocean. Sailors navigating across the oceans long ago noticed predictable ocean currents such as the Kuroshio and Gulf Stream. Sailors discovered they could make much better time sailing from North America to Europe using the Gulf Stream and the westward moving winds than they could during the return trip. The map on the next page identifies some major currents.

Notice that the currents in the Northern Hemisphere move in a clockwise direction, while the currents in the Southern Hemisphere move in a counterclockwise direction. When the wind blows over the oceans, water is deflected to the right in the Northern Hemisphere and to the left in the Southern Hemisphere. This deflection is caused by Earth's rotation; it is called the *Coriolis Effect*.

Currents can also move vertically in a process called *upwelling*. Upwelling near the coast occurs when wind blows warm surface water offshore, allowing deeper, colder water to reach the surface. This deeper, colder water tends to be rich in nutrients because dead organic

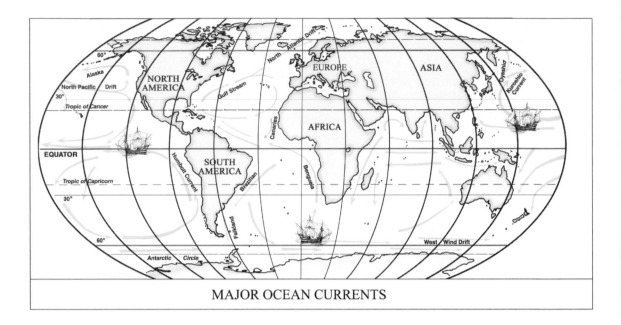

MAJOR OCEAN CURRENTS

matter is constantly sinking to the bottom of the ocean. When an upwelling brings cold, nutrient-rich water to the surface, microscopic algae, called *phytoplankton*, consume the nutrients and flourish. Larger marine animals then feed on the phytoplankton. This is why upwellings often support large fisheries, such as those off the west coast of South America.

Ocean water is continuously on the go, rising and sinking. Imagine a giant ocean conveyor belt moving water through the ocean. It can take 1,000 years for a drop of ocean water to sink to the ocean bottom, resurface, and sink again. Deep ocean circulation is driven by differences in water density. *Density* is the mass, or amount of matter, packed into a certain volume. You may have studied the equation $D = M/V$ (density is equal to mass divided by volume).

Both temperature and salinity affect the density of water. Cold water is denser than warm water, and saltier water is denser than less salty

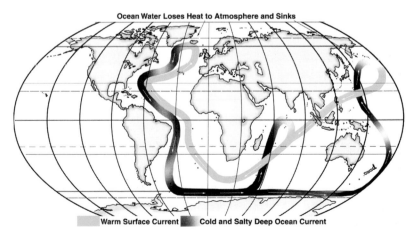

Ocean water is circulated all around Earth, rising and falling as it is heated or cooled, as if riding on a giant conveyer belt.

water. More salt means more dissolved matter and higher density. Salt also lowers the freezing point of water, so ocean temperatures can drop below 0° Celsius (32° Fahrenheit) without the water freezing. Therefore, ocean water becomes denser with decreasing temperatures or increasing salinities.

Here's one example of how these two factors can help create movement beneath the water. At the poles, frigid air cools the ocean surface. When ice forms, most of the dissolved salts in the ocean water do not get frozen into the ice crystals. They are left behind in the water. So the formation of sea ice further increases the salt concentration and therefore the density of the remaining cold surface water. As a result, a blob of very cold, very salty, and very dense surface water forms. This dense surface water near the poles then begins to sink. As it sinks, it is replaced by surface water that has been warmed near the equator and transported to the poles by currents. On the ocean's conveyor belt, warm surface water continuously circulates to the poles where it cools, becomes very dense, and sinks to start another cycle.

The Ocean Floor

Ocean circulation is also affected by the ocean floor. Deep water changes direction when it encounters features similar to those found on land. Just as rivers meander between riverbanks, so currents make their way among chains of underwater mountains. These submarine mountain chains are the riverbanks of the ocean.

Imagine you are navigating a tiny submarine from near shore toward the open ocean, known as the *pelagic zone*. The first thing you notice is the nearly flat plain called the *continental shelf*. The shelf is the shallow edge of a submerged continent, reaching depths of about 200m (660 ft). As you motor on, you notice the seafloor dropping away. You have reached the *continental slope*. As you reach the bottom of the slope, your sub hovers above the *continental rise*, a wedge of sediment several kilometers thick. These sediments washed from the land, across the shelf, and down the slope to settle at the bottom. At the end of the rise, a huge expanse of flat ocean floor is before you.

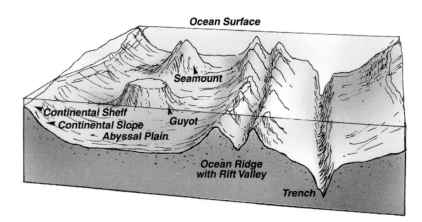

The ocean floor has geographical features, just like the continents.

You are now in the deep ocean basin about 4 km (2.5 miles) deep, gliding over an abyssal plain. An *abyssal plain* is an extremely flat, broad area. If your sub's robotic arm could scrape away about 500 m (1,600 ft) of sediment, you'd find jagged volcanic rocks. Originating from the land and from the remains of marine life from above, these sediments buried the original volcanic ocean floor to form Earth's flattest areas.

Before you go too far, you cruise over a deep-sea trench. A *trench* is a long, narrow, steep-sided depression in the ocean bottom. Deep-sea trenches are the deepest places in the ocean. The Marianas Trench in the Pacific is the deepest at about 11 km (7 miles). Deep-sea trenches form at convergent boundaries between plates.

In the distance, a mid-ocean ridge, an underwater volcanic mountain range, looms up over the abyssal plain, just as the Rocky Mountains overlook the prairies. Mid-ocean ridges form an almost continuous chain through the ocean basins. The Mid-Atlantic Ridge is the longest mountain range in the world, longer than any mountain range on land. It runs right down the middle of the Atlantic Ocean, and it is almost entirely submerged. There are a few places, such as Iceland and the Azores, where the ridge pokes above the ocean's surface.

It is in the Pacific Ocean where you will find the tallest mountain on the planet. Most of this mountain is under the ocean. Only the top of Mauna Kea, in Hawaii, sticks above the ocean's surface. Mauna Kea is about 9.5 km (about 6 miles) high. That is about 1 km (0.6 miles) taller than Mount Everest, the tallest mountain on land.

In tropical areas, coral reefs can build up around a volcanic island. Over tens of thousands of years, the island can weather, erode, and completely submerge, leaving behind a ring-shaped reef called a *coral atoll*.

This coral atoll in the Pacific Ocean has a ring of coral reefs just below the surface enclosing a deeper lagoon.

Ocean Life

The ocean is teeming with life. Marine life can be categorized into three kinds of organisms. *Benthos* are organisms living on, under, or attached to the bottom. Giant kelp and snails are two examples. *Nekton* are free-swimming animals. Fish and whales are examples.

Lastly, *plankton*, are small, drifting organisms. Plantlike plankton are called *phytoplankton* and animal-like plankton are called *zooplankton*. Plankton, nekton, and benthic organisms live throughout the ocean—from shallow coastal regions to deep-sea trenches.

Two four-eyed butterfly fish.

All organisms need energy to live and grow. Food energy is passed from one organism to another through a *food chain*. Most food chains start with energy from the sun. Phytoplankton living near the surface use the sun's energy to produce their own food through photosynthesis. However, most organisms cannot make their own food; they must eat other plants or animals, or scavenge the bodies of dead organisms. Here is a simple marine food chain.

sunlight → phytoplankton (diatom) → zooplankton (copepod) → small fish (anchovy) → larger predator (squid)

A sea horse.

Because most organisms eat and are eaten by more than one kind of organism, many different food chains interconnect to form *food webs*. In marine ecosystems, phytoplankton form the base of most food webs. Large populations of phytoplankton can support healthy marine ecosystems.

Like plants on land, phytoplankton require sunlight to carry out photosynthesis, but they also need nutrients. On land, nutrients are provided by the soil. In the ocean, the nutrients are found in the surrounding water. Recall that ocean water carries essential nutrients such as phosphorus and nitrogen. Phytoplankton thrive only where there is adequate light and an adequate supply of nutrients. Surface waters of the pelagic zone have plenty of sunlight but are usually low in nutrients. Deeper parts of the ocean contain nutrients but very little or no sunlight. Nutrients trapped deep in the ocean cannot be used by the phytoplankton unless they are brought to the surface. Shallow coastal areas often have both light and nutrients. The water may be enriched with nutrients brought in by rivers or by upwelling from below. This is why these coastal areas are home to 90 percent of marine species.

Does that mean there is no life in the deep ocean? Definitely not! Deep-water organisms are quite successful at living on the decaying marine life that is always raining down. Benthic organisms, such as sponges and scallops, filter decaying particles from the water. Crabs and worms scavenge the bottom for food. Deep-sea fish take another approach. Jawfish have huge mouths to gobble up large prey, and anglerfish have a glowing or bioluminescent fin shaped to lure in prey.

Fish swimming along the ocean floor in the Florida Keys National Marine Sanctuary.

ASTRONOMY

Newton and Gravity

There is an old saying, "What goes up must come down." From the earliest times, people have known that any object thrown up into the air will fall down. The force that makes objects fall back to Earth is called gravity.

We owe a great deal of what we know about gravity to Isaac Newton, whom you read about in the history section on the Enlightenment. According to one story, Newton began thinking about gravity after an apple fell off a tree and hit him on the head. That story may not be true, but Newton did go on to show that gravity was responsible not only for falling apples but also for the motions of Earth, the moon, and the other planets in our solar system and for the rising and falling of Earth's tides. Newton discovered that there is an attractive force (gravity) between any two objects in the universe, and that this force grows greater when the objects contain more mass or are closer to one another. Newton wrote an equation that allows us to calculate the force of gravity between any two objects in the universe:

$$F_g = G \ \frac{m_1 \, m_1}{r^2}$$

This famous equation says that the force of gravity (F_g) between any two objects can be calculated if you know the mass of the first object (m_1), the mass of the second object (m_2), and the distance between them (r). (G is what is called the "universal gravitational constant.")

Gravity is a force of attraction between any two objects that have mass. *Mass* is a measure of how much matter an object has. All things are made of matter, from the family goldfish to the fork in the kitchen to the stars in the farthest reaches of the universe. All these things take up space and have mass. Is there a gravitational force between the goldfish and the fork? Yes, there is. Remember: gravity is always working between any two things. Then why don't you see the goldfish and fork gravitating toward each other? This is because gravity is a relatively weak force between objects with small masses. We only notice gravitational forces exerted by massive objects, such as Earth.

Isaac Newton.

When you jump into the air, you feel the force of Earth's gravity pull you down. That force is *weight*. But as Earth pulls on you, you also pull on Earth. You just don't feel your gravitational force pulling back on Earth because your mass is so incredibly small in comparison to the mass of Earth. Your weight, or the weight of any object, is a measure of how strongly Earth's gravity pulls on it.

The fact that every object in the universe, from the smallest atom to the largest star, attracts every other object is one of Newton's most astonishing discoveries. According to Newton's law of universal gravitation, any two objects attract each other with a force that depends on two factors—the masses of the two objects and the distance between the two objects. Let's look at each of these factors.

Newton's Two Factors

The first factor Newton identified is mass. Objects with larger masses exert greater gravitational forces. For example, an elephant is much more massive than a mouse. That's easy to see. Imagine lifting an elephant. Ouff! Only cartoon characters with superpowers can lift an elephant. Now imagine lifting a mouse. When you pick up the mouse, you are pulling against the gravitational attraction between the mouse and Earth. The gravitational attraction between the mouse and Earth is less than the attraction between the elephant and Earth. Hence, the mouse weighs less. You can probably generate enough force to lift the mouse.

Now pretend you have flown to the moon. The moon is less massive than Earth, so it has a weaker gravitational force. Because the pull of the moon's gravity is weaker, you, the elephant, and the mouse would all weigh less than on Earth. Even the elephant could make giant leaps on the moon, just as the astronauts did when they walked on the moon. However, the mass of you and the mouse and the elephant would stay the same because you are all still made up of the same amount of matter. Mass remains constant no matter where the object is in the universe. The weight of an object changes depending on its location.

Because the moon has less mass than Earth, a can of soda weighed on the moon would weigh less than it would if weighed on Earth.

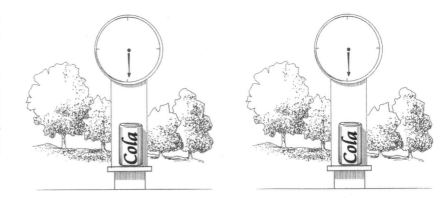

Imagine you could rocket over to Jupiter, the largest planet in our solar system. Would you weigh more or less than on the moon? Remember, according to Newton's law of universal gravitation, the larger the mass, the greater the gravitational force. On Jupiter you would weigh a great deal more, but your mass would still be the same.

The second part of Newton's law of universal gravitation states that the closer two objects are, the greater the gravitational force is between them. The opposite is true as well. As the distance between two objects increases, the amount of gravitational force decreases.

Jupiter.

One of the things Newton demonstrated was that the rise of the ocean tides is caused primarily by the pull of the moon and not the sun. At first, this may seem to contradict Newton's law. After all, the sun is about 300,000 times more massive than the moon. Shouldn't it therefore exert a much greater gravitational force? Yes, but remember: the sun is much farther away from Earth than the moon. Therefore, the moon's gravitational pull on Earth's ocean water is greater than that of the sun's.

Newton also saw that the force of gravity keeps the moon circling Earth and all the planets orbiting the sun. In his book *Principia*, Newton asked his readers to imagine a large mountain with a very powerful cannon on top. Each time the cannon blasted, it would use larger and larger amounts of gunpowder. With each explosion the cannonball would travel farther and farther before gravity pulled the ball to the ground. Newton then told his readers to think about the cannon being so powerful when fired that the cannonball would travel fast enough to "fall" completely around Earth. The ball never lands because Earth's surface curves away from the ball as it falls. Newton said this is how planets stay in orbit around the sun. Newton also concluded that if the cannonball were shot fast enough, it would escape the pull of Earth's gravity and travel through space.

Of course there were no space rockets in the 1600s, but spacecraft today have engines powerful enough to place them in orbit around Earth or launch them into space in just the way Newton described.

Newton imagined what would happen if a cannon could fire a cannonball with enough power to overcome Earth's gravitational pull. He concluded that a cannonball fired with enough force would go into orbit around the Earth.

During liftoff, the space shuttle fires powerful rockets to overcome Earth's gravitational pull.

Stars

The sun is the most massive object in our solar system and the brightest star in our sky. You may not be used to thinking of the sun as a star because all the other stars are so far away they appear as tiny twinkles of light. In reality, stars are extremely large, extremely hot balls of gases, mostly hydrogen and helium. Stars are held together by gravity and give off enormous amounts of heat and light.

The sun gives Earth energy for life. Almost all living organisms depend, in one way or another, on the sun's energy. We see and feel the intensity of the sun's energy because it is relatively close. Although the sun is 150 million km (93 million miles) away and its light takes 8 minutes to reach us, other stars are so far away that astronomers had to invent a new unit of measurement, the *light-year*, in order to measure their distance. One light-year is the distance light travels in one year—about 9.6 trillion km (6 trillion miles).

After the sun, the next closest star is Alpha Centauri, which is about 4 light-years away. By the time light from Alpha Centauri reaches Earth, it has already traveled through space for 4 years! Many stars are hundreds, thousands, even millions of light-years away.

To us the sun is life giving and special. But as far as stars go, it's just average. It's average in size, brightness, and temperature. Astronomers have determined that you can tell how hot a star is by its color. You may have noticed the metal elements inside a toaster turn red-hot as they toast a slice of bread. Just as a piece of metal glows red or orange when heated, so a star's color indicates its temperature. Blue stars are the hottest; then come white, yellow, orange, and red. Like most stars, the sun is a yellow star.

A Star Is Born

All organisms have a life cycle: they are born, they grow up, they age, and finally they die. Did you know stars have life cycles, too? Stars are "born," burn, then run out of fuel and "die." A star begins its life as a *nebula*, a cloud of mostly hydrogen gas and dust floating in space. Gravity causes the cloud to coalesce, or come together. As the particles are forced closer together, the cloud heats up and begins to glow. When temperatures get hot enough, fusion begins. *Fusion* [FEW-zhun] is a process in which two atoms combine—or fuse—to make a new atom. In this case, two atoms of hydrogen combine to make a single atom of helium. In the process, a portion of the mass of the hydrogen is converted into energy. Fusion generates such a tremendous amount of energy that the cloud actually explodes. However, the star is very massive, and the force of gravity is so great that the burning gases do not blow apart and spread out in all directions. Rather the burning material hangs together—and a star is born.

What happens afterward depends on the star's size. All stars keep fusing hydrogen atoms into helium until they run out of fuel, but very large stars pass through different phases than smaller and average-size stars. Medium-size stars, like our sun, use up their hydrogen fuel in about 10 billion years. But don't worry: there is little chance our sun will run out of fuel anytime soon. Astronomers figure it has about another three billion years of fuel left. When a star begins to run out of hydrogen fuel, it begins to collapse. As it does, the star generates even more heat and becomes so hot that it starts fusing helium. (Remember: previously the star had been fusing hydrogen.) Refueled, the star expands again, this time into a *red giant*. When a red giant runs out of fuel, this time it collapses into a small, dense *white dwarf*. A white dwarf appears very dim because of its small size, but it is extremely hot.

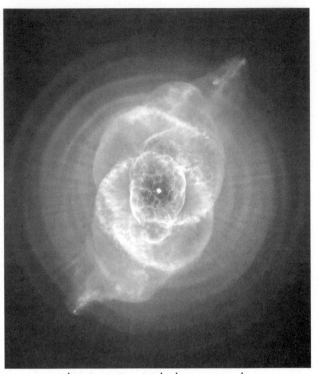

The Cat's Eye Nebula, as seen by the Hubble Space Telescope.

For very large stars, the stages are a little different. These stars develop into Red Supergiants. When a Red Supergiant dies, it goes out with a bang. The collapsing Red Supergiant generates so much energy that the star explodes. The explosion is called a *supernova* and is millions of times brighter than an ordinary star.

The stuff that is left over after the explosion collapses down to a very dense object known as a *neutron star*, and sometimes even to the super-dense object known as a *black hole*. Neutron stars spin rapidly and often send radio waves into space. Radio telescopes detect the waves as a pulsing signal. There is a pulse for every time the neutron star rotates. Because of these pulses, neutron stars are also called *pulsars*.

When particularly massive stars die and "go nova," they collapse into what astronomers call a black hole. Do you remember the description of cannons firing cannonballs higher and higher until one of them finally escapes the gravitational pull of Earth? A black hole is so dense, and its gravitational force so strong, that nothing—not a cannonball, not even light —can escape from it. Because no light can escape, black holes are invisible. How then do we know that black holes exist? Astronomers use special X-ray telescopes to investigate these gigantic vacuum cleaners in space.

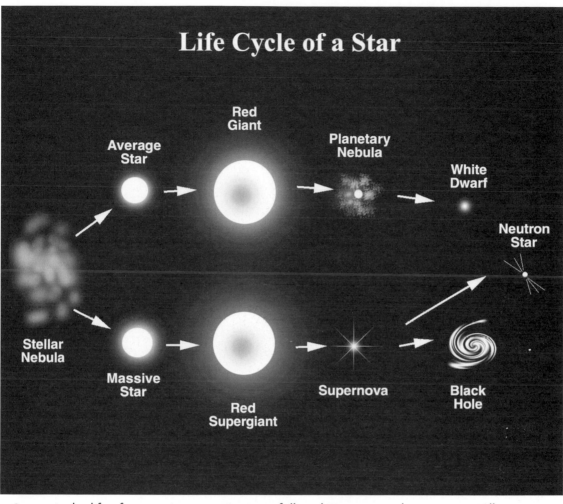

Life Cycle of a Star

Stellar Nebula

Average Star

Red Giant

Planetary Nebula

White Dwarf

Neutron Star

Massive Star

Red Supergiant

Supernova

Black Hole

Stages in the life of a star. Average-size stars follow the stages on the top; especially massive stars follow the stages on the bottom.

Constellations

Long before telescopes were invented, people spent hours watching the night sky. They noticed that stars seem to rise in the east, move across the sky, and set in the west. We know now that stars only *seem* to move across the night sky. In fact, it is the rotation of Earth that accounts for the movements. As Earth spins on its axis, the stars seem to rise and set, just as the sun seems to rise and set.

Ancient people saw star patterns in the sky called *constellations*, from the Latin word meaning "clusters of stars." Constellations were named thousands of years ago after mythological gods and heroes, animals, and familiar objects. Sometimes constellations really do look like connect-the-dot tracings of objects or animals they represent. The Big Dipper and the Little Dipper actually look like soup ladles, or dippers. If you use your imagination on a winter's night, you may also be able to see the ancient Greek hunter, Orion. Look for his club in the air, his shield in front, and his sword dangling from his belt.

There is one famous star that has been particularly important to people over the years. Polaris (the North Star) is located at the tip of the Little Dipper. When you look at Polaris, you are facing north. People have used the North Star to navigate for centuries. It's the only star that does not change its location during the night. From Earth, the North Star is located in space above the North Pole. Unlike the rest of the stars, it maintains its position as Earth spins. The next time you step outside at night, look for Polaris.

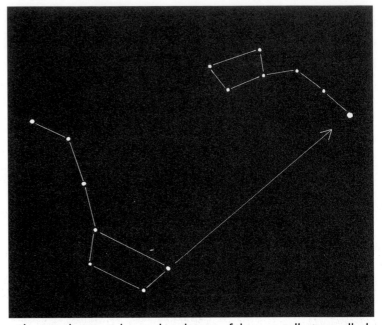

The North Star is located at the tip of the constellation called the Little Dipper. You can find the North Star by locating the constellation known as the Big Dipper and tracing a line across to the tip of the Little Dipper, as shown here.

The North Star: A Fixed Point

Unlike the rest of the stars, the North Star maintains its position as the earth spins. Make a little dot in the center of this book. Then have somebody hold the book over your head, with the dot directly overhead. Focus on the dot. That's your "North Star." You are the Earth, and your head is the North Pole. Now slowly turn around in a circle. Can you see how your "North Star" stays pretty much in the same spot and the other words seem to swirl around it?

Galaxies

A *galaxy* is a cluster of stars—billions of stars. The galaxy that we live in is called the Milky Way. On a clear, dark night you can look up into the sky and see a faint band of light curving across the night sky. The Vikings and the ancient Maya thought this band of light was a path souls traveled to the afterlife; the ancient Greeks thought it was milk spilled across the sky by a goddess. This is where we got the name "Milky Way." But it was the great Italian astronomer Galileo who solved the mystery of the Milky Way. As he gazed through his telescope around 1610, he discovered that the Milky Way is actually thousands and thousands of stars. The stars are just too faint to be seen individually by the naked eye. Without a telescope, the stars look like a faint ribbon of light.

What Galileo didn't know was that the shimmering band of starlight is only a tiny part of our galaxy. Astronomers today estimate that the Milky Way galaxy contains more than 300,000 billion stars. The Milky Way swirls in a spiral, similar to a pinwheel, and is about 100,000 light-years across.

Our solar system is only a tiny part of the Milky Way galaxy, and our galaxy is only one of many galaxies in the universe. The Andromeda Galaxy is the next closest, over two million light-years away. Compared to the Milky Way, Andromeda is huge and contains more than

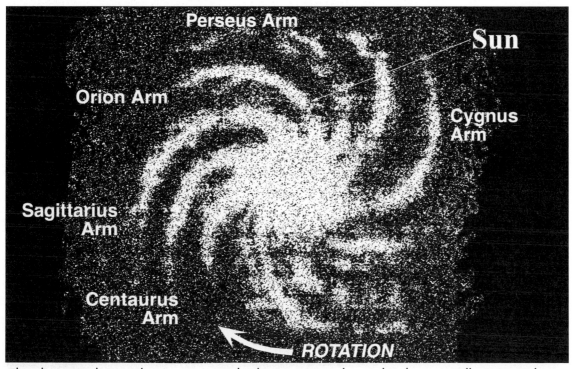

This diagram shows where our sun and solar system are located in the vast Milky Way galaxy.

twice the number of stars. Both Andromeda and the Milky Way are spirals, but galaxies may also be elliptical (oval) or irregular in shape.

Billions of light-years away, *quasars*, or quasi-stellar objects, are the most distant objects astronomers can detect. Quasars can be seen only because they are so bright. They may be the early stages of newly forming galaxies at the edge of the known universe.

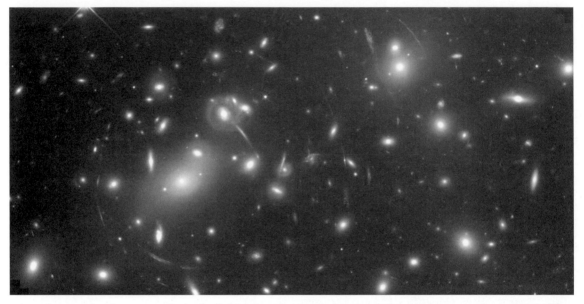

This cluster of galaxies, called Abell 2218, is located about 2 billion light-years from Earth. The picture was taken by the Hubble Space Telescope.

This spiral galaxy, known to astronomers as NGC 4414 and seen here by the Hubble Space Telescope, is about 60 million light-years away from Earth.

ENERGY, HEAT, AND ENERGY TRANSFER

Atoms

If you read the previous book in this series, you know that everything in our world is made up of matter. All matter is made up of tiny particles called *atoms*. Atoms can be broken up further into unimaginably small particles called *protons, neutrons,* and *electrons*. Atoms can also combine to make clusters, called *molecules*. For example, two atoms of hydrogen and one atom of oxygen can combine to make a molecule of H_2O, or water.

All of the matter in the world—including water, air, wood, plastic, steel, clay, blood, and bone—is made up of atoms. Just as we can form millions of words from the 26 letters of the alphabet, so we can form millions of different kinds of matter from the 90 or so kinds of atoms that occur in nature.

A Matter of State

Most kinds of matter can exist in three states: as a solid, a liquid, and a gas. These states are also known as *phases*.

Any piece of matter that tends to keep its shape is a solid. An iron nail is solid; so are clay, brass, and ice. The particles (atoms and molecules) that make up solids are packed tightly together. Because they are already so close together, they cannot be easily squeezed into a smaller space or volume.

Unlike solids, liquids flow and take on the shape of their containers, whether the container is a fish bowl, a milk jug, or a swimming pool. Water, milk, and mercury are all liquids at room temperature. The particles in liquids are not as rigidly packed as solids, but they do remain close together. Like solids, liquids are difficult to squeeze or compress into smaller volumes.

Water can change state from solid to liquid, and from liquid to gas. Energy in the form of heat causes molecules to vibrate more rapidly. When the molecules in the ice vibrate more rapidly, the ice melts into liquid water. Adding more heat makes the molecules vibrate even more and the liquid water turns into steam.

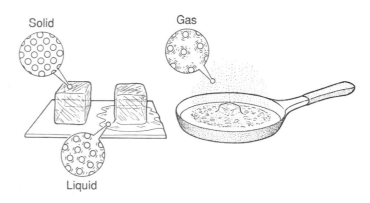

Solid   Gas

Liquid

Like liquids, gases flow and have no definite shape. But unlike liquids, gases can be squeezed or compressed into much smaller volumes. For example, a great deal of oxygen gas can be compacted into a relatively small tank—provided the tank is strong enough to hold it all!

Temperature and Phase Changes

Substances can change phases, or states, when they are heated or cooled. Many substances are solid at low temperatures, liquid at medium temperatures, and gaseous at high temperatures.

In order to understand why substances change from one state to another, it is important to understand that atoms and molecules are constantly vibrating. Even the atoms and molecules of a solid, although packed tightly together, vibrate a little. The amount of vibration is connected with temperature. In fact, temperature is a measure of the average amount of vibration, or *kinetic energy*, in a substance. The higher the temperature, the more energetically the particles in a substance are vibrating. A low temperature means the particles are vibrating rather little. A high temperature means the particles are vibrating more vigorously.

When the temperature of a solid climbs high enough, the vibrations become so vigorous that they overcome the attractive forces that had previously held the atoms and molecules close to one another. The particles break out of formation and begin to slide around more freely. The solid then *melts* and becomes a liquid. The temperature at which this occurs for a particular substance is called the *melting point*. Each pure solid has its own melting point. Under normal atmospheric pressure, ice melts at 0°C (32°F), but iron doesn't melt until the temperature reaches 1535°C (2795°F).

The transformation from liquid to gas occurs for the same reasons. When a liquid is heated, its molecules start bouncing around more rapidly and moving farther apart. When the molecules are far enough apart, the intermolecular forces are too weak to pull them back together. At that point the molecules turn into a gas, or vapor. When a liquid is heated to its *boiling point,* bubbles of vapor form within the liquid and rise to the surface. A liquid that is boiling is turning to a gas at a rapid rate. Under normal atmospheric pressure, water will boil at 100°C (212°F), liquid helium at –269° C (–452° F), and liquid platinum at 3825° C (6917° F).

The same processes also work in reverse. If you take a gas and cool it, the vibrations of the particles will slow down until, at a certain point, the gas *condenses* into a liquid. You may have noticed that the bathroom mirror gets "fogged up" after a long, hot shower. This is because the warm water vapor in the air touches the cool mirror and condenses, forming water droplets.

If you take a liquid and cool it, the vibrations will slow down until, eventually, the liquid will freeze into a solid. The temperature at which this occurs is called the *freezing point*. The freezing point for a particular substance is always the same as its melting point. Water freezes at 0° C (32° F), milk freezes at –0.5°C (31° F), and mercury freezes at about –39° C (–38° F).

Note that all of these changes are *physical* changes, rather than *chemical* changes. When water changes phase, no new substance is produced. Ice is the same substance as water, but in a solid state. Likewise, water vapor is still water, but in a gaseous state.

Even though a phase change (e.g., from solid to liquid) does not create a new substance, phase changes can be very useful. If you've ever made ice cubes or popsicles in a freezer, you have taken advantage of phase changes. Another example of the usefulness of phase changes is the process of distillation. To purify, or distill, impure water, you heat the impure water to the boiling point in a container such as a flask. When the water is heated to the boiling point, it turns into vapor and rises into the neck of the flask. Then it passes into a second chamber, where it is cooled and condenses. Finally, a second flask collects the purified water. During this process, the water moves from one flask to the other by boiling and then condensing; the impurities, however, are left behind—because they have a much higher boiling point.

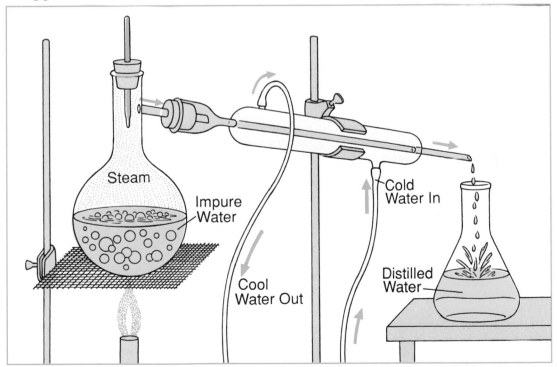

Distillation can be used to purify water by separating the water from materials dissolved in it. The impure water is heated until it vaporizes. Then the vapor is passed through a cooling tube so it will condense, and the distilled, or purified, water is collected on the right. The impurities remain in the bottle on the left since they have a much higher boiling point than the water.

Expansion and Contraction

Solids and liquids are difficult to compress. However, when you add or remove heat energy, the volume of the object almost always changes, even if it's just a little. When a substance is heated, its particles gain energy, move more vigorously, and move farther apart. Thus the substance occupies a bit more space. When a substance is cooled, the particles slow down, move with less energy, and move closer together. Thus the substance occupies a bit less space.

You can observe these changes in a liquid using a thermometer. Place the end of the bulb between two fingers and hold it. Heat energy from your body will transfer to the bulb, warming the liquid inside the glass tube. As the temperature increases, the particles in the tube will move more vigorously and the liquid will expand and rise higher in the tube. Now take your hand away. As the liquid cools, the particles will move less vigorously and occupy less space, so the level will drop.

Water is an exception to the general rules concerning expansion and contraction with temperature shifts. As water cools, it contracts slightly and its density increases, just like a typical liquid. However, when water cools to 4° C (39° F) it reaches its maximum density. At lower temperatures, water molecules begin to align in a honeycomb shape. As ice forms, this honeycomb framework of ice crystals holds the water molecules farther apart than they were when they were a liquid. Therefore, ice is less dense than liquid water: it is one of only a few solids that float in their own liquid.

Conduction, Convection, and Radiation

Heat energy is transferred from one place to another in three main ways: by conduction, by convection, and by radiation.

Conduction is the movement of heat energy through a material or between objects when they are in contact. When you hold the bulb of a thermometer between your fingers, some of the heat energy is transferred from your fingers to the thermometer and the liquid inside. Conduction also takes place when you place a metal spoon in a cup of hot chocolate. The hot chocolate warms the particles in the spoon it comes in contact with, and those particles warm the particles next to them, and so on. The particles in the hot chocolate are vibrating rapidly, colliding with their neighbors both in the cocoa and on the outside of the spoon. Then the particles in the lower part of the spoon begin to vibrate and collide with their neighbors, causing them to vibrate as well. The heat energy travels from particle to particle until it reaches the other end of the spoon. Note that the particles themselves do not move from one end to the other; rather, each particle transfers some of its heat energy to the particle next to it.

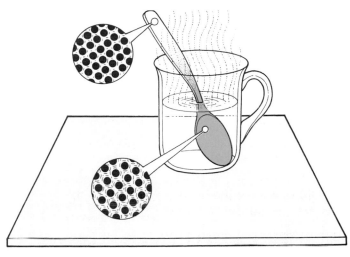

Molecules in the immersed section of the spoon vibrate more rapidly because energy has been transferred to them from the hot cocoa. Eventually energy will be conducted throughout the spoon.

A second way in which heat is transferred is *convection*. Convection is the transfer of heat energy by the movement of a heated material. You learned something about convection earlier (page 313), when you read about the slow cyclical movements in Earth's mantle. Think again of that pot of thick pea soup, in which the warmed soup rises to the surface, spreads out, cools, and then sinks back to the bottom. Convection occurs in gases as well as liquids. For example, a woodstove or a radiator can heat the air around it. The heated air then expands and rises, and cooler air replaces it.

In both conduction and convection, vibrating particles transmit heat energy. *Radiation* is a little different. Radiation transfers energy as waves. Most radiation on Earth travels through space from the sun. The sun gives off waves of light and also heat—also known as *infrared rays*, or *radiant energy*. When these infrared rays strike an object, the object absorbs heat energy. When you step into the sunlight, you can feel its radiation warm your skin.

Forms of Energy

So far we've been discussing heat energy, but there are many other forms of energy. Indeed, energy is all around us. However, unless you know what to look for, it can be hard to recognize because it takes so many different forms and is constantly being transformed from one form to another. Scientists classify energy into several categories:

- *Mechanical energy* is energy related to motion and movement; it is the energy that moves things from place to place. Mechanical energy is also known as kinetic energy.
- *Chemical energy* is energy stored in the form of chemical bonds, or the attractions that bind atoms together into molecules. Chemical energy is released during chemical reactions.
- *Electrical energy* is a stream of electrons moving through a substance.
- *Radiant energy* is wave energy from the sun that travels to Earth. It includes heat energy and light (solar) energy.
- *Nuclear energy* is produced by *fission*, or the splitting of the atoms of certain elements, like uranium. It is also produced by fusion, which was discussed earlier.

Energy can be transformed from one form to another. For example, a car burns gasoline to turn its wheels; what the car is doing is transforming the chemical energy in the gasoline into the mechanical energy of motion. Another example would be a hydroelectric power plant, which uses moving water to turn a turbine and generate electricity—it turns the mechanical energy of the moving water into the electrical energy that powers our lamps and televisions.

Grand Coulee Dam is one of many hydroelectric power plants in the United States.

Energy Resources

We humans rely on energy for just about everything. Energy is needed to lift objects, power machines, light and heat homes, power computers, and run businesses. Where does all this energy come from? Much of it comes from natural resources found on (or within) Earth.

Carbon-based chemical energy resources such as coal, oil, and natural gas are called *fossil fuels* because they were formed millions of years ago from the remains of decaying plants and animals. Fossil fuels are considered *nonrenewable resources* because we have only a limited supply—they cannot last forever. Uranium is another nonrenewable fuel mined from limited supplies. Approximately 94 percent of the energy in the United States comes from nonrenewable energy sources. Only about 6 percent comes from replaceable or *renewable resources*, such as sunlight, wind, moving water, wood, and geothermal heat. *Geothermal heat* comes from water heated beneath Earth's surface near tectonic plate boundaries.

Without electricity, life as we know it would not be possible. Most of our electricity comes from power plants. Power plants generate electricity by converting energy resources into electrical energy.

Windmills and wind turbines convert the mechanical energy of wind into electrical energy. The wind turns a *turbine* —a machine with rotating blades, like propellers. The turbine is attached to a generator, which converts the mechanical energy of turning into electrical energy. This electrical energy then passes along electric lines to homes and businesses.

Hydroelectric power plants work in much the same way, but in this case the turbines are driven by water. The mechanical energy of water released from behind a dam, or over a waterfall, turns the blades of the turbines. Then generators convert the mechanical energy of the turning blades into electrical energy.

In a coal-burning power plant, heat energy generated by burning coal heats water to the boiling point, creating steam. The expanding steam is then used to power generators that produce electricity.

Nuclear power plants also use steam to

A natural gas well.

This man is adjusting a solar panel that turns energy from the sun into electrical energy.

generate electricity, but they use nuclear fission to create the steam. *Nuclear fission* is the splitting of naturally unstable or *radioactive* atoms, such as uranium. First, uranium is mined and concentrated into special pellets. Then these pellets are placed in a *nuclear reactor*, where a controlled chain reaction is initiated. A *chain reaction* is a series of reactions that occur one after another, like a series of falling dominos, each knocking over the next. In an atomic chain reaction, the release of neutrons from the splitting of one atom leads to the splitting of others. These chain reactions release tremendous heat energy. Inside the nuclear reactor, water is heated by these nuclear reactions, creating steam. The steam flows through a pipe to generators that transform the heat energy into electricity.

Environmental Risks

Humans have come to depend heavily on electrical energy. But some of the ways we produce electricity can lead to environmental problems and safety issues. For example, many people worry that nuclear power plants might malfunction and release harmful radioactive material into the environment. Nuclear accidents are rare, but they have occurred. An accident at Three Mile Island in Pennsylvania in 1979 scared many Americans, but this was minor compared to the accident that took place in Chernobyl, Ukraine, in 1989. The fire and subsequent fallout at the Chernobyl reactor left more than 40,000 people ill or disabled, caused horrible deformities in farm animals, and left tens of thousands of acres of land contaminated with nuclear radiation. Although these accidents have led to improved safety standards and safer reactor designs, some people still think nuclear power is inherently unsafe.

Another problem associated with nuclear power is the problem of *radioactive waste*. Nuclear plants create waste that can remain hazardous for millions of years. This waste must be stored in safe locations and secure containers to avoid contamination of land and water.

Fossil fuels can also harm the environment. Oil has to be transported to the areas that need it. If a ship carrying oil

Two cooling towers of a nuclear power plant along the Ohio River.

runs aground, it can dump millions of gallons of oil into the ocean, killing plants and animals and damaging the environment.

Fossil fuels also introduce chemicals into the air we breathe. When fossil fuels are burned, they release smoke, ash, and carbon dioxide gas. Many types of coal also contain a great deal of sulfur. If the coal is burned without removing the sulfur, sulfur dioxide gas reacts with water vapor in the air to form sulfuric acid. When this acid dissolves in

This stand of spruce trees in Poland was devastated by acid rain.

water droplets, it falls to the earth as *acid rain*. Acid rain can poison animals in lakes and rivers, destroy vegetation, and damage buildings and sculptures.

The Greenhouse Effect

A greenhouse is a building with glass walls and a glass ceiling. Greenhouses help people grow plants in the winter. The glass panels of the greenhouse let sunlight in but keep heat from escaping. This makes the greenhouse heat up, like a car parked in the sun. Certain gases in our atmosphere are called greenhouse gases because, like the panes of glass in a greenhouse, they allow light to enter our atmosphere but prevent heat from escaping. Without greenhouse

gases, our planet would be much colder. However, if greenhouse gases increase much more, Earth will get too hot. Many scientists are worried about this possibility.

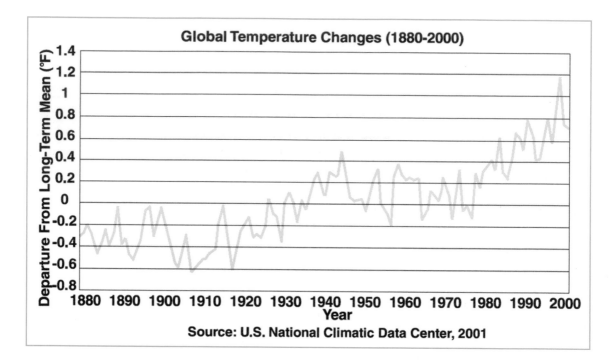

Global temperatures have risen in recent years. Scientists and others are increasingly worried about global warming.

Another by-product of burning fossil fuels is the introduction of large amounts of carbon dioxide into the atmosphere. Carbon dioxide emissions have been increasing ever since the Industrial Revolution got underway. In recent years global temperatures have also been increasing. Many scientists believe there is a connection between the burning of fossil fuels and increasing global temperatures. Most scientists now agree that global warming is occurring and that an increase in the greenhouse effect (see box on page 345) may be the cause. However, scientists cannot tell whether these changes will have serious consequences for Earth's climate.

Energy and the threats posed to the environment by various kinds of energy are likely to be important issues throughout your lives. So be sure to think about the ways in which you use electricity and look for ways to conserve energy.

THE HUMAN BODY

The Circulatory System

If you've read the earlier books in this series, you know that the *circulatory system* is made up of the heart, blood vessels, and blood. Blood vessels carry blood from the heart out to all the organs and limbs of the body, and then back to the heart.

The heart pumps blood through blood vessels to the lungs, where red blood cells are loaded up with oxygen. Arteries then carry these oxygen-rich blood cells away from the heart and out to all of the parts of the body that need oxygen. The arteries divide and subdivide until eventually they turn into *capillaries*—tiny blood vessels so small that red blood cells must squeeze through them one at a time. While in the capillaries, the blood cells drop off oxygen and other nutrients needed by the body and collect waste products, including carbon dioxide. The blood then travels back to the heart and lungs along blood vessels called veins. Red blood cells deposit the unneeded carbon dioxide in the lungs, and it is breathed out when you exhale. Then, when you

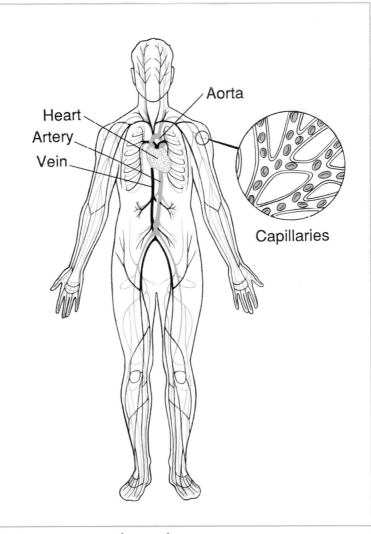

Heart

Artery

Vein

Aorta

Capillaries

The circulatory system.

inhale, you bring in more oxygen that can be distributed throughout the body by the circulatory system.

Blood

Your blood is a mixture of liquid *plasma* and various kinds of blood cells. *Red blood cells* carry oxygen out to the body. *White blood cells* fight disease by attacking microorganisms, or microbes, that cause disease.

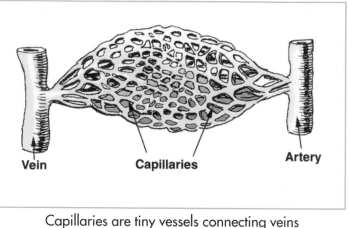

Capillaries are tiny vessels connecting veins and arteries.

Platelets help the body to stop bleeding. Platelets clog openings and form a scab to protect wounds until they heal. This is called *clotting*.

If it weren't for red blood cells, the cells in our bodies couldn't get the nutrients and oxygen they need or get rid of waste products. If it weren't for white blood cells, the body could not fight off diseases. And, if it weren't for platelets, a cut or laceration would never heal.

Clogging up the System

The circulatory system is like a complicated system of pipes, and those pipes can become clogged. Fat carried in the blood can stick to the sides of arteries and limit the amount of blood that can pass through. Such clogs can cause high blood pressure because the heart has to work harder than normal to pump blood through the arteries.

If an artery leading to the brain becomes completely clogged, brain cells starve and die for lack of oxygen. This is called a *stroke*. When the blocked artery is in the heart, some of the heart muscles die and the person experiences a *heart attack*. You can decrease the chances of having a stroke or heart attack by exercising regularly and eating a healthy diet.

The Lymphatic System

The *lymphatic system* is a collection of tissues, organs, and vessels that help protect the body from disease, chiefly by producing white blood cells and trapping foreign particles. As you've already learned, white blood cells are important because they fight germs and infections in the body. White blood cells are transported to various parts of the body in a pale fluid called *lymph*. The lymph flows through a complicated network of lymphatic vessels, much as blood flows through blood vessels. In fact, the lymphatic system works closely with the circulatory system by collecting fluid and white blood cells from the body's tissues and returning them to the bloodstream.

Lymph nodes are oval masses of tissue filled with specialized white blood cells. These nodes are located in strategic locations throughout the body, especially in the neck, the abdomen, the groin, and the armpits. As lymph circulates through the body, the nodes filter and destroy foreign matter like bacteria.

When the lymphatic system is waging war against a serious infection, the lymph nodes swell up. If you've ever heard someone complaining of sinus problems or swollen glands, this is what the person is referring to.

Several other parts of the body also play important roles in the lymphatic system. Bone marrow inside your bones helps create white blood cells. And those funny little things in the back of your throat—your tonsils—are also part of the lymphatic system: they are designed to prevent germs and microbes from entering your body by coming down your throat.

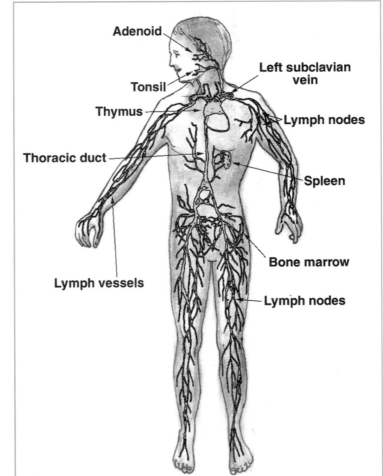

The lymphatic system.

Noncommunicable Diseases

The lymphatic system is important because there are lots of diseases that need to be resisted. Diseases can be divided into two types: communicable diseases and non-communicable diseases.

Noncommunicable diseases cannot be communicated or spread directly from person to person. This kind of disease is usually caused by something going wrong with organs or other parts of the body.

Some noncommunicable diseases are hereditary— they are passed from parent to child through the genes. Hemophilia, a disease in which the blood does not clot correctly, is a hereditary noncommunicable disease.

Other noncommunicable diseases can be caused by poor nutrition. Scurvy, a disease caused by a lack of vitamin C, causes bleeding gums and exhaustion. Heart disease can be brought on by an excess of fat and cholesterol in the diet, coupled with a lack of vegetables, fruit, and fiber.

Still other noncommunicable diseases are closely linked with risky behaviors. Smoking tobacco is a risky behavior that can lead to lung cancer, and spending lots of time in the sun without wearing sunscreen is a risky behavior that can lead to skin cancer.

Smoking is no joke. It can lead to lung cancer and other diseases.

Communicable Diseases

A second kind of disease is a communicable disease. A *communicable* disease can be communicated, or passed, from one organism to another. A sick person can infect his friends, neighbors, or classmates. That is why communicable diseases are also called *infectious* diseases. If someone has an infectious disease and is at risk for giving that disease to other people, we say the person is *contagious*.

The common cold is an infectious disease. So is influenza, or the flu. When people say the flu is going around, they mean the disease is spreading from one person to another. When a disease is spreading very rapidly and making many people sick, we say an *epidemic* has broken out.

Diseases can be spread by humans or by other animals. Rabies is a communicable disease that is spread from animals to humans. Rabies is spread when an infected animal, such as a dog, bites a human. The virus that causes the disease is transferred from the dog's saliva to the person's blood.

Diseases can spread among humans in a variety of ways. Many diseases, including colds and flus, can be spread by coughing and sneezing. Other microorganisms can pass from one person to another when people shake hands or share drinking glasses and eating utensils. Simple precautions, such as staying home when you are sick and washing your hands frequently, can help prevent the spread of contagious diseases.

Germs can be spread by sneezing. Be sure to cover your mouth when you sneeze.

Bacterial and Viral Diseases

Many diseases are caused by tiny organisms called bacteria. Tetanus is a bacterial disease you can get from stepping on a rusty nail. Tuberculosis is a bacterial disease that usually affects the lungs. It can lead to severe coughing and, ultimately, death. Typhoid fever is a disease caused by bacteria in food; it leads to high fevers and can cause death.

Diseases can also be caused by *viruses*. Viruses invade living cells and inject their DNA into the host cell. They then use the host cell to produce more viruses. The viruses multiply until they use up the cell's food. Then the cell bursts, and the viruses are released. These new viruses invade other cells and destroy them. In this way, a virus can rapidly weaken an organism.

A disease caused by a virus is called a *viral* disease. The common cold is a viral disease; so are rabies and the chicken pox. Mononucleosis is a viral disease that leaves the patient listless and exhausted. Polio is a viral disease that can lead to paralysis. U.S. President Franklin Delano Roosevelt was left paralyzed from the waist down by polio.

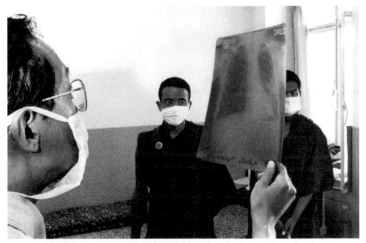

A doctor in India checks a chest X-ray for dark patches caused by the bacterial disease tuberculosis. The doctor and the patients wear masks to prevent the spread of the disease.

The Immune System

Earlier you learned a little about white blood cells. When a bacterium or virus invades the body, the white blood cells go into action, attacking foreign microorganisms in the blood, lymph, and tissues.

Some white blood cells also produce antibodies. An *antibody* is a kind of secret weapon specially designed to defeat a specific virus or bacterium. Each kind of bacterium or virus has its own distinctive chemical label called an *antigen*. Once the immune system determines the chemical identity of a specific virus or bacterium, white blood cells build a unique antibody to help neutralize the invader.

The antibody works by attaching itself to a specific location on the antigen and then disabling the virus or bacterium. The antibody and antigen fit together like a lock and key. Once they are locked together, the invader is deactivated and loses its ability to cause harm.

Even after the antigens have been deactivated and the disease has been overcome, the antibodies that were made to attack that disease remain in the blood. If the same invader appears in the future, the antibodies already in the body can immediately attack the invading microbes and keep them from causing a disease or infection. Some antibodies can protect you from getting the same disease twice. Have you ever had the chicken pox? If you have, you will not get it again, because your body has built up a lifetime immunity. We say you are *immune* to chicken pox.

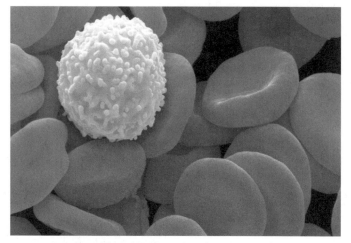

A single white blood cell, with a bumpy surface, stands out against a number of smoother red blood cells. These tiny cells have been magnified many times by a scanning electron microscope.

Unfortunately, there are some diseases that you can get again and again. One of these is the flu. The reason your immune system cannot protect you from multiple cases of the flu is because the viruses that cause flu are constantly changing. Each new version is a little different from the previous version, so the antibody the body developed the last time you had the flu will probably not be effective against the new antigen. That means you will be sick with the flu until your body makes enough white blood cells with the proper antibodies to destroy the new virus.

Antibiotics

The human body has an amazing ability to fight diseases, but modern medicine has discovered some additional ways to fight diseases. One of the most important weapons in our ongoing struggle against disease is antibiotic medicines.

Antibiotics are drugs that kill bacteria, or slow bacterial growth, without killing healthy body cells. Penicillin, one well-known kind of antibiotic, was discovered in 1928 and is produced by a particular kind of mold.

Penicillin was discovered by Dr. Alexander Fleming (1881–1955). During World War I, Dr. Fleming treated infected wounds with *antiseptics*—medicines that stop infection. But Fleming noticed that antiseptics killed white blood cells as well as bacteria. This discovery fueled Fleming's lifelong search for a substance that would destroy bacteria without weakening the body's natural defenses.

After the war, Fleming worked in a laboratory growing deadly bacteria and possible antidotes in shallow petri dishes. For years he was unsuccessful. But on a hot September afternoon in 1928, he noticed that the bacteria cultures on one petri dish had been invaded by a mold. Ordinarily, Fleming's next step would have been to toss the contaminated dish into the sink, but something caught his attention. There was an empty zone around the mold where bacteria colonies were not growing. Fleming investigated and found that the mold was stopping, even destroying, the lethal bacteria!

The mold turned out to be an antibiotic, or bacteria killer. Fleming named the antibiotic mold *penicillin*. Further tests revealed that penicillin destroyed many types of bacterial infections but did not harm white blood cells.

By 1944, English and American factories were mass-producing penicillin for medical use. Since then, penicillin and other antibiotics have been used to save millions of lives. Antibiotics are used in the treatment of pneumonia and strep throat, as well as many other bacterial diseases. Unfortunately, antibiotics are not helpful in fighting viruses.

Alexander Fleming in his laboratory.

Vaccines

Another weapon modern medicine has developed to fight disease is the vaccination. A *vaccination* is a procedure that protects people against a particular disease. Vaccinations are usually given as injections (or shots) through the skin with a needle. Other vaccinations are given by mouth. You may remember receiving vaccinations when you were a young child.

The first modern vaccination was developed by an English country doctor named Edward Jenner (1749–1823). Jenner noticed that people who had been infected with cowpox, a mild viral disease usually affecting cows, seemed never to get smallpox. Smallpox was a much more serious and often fatal disease. Jenner had the idea that a person might be given cowpox in order to protect him from smallpox. A young boy was Jenner's first patient. Jenner injected the boy with the cowpox, or vaccinia, virus. The boy did

Edward Jenner.

not contract smallpox—and neither did others tested later. Jenner's method of infecting people with cowpox to protect them from smallpox worked!

Although Jenner himself did not understand the details, we now know that vaccinations work because they stimulate the body's immune system to build antibodies that protect the body against infections.

The term *vaccination* originally meant injection with the vaccinia (cowpox) virus. But today vaccination can offer us protection from many diseases that were frequently fatal to our ancestors. We now have vaccines for tetanus, typhoid, polio, and rabies.

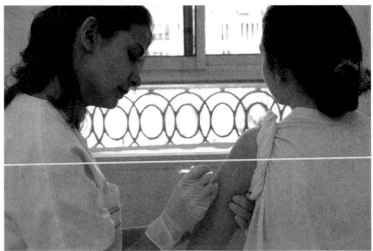

A young girl receives a vaccination.

Scientists continue to study the immune system and develop new vaccines, but there are a number of viral diseases for which we still have no vaccination. AIDS (Acquired Immune Deficiency Syndrome) is one example. AIDS is a deadly viral disease that has become a serious health problem in recent years. The AIDS virus attacks the immune system, making it difficult, and sometimes impossible, for a person to resist and fight off other diseases. People with AIDS become very susceptible to infections such as pneumonia.

In many parts of the world, AIDS has reached epidemic proportions. Some scientists estimate that as many as 40 million people may already have this disease. At this time there is no cure for AIDS although the disease can be treated and sometimes held at bay using expensive medicines. The only way to avoid getting AIDS is to avoid contact with infected blood or other bodily fluids. That means avoiding drugs that encourage needle-sharing (like heroin), avoiding promiscuous sexual behavior, and/or practicing safe sex.

An AIDS researcher conducts DNA analysis. Scientists are working to find a cure for the disease.

SCIENCE BIOGRAPHIES

Marie Curie

Marie Curie (1867–1934) was born in Warsaw, Poland. As a young woman she was interested in math and science, but at the time no Polish university would accept female students. Marie saved her money for several years. Then, at age 24, she went to Paris, France, to study science. While in Paris, she met and married Pierre Curie, a well-known physicist.

In 1895, a German scientist discovered rays that could pass through solid wood or flesh. These were called *X-rays*. About the same time another scientist discovered that the element called uranium also gave off rays. Marie Curie decided to focus her research on the rays produced by uranium. To describe uranium's ability to emit rays, Curie coined the term *radioactive*.

A little later Curie discovered that other substances emit the same kind of rays as uranium. She was particularly excited about a

Marie Curie.

mineral known as pitchblende. This mineral was strongly radioactive but contained only a small amount of uranium. Curie guessed that it must contain some other element—a fiercely radioactive element previously unknown to science.

Curie convinced her husband Pierre to set aside his own work and help her isolate this new element in a pure form. They worked together as a team, in a cold, drafty shed. The goal was to separate the radioactive element from tons of pitchblende. Marie dissolved the powdered mineral and boiled it in huge metal pots for hours at a time. Pierre used chemicals to separate the compounds, discarding whatever was not radioactive. They soon discovered that the radioactive element made up only a tiny portion of the pitchblende—less than one part in a million!

As they worked with the pitchblende, the Curies developed some unusual physical symptoms. They suffered from extreme fatigue, experienced pains in their limbs, and developed burns that wouldn't heal. But they pressed on. Finally, in 1898, they announced the discovery of not one but two new elements. The Curies named one *polonium*, in honor of Marie's native Poland. They called the other element *radium*.

Later, Pierre Curie demonstrated that high doses of radium could damage flesh. Gradually people realized that radioactivity might have medical uses—it could be used to kill cancerous cells, for example. But it had to be used with caution because radioactivity could also kill healthy cells. Today radioactive materials are widely used in medicine.

Doctors now feel confident that the reason why the Curies suffered those mysterious symptoms was because they had spent many hours in close proximity to highly radioactive radium. The Curies breathed radioactive gas, ate radium in their food, and handled it with their bare hands. Scientists estimate that the radiation in their laboratory was 100 times the amount considered safe today; Marie Curie's notebooks are *still* too radioactive to handle!

Marie Curie went on to do more amazing things. She became the first woman professor at the Sorbonne in Paris. She and Pierre received a Nobel Prize in 1903, and Marie received another one in 1911. During World War I, she equipped a fleet of cars and vans with X-ray equipment that could be transported to the edge of a battlefield. This saved many lives. Marie Curie's life is a shining example of what curiosity and determination can achieve.

Lewis Howard Latimer

Lewis Howard Latimer (1848–1928) was an African-American scientist who made many important scientific discoveries at a time when it was difficult for African Americans to excel. Latimer was born in Chelsea, Massachusetts, in 1848, to parents who were escaped slaves. At the age of 15, he altered the age on his birth certificate in order to join the Union navy during the Civil War.

After his military discharge in 1865, Latimer was employed as an office boy at the patent attorney office of Crosby and Gould in Boston, where he learned mechanical drawing. He displayed great talent and was eventually promoted to head draftsman.

In 1876, Latimer was hired by Alexander Graham Bell to create the drawings necessary for a patent application for Bell's new invention, the telephone. Latimer completed these drawings and rushed them to the patent

Lewis Howard Latimer.

office, where they arrived only a few hours before the blueprints of a competitor. Thus, Bell secured the patent for the telephone.

While working for the U.S. Electric Lighting Company, Latimer and his employers looked for a way to improve upon the incandescent lightbulb that was being marketed by Thomas Edison. Edison's lightbulbs lasted only a few days. By inventing a cardboard envelope that surrounded the carbon filament in the lightbulb, Latimer was able to make lightbulbs longer lasting and less expensive. As a result, many cities saw electrical lighting as a better and cleaner way to light their streets and homes. Cities like New York, London, Montreal, and Philadelphia installed this kind of lighting, and Latimer was dispatched to plan and supervise the installation of the systems.

In 1890, Latimer was hired by Thomas Edison at the Edison Electric Light Company, which would eventually become General Electric. There he made more important discoveries and wrote a well-known book. He was also the only African-American member of the Edison Pioneers, a group of men who virtually created the electric industry.

In addition to his achievements in electricity, Latimer invented a bathroom compartment for trains, a locking rack for hats, coats, and umbrellas, and a new improved book holder for bookshelves. He died in 1928.

Illustration and Photo Credits

Every effort has been taken to trace and acknowledge copyrights. The editors tender their apologies for any accidental infringement where copyright has proved untraceable. They would be pleased to insert the appropriate acknowledgement in any subsequent edition of this book. Trademarks and trade names are shown in this book for illustrative purposes only and are the property of their respective owners. The references to trademarks and trade names given herein do not affect their validity.

Art Resource

Apollo Belvedere. Museo Pio Clementino, Vatican Museums, Vatican State/Scala/Art Resource, NY: 175(b)

Caravaggio, *Calling of St. Matthew*. S. Luigi dei Francesi, Rome, Italy/Scala/Art Resource, NY: 181

David, *Oath of the Horatii*. Réunion des Musées Nationaux/Louvre, Paris, France/Art Resource, NY: 185

Eugene Delacroix, *Liberty Leading the People*. The Louvre, Paris, France/Erich Lessing/Art Resource, NY: 188

Jean Millet, *The Gleaners*. Musée d'Orsay, Paris, France/Scala/Art Resource, NY: 190

Michelangelo's *David*. Accademia, Florence, Italy/Scala/Art Resource, NY: 177

Myron of Athens, Discobolus. Museo Nazionale Romano (Terme di Diocleziano), Rome, Italy/Scala/Art Resource, NY: 175(a)

Notre Dame Cathedral. Notre-Dame, Paris, France/Scala/Art Resource, NY: 176

Raphael, *School of Athens*: Stanza della Segnatura, Vatican Palace, Vatican State/Scala/Art Resource, NY: 178

Reconstruction drawing of the Colosseum. Alinari/Art Resource, NY: 104

Three participants in a foot race at the Panathenaic Games: Musée Vivenel, Compiegne, France/Erich Lessing/Art Resource, NY: 93(a)

Bridgewater State College/Office of Public Affairs

Lewis Howard Latimer-African-American scientist. Portrait by T. A. "Ted" Charron, Courtesy of Bridgewater State College: 357

Corbis

Engraving of the Death of Robespierre. © Bettmann/CORBIS: 116

Julius Caesar Murdered in Cleopatra. © Bettmann/CORBIS: 102

Louis XVI and mob during French Revolution. © Leonard de Selva/CORBIS: 114(b)

Manchester Print Works Factory. © CORBIS: 126

Three camels with riders in the desert. © Frans Lemmens/zefa/CORBIS: 81

Vanderbilts' Biltmore Estate. © Neil Rabinowitz/CORBIS: 157

Visitors surround the Fountain of Latona at the Palais de Versailles. © Bill Ross/CORBIS: 111

Edgar Allen Poe. LC-USZC4-8266: 15

Edison Kinetoscopioc record of a sneeze. LC-USZ62-44602: 351(a)

Emiliano Zapata and staff. LC-USZ62-73425: 140(a)

Eugene Debs. LC-USZC4-6885: 163(b)

Frederic Chopin. LC-USZ62-103898: 217(b)

Fritz Kreisler. LC-USZ62-102200: 206

Grand Coulee Dam. LC-USZ62-60012: 342

Greenhouse. LC-USZ62-42984: 345(b)

Hannibal. LC-USZ61-1376: 101(a)

Homeless boys. LC-USZ62-39057: 162

Homestead Strike. LC-USZ62-75205: 155

Ida Tarbell. LC-USZ62-117944: 163(a)

Immigrants at Ellis Island. LC-B2-2109-14: 145

Irving Berlin. LC-USZ62-37541: 149(b)

Isaac Newton. LC-USZ62-101363: 327

Italian Immigrants at Ellis Island. LC-USZ62-67910: 143

J. P. Morgan. LC-B2-4379-2[P&P]: 159

Jane Addams. LC-USZ62-37768: 164

Johann Sebastian Bach. LC-USZ62-48740: 208

José de San Martín. LC-USZ62-101690: 141

Karl Marx. LC-USZ62-16530: 130

Louis XIV. LC-USZ62-124397: 111A

Marie Antoinette. LC-USZ62-70975: 113

Marie Curie. LC-USZ62-91224: 356

Mark Twain. LC-USZ62-5513: 150

Miguel Hidalgo. LC-USZ62-98851: 135

Mojave Desert. LC-USW36-701: 82

Moses. LC-USZC4-7341: 86

Mozart performing. LC-USZ62-107147: 213

N.A.A.C.P. picketers. LC-USZ62-33784: 167(b)

Nativist newspaper, *American Citizen*. LC-USZ62-96392: 147

Natural gas well. LC-USZ62-85356: 343

New York city street. LC-USZ62-107835: 146(b)

Plato. LC-USZ61-1310: 97

Rebel Fighters during Mexican Revolution. LC-USZ62-80779: 139

Samuel Gompers. LC-USZ62-19862: 159(b)

San Francisco earthquake. LC-USZ62-64746: 318

Santa Anna. LC-USZ62-21276: 137

Sermon on the Mount, Currier & Ives. LC-USZ62-36517: 90(a)

Simón Bolívar. LC-USZ62-102147: 140(b)

Smoking. POS-TH-1900.j4, no2: 350

Solar panel. LC-USZ62-84821: 343

Statue of Liberty. LC-USZ62-1005: 144(b)

Statue of Augustus Caesar in the Vatican museum. LC-USZ62-97803: 103

String Quartet. LC-H815-1438-002: 212

Teddy Roosevelt. LC-USZ62-46716: 165

Temple of Theseus. LC-USZ62-108911: 93(b)

Tenement apartment, NYC, National Child Labor Committee Collection. LC-DIG-nclc-04105: 149(a)

Thomas Edison. LC-USZ62-67859: 151

Toussaint L'Ouverture. LC-USZ62-7862: 132

William Jennings Bryan. LC-USZ6-831: 161

Woman Suffrage Headquarters. LC-USZ62-30776: 168

G. B. McIntosh

Original art: ii, iii, 1, 73, 169, 195, 219, 303, 334

Gayle Sherwood Magee
Original art: 198, 199, 200 (all), 201, 202, 205, 209, 214(b)

Metropolitan Museum of Art
El Greco (Domenikos Theotokopoulos) (Greek, 1541-1614), *View of Toledo*, Oil on canvas; 47 3/4 x 42 3/4 in. (121.3 x 108.6 cm): The Metropolitan Museum of Art, H. O. Havemeyer Collection, Bequest of Mrs. H. O. Havemeyer, 1929 (29.100.6). Photograph © 1992 The Metropolitan Museum of Art: 180
Jacques-Louis David (French, 1748-1825), *The Death of Socrates*, 1787. Oil on canvas; 51 x 77 1/4 in. (129.5 x 196.2 cm): The Metropolitan Museum of Art, Catharine Lorillard Wolfe Collection, Wolfe Fund, 1931 (31.45). Photograph © 1995 The Metropolitan Museum of Art: 186
Winslow Homer (American, 1836-1910), *Northeaster*, 1895. Oil on canvas; 34 1/2 x 50 in. (87.6 x 127 cm): The Metropolitan Museum of Art, Gift of George A. Hearn, 1910 (10.64.5) Photograph © 1995 The Metropolitan Museum of Art: 194

Museum Oskar Reinhart am Stadtgarten, Winterthur
Caspar David Friedrich, *Chalk Cliffs on Rügen*, 1818-19, Oil on canvas, 90 x 70 cm, Museum Oskar Reinhart am Stadtgarten, Winterthur. Used with permission: 189

NASA
Space Shuttle liftoff 7/26/05. NASA: 330(b)

National Gallery of Art
1937.1.72.(72)/PA: Rembrandt van Rijn, *Self-Portrait*, 1659, oil on canvas, .845 x .660 (33 1/4 x 26) Andrew W. Mellon Collection, Image © 2005 Board of Trustees, National Gallery of Art, Washington: 182
1939.1.24.(135)/PA: Panini, Giovanni Paolo, *Interior of the Pantheon, Rome*, c. 1734, oil on canvas, 1.280 x .990 (50 1/2 x 39); framed: 1.441 x 1.143 (56 3/4 x 45) Samuel H. Kress Collection, Image © 2005 Board of Trustees, National Gallery of Art, Washington: 174

New York Public Library
Jewish immigrant. Photography Collection, Miriam and Ira D. Wallach Division of Art, Prints and Photographs, The New York Public Library, Astor, Lenox and Tilden Foundations: 144(a)

NOAA
Fish. National Oceanic and Atmospheric Administration/Department of Commerce: 326
High tide. National Oceanic and Atmospheric Administration/ Department of Commerce: 321(b)
Low tide. National Oceanic and Atmospheric Administration/ Department of Commerce: 321(a)
Seahorse. National Oceanic and Atmospheric Administration/ Department of Commerce: 325(b)
Ship in stormy sea. National Oceanic and Atmospheric Administration/ Department of Commerce: 319
Two four-eyed butterfly fish. National Oceanic and Atmospheric

Poetry Credits and Sources

Index

Page numbers in *italics* refer to illustrations.

11-21-06

372.19 WHAT

What your sixth grader needs
   to know